Mutual Aid and Union Renewal

Mutual Aid
and
Union Renewal

Cycles of Logics of Action

Samuel B. Bacharach

Peter A. Bamberger

William J. Sonnenstuhl

ILR Press *an imprint of*

Cornell University Press   ITHACA AND LONDON

Copyright © 2001 by Cornell University

All rights reserved. Except for brief quotations in a review, this
book, or parts thereof, must not be reproduced in any form without
permission in writing from the publisher. For information, address
Cornell University Press, Sage House, 512 East State Street, Ithaca,
New York 14850.

First published 2001 by Cornell University Press
First printing, Cornell Paperbacks, 2001

Printed in the United States of America

Library of Congress Cataloging-in-Publication Data

Bacharach, Samuel B., b. 1945
   Mutual aid and union renewal : cycles of logics of action / Samuel B.
Bacharach, Peter A. Bamberger, William J. Sonnenstuhl.
      p. cm.
Includes bibliographical references and index.
   ISBN 0-8014-3842-X (acid free) — ISBN 0-8014-8734-X (pbk. :
acid free)
   1. Labor unions—United States. I. Bamberger, Peter A., b. 1960.
II. Sonnenstuhl, William J., b. 1946. III. Title.
   HD6508 .B244 2001
   331.88'0973—dc21
                                                    00-012151

Cornell University Press strives to utilize environmentally responsible
suppliers and materials to the fullest extent possible in the publishing
of its books. Such materials include vegetable-based, low-voc inks,
and acid-free papers that are recycled, totally chlorine-free, or partly
composed of nonwood fibers. Books that bear the logo of the FSC
(Forest Stewardship Council) use paper taken from forests that have
been inspected and certified as meeting the highest standards for
environmental and social responsibility. For further information, visit
our website at www.cornellpress.cornell.edu.

Cloth printing   10   9   8   7   6   5   4   3   2   1

Paperback printing   10   9   8   7   6   5   4   3   2   1

This book is dedicated to the memory of R. Brinkley Smithers and Harrison M. Trice, a philanthropist and an academic, whose relationship made this book possible.

Contents

Preface

Unions are dead. At least that is what employers would like to believe and many Americans accept as the truth. The litany of reasons for the demise of unions is familiar:

- Unions protect and encourage unproductive workers.
- Unions make it difficult for American companies to compete globally.
- Unions are corrupt.
- Unions institutionalize conflict between employers and workers.
- Unions are no longer necessary to protect workers because today's employers are enlightened and laws protect workers from employer abuse.

In this book, we argue that unions are not dead. They are under sharp attack from employers and an increasingly hostile legal environment. Nevertheless, we argue that unions may be poised to renew themselves, if they can create a new logic of action for legitimating themselves and regaining their members' commitment. Originally, unions were organized around a logic of mutual aid, which emphasizes that, like an extended family, the union is a corporate entity whose members have multiple obligations to one another and share a collective responsibility for the well-being of one another. This logic enabled unions to survive in a hostile environment characterized by employer and legal opposition. Over time, unions lost their legitimate authority to command members' commitment because they shifted their orientation from involving members in the lives of their unions to a servicing logic, which emphasizes the role of leadership in negotiating material gains through a bureaucratic process, especially providing members with good wages and benefits. In today's hostile environment, this logic is no longer effective. In order to survive, many unions are attempting to re-create their old mutual-aid logic by implementing a variety of programs that involve members in their unions and rekindle feelings of brotherhood and sisterhood. In the following pages, we examine these shifts within the American labor movement and within three unions.

In writing this book, we have incurred many debts. We want to thank several people for their generous support and encouragement. In particular, we want to acknowledge the generous support for this project provided by the National Institute on Drugs (DA 06995–03) and by the Christopher D. Smithers Foundation. In addition, we owe a great debt to the unions and members who shared their experiences with us. Without their generosity, this book would never have been written. We would also like to thank

Colleen Clauson, who watched over our budgets and kept this project on track from its inception to completion. We owe a debt to our former students who helped us by collecting data as well as reading and commenting on drafts: Many thanks to Valerie Kennedy, Fil Sanna, Valerie McKinney, Bryan Booth, Deb Balser, and John Ontiveros. In addition, we gratefully acknowledge the support and encouragement received from our colleagues Clete Daniel and Harry Katz, who read and commented on earlier drafts. We also thank the anonymous reviewers for their timely and generous comments on an earlier draft.

Finally, we wish to acknowledge our great debt to R. Brinkley Smithers and Harrison M. Trice. Brink, a philanthropist, was dedicated to helping suffering alcoholics, especially in the workplace. Harry, an academic, was a pioneer in workplace substance abuse, striving to make sociological thinking an integral part of his studies. Through the R. Brinkley Smithers Institute on Alcohol-Related Workplace Studies, we are working to continue their vision of theory and practice. Therefore, we dedicate this book to their memory.

Samuel B. Bacharach
Peter A. Bamberger
William J. Sonnenstuhl

New York

Mutual Aid and Union Renewal

1 Mutual-Aid and Servicing Logics in American Labor

As an institution, American unions are in crisis. Union member-ship in the United States has declined from an all time high of 36 percent of the national labor force in 1945 to approximately 16 percent in 1989 and approximately 14.5 percent in 1997.

Social scientists have suggested a number of explanations for this decline. According to one line of argument, the individualistic culture of the United States and negative public opinion about unions discourage workers, particu-larly those in the growing, nonmanufacturing sectors, from participating in the labor movement. A second line of argument places the blame on chang-ing economic and political conditions, which have enabled employers to become more resistant to workers' efforts to unionize. According to this rea-soning, antilabor laws, pro-employer regulatory decisions, and the global economy have emboldened employers, who are increasingly likely to use both legal and illegal methods to undercut workers' organizing efforts. Strategies designed to resist unionization include the adoption of "high commitment" human resource policies, the threatened or actual closing of union plants, and the threatened or actual relocation of jobs to nonunion areas, often offshore. Within this context, American unions have found it increasingly difficult to stem the decline in membership and achieve such basic bargaining objectives as job security and the maintenance of a union wage advantage.[1]

1. For useful discussions of union decline see the "Labor Symposia" in the March 1994 and March 1998 issues of *Contemporary Sociology* and the August 1997 special issue of *Work and Occupations*, "Labor in the Americas." See also Clawson and Clawson (1999); Masters and Atkin (1999); Bronfenbrenner et al. (1998); Lipset (1998, 1996); Kochan, Katz, and McKersie (1994); Appelbaum and Batt (1994); and Cornfield (1999).

Some social scientists argue that unions must have committed members to rebuild themselves. As Gordon et al. (1980, 481) note:

> Since the ability of union locals to attain their goals is generally based on the members' loyalty, belief in the objectives of organized labor, and willingness to perform services voluntarily, commitment is part of the very fabric of unions.

Members' commitment provides unions with the potential for mobilizing collective power. To attain union goals, leaders rely on local members to act in their collective interest by complying with bargaining agreements, acting as shop stewards, educating newcomers, and if necessary, striking to force management to bargain in good faith. When members are unwilling to become involved in their union and take personal risks for its collective interests, collective bargaining outcomes are likely to be less favorable to the union. Unfortunately, this creates a vicious cycle because a union perceived to offer few instrumental benefits to its members has difficulty retaining old members and attracting new ones.

We argue that labor's current problems reflect more than a loss of commitment. It also reflects a legitimacy crisis, in which unions have lost their authority. In order to feel committed to an organization, members must first regard its authority as legitimate. According to Weber, legitimate authority "enjoys the prestige of being binding, or, as it may be expressed, of *legitimacy*" ([1922] 1964, 125; emphasis in original). As Weber observed, social systems are based on different principles of legitimacy. For instance, rational authority rests on a belief that rules and commands are binding elements of an impersonal order. Members obey the rules because they believe in the system of rules rather than a particular individual, and leaders elicit obedience by likewise demonstrating their belief in the impersonal system of rules. Many other principles of legitimacy are familiar, including divine will, seniority, and special competency (Selznick 1992).

Social theorists who have examined institutions, such as unions, argue that exchange relationships are institutionalized to the extent that systems of rules provide the parties with shared knowledge that orients their behavior toward one another (Berger and Luckmann 1967). For instance, Ostrom (1986, 5) views institutions as rules prescribing which actions are "required, prohibited, or permitted." Rules are the normative pillar, constraining social behavior, conferring responsibilities, privileges, and duties, and thus specifying social obligations that enable social action (Scott

1995). Rules, then, constrain exchange relations by specifying the rights and obligations of each party.

In studying the evolution of institutionalized exchange relationships, theorists such as Commons (1970) argue that institutions are working rules that change gradually as the parties reach pragmatic but temporary agreements on what constitutes reasonable accommodation to the interests of each. This perspective implies that institutional change occurs through a process of rule accumulation and that the rules comprising the institutionalized exchange relationship may be understood by examining the particular but constantly evolving characteristics of the technical environment of the actors (i.e., labor markets, product markets, and technologies).

In this context, we argue that the exchange relationship between members and their representatives is currently organized around a servicing logic and that the authority of unions is based on their ability to provide members with good wages and benefits. We also argue that this logic of union-member relations is inconsistent with labor's current political and economic environment. In this hostile environment, unions increasingly have been unable to provide the services that members have come to expect, prompting a loss of union legitimacy and member commitment. In addition, we argue that to renew itself the labor movement must generate an alternative logic of union-member relations, the mutual-aid logic.

Our analysis suggests that to renew themselves unions must solve two problems simultaneously. At the microlevel of analysis, they must solve the problem of commitment. At the macrolevel of analysis, they must solve the problem of legitimacy. These problems are closely related. In the remainder of this chapter, we examine their implications for the labor movement.

The Problem of Commitment

Union commitment refers to "the strength of an individual's identification with and involvement in a particular organization" (Porter et al. 1974, 604). Most researchers employ Gordon et al.'s (1980) definition of union commitment as the extent to which a person (a) has a strong desire to retain union membership, (b) is willing to exert effort for the union, and (c) believes in the objectives of organized labor. This definition casts union commitment in terms of a combination of union-related attitudes, beliefs, and behavioral intentions. In the last two decades, researchers have conducted a large number of studies on union commitment, and they have demonstrated a relationship between union commitment and engaging in a variety of union activities (Barling, Fullagar, and Kelloway 1992). In their seminal work, for instance, Gordon et al. found that union commitment was strongly correlated with engaging in such activities as serving in an elected office, voting, attending membership meetings, understanding the contract, and filing grievances. Union commitment has also been shown to predict members' willingness to strike and members' willingness to support the union's political activities. Thus, there is strong empirical evidence supporting the notion that commitment is the key to collective power mobilization.

Researchers have also examined the antecedents of union commitment; the two most widely studied antecedents have been members' perceptions of their union's instrumentality and members' attitudes toward the union generally (Barling, Fullagar, and Kelloway 1992). Researchers are divided about the extent to which instrumentality and union attitudes contribute to members' commitment to their unions and the extent to which unions should focus on them in order to enhance members' commitment. Researchers have taken several approaches to these questions (Shore et al. 1994). The first approach, which is consistent with an economic-exchange perspective, focuses on enhancing members' perceptions of their union's instrumentality. The second approach, which is consistent with a social-exchange perspective, focuses on enhancing members' beliefs in unionism and developing the union as a source of support and community. Given the lack of research regarding the relative impact of instrumentality and beliefs on union commitment, theorists remain divided about the relative contribution of the two. Tetrick (1995) argues that maintaining a relationship based on economic exchange will not foster commitment because only social exchange tends to engender feelings of personal obligation, gratitude, and trust. Purely economic exchange does not. Therefore, Tetrick urges unions to make a greater investment in developing prounion attitudes in order to enhance member commitment. Findings on faculty union commitment are consistent with this approach (Sinclair and Tetrick 1995). On the other hand, Kochan (1980) suggests that instrumental-based approaches are likely to offer unions a higher degree of utility than the more "traditional," ideological-based approaches. He found that an interest in enhancing the material and economic benefits of work was the primary factor motivating a prounion vote and that prounion attitudes were not even cited as a cause for a prounion vote.

Newton and Shore (1992, 285) attempt to bridge the gap between the two approaches, arguing unions "need to emphasize both ideological and instrumental issues to promote the kind of active support needed to maintain them." Implicit in Newton and Shore's argument is the notion that attitudes are founded in part on beliefs. Their theory suggests that member attachment to the union is a process that begins with the establishment of instrumentality beliefs. Over time, however, building on these instrumentality beliefs, members develop prounion attitudes, and it is these attitudes that are the most directly predictive of union commitment. This model suggests that the impact of union instrumentality on union commitment may be indirect, mediated by union attitudes; a number of studies provide indirect, empirical support for this model (Shore and Newton 1995; Sverke and Sjoberg 1995). Recently, Bamberger, Kluger, and Suchard (1999) tested such a multivariate model. In a meta-analysis of dozens of union commitment studies, they found union attitudes to be the strongest single predictor of union commitment with an effect size that was approximately double that of union instrumentality.

Overall, the research suggests two dimensions of commitment: one value- or normative-based and the other instrumental-based (Newton and Shore 1992; Sverke and Kuruvilla 1995).

Value- or normative-based commitment refers to the degree of value congruence between the member and the union. The individual's attachment to the union is likely to be higher when his or her values are consistent with the goals of the union than when they are inconsistent with them. Instrumental-based commitment reflects a utilitarian relationship between members and the union, and it is based on the individual member's calculations of the costs and benefits associated with membership. The individual's feelings of loyalty to the union are likely to be high when the benefits of membership are perceived as outweighing its costs, and they are likely to be low when he or she perceives the costs of membership as outweighing the benefits.

Thus research findings on union commitment reflect the two basic ways in which people participate in social life (Selznick 1992). On one hand, people may intensively participate in particular groups, building their life experiences and sense of self around their relationships with group members. Intensive involvement fosters a strong sense of social obligation among group members and makes them normatively committed to the group. Such core participation is exemplified in occupational communities (Salaman 1974). On the other hand, people may participate on a limited basis. Limited involvement fosters a weak sense of social obligation among members and weakens individuals' commitment to the group. Such segmental participation is well exemplified by the modern commercial contract, which limits parties' obligations to one another and provides them with a mechanism for withdrawing from the relationship when things go wrong. Modern life is characterized by a tension between these two modes of participation and commitment. The tension is most difficult in organizations such as trade unions that are dependent on highly committed members who do not have the freedom to leave when they are dissatisfied with the organization and its leaders (Selznick 1992, 186).[2]

Within this context, we argue that members may be committed to their unions in two ways. First they may experience segmented commitment, which is driven by an instrumental orientation to the union and is characterized by their limited involvement in the union. Alternatively, they may experience core commitment, which is driven by a normative orientation to the union and characterized by their intensive involvement with the union. At any point in time, unions are composed of members with both orientations. The problem of viewing commitment as the central point in the analysis of union renewal is that commitment is a micropsychological variable. It involves only the orientation of the member toward the union. The relationship between a union and its members is not determined solely by the attitudes of the members; the relationship is also determined by the mechanisms through which unions secure member commitment.

Logics of Action and Legitimacy

In order to understand the exchange relationship between members and their union, it is necessary to place the findings on commitment within the context of how unions legitimize themselves and elicit commitment from members. As suggested above, we argue that the exchange relationship between unions and their members may be viewed as being organized around alternative logics of union-member relations. Organizations use logics of action to legitimize their authority and elicit commitment from members. A number of theorists use the term "logics of action" to refer to "an interdependent set of representations or constraints that influence action in a given domain" (DiMaggio 1997, 277). Logics are

2. Under the current rules of collective bargaining, all workers employed in a union shop must join the union. If they withdraw from the union, they lose their job. Therefore, they do not have the option of expressing their displeasure with the union by withholding their membership dues or quitting it.

cognitive frameworks that individuals and groups use to guide their behavior as they confront the practical constraints on their lives (Bourdieu 1990). In the context of this book, logics are the cognitive frame that unions use to guide the relationship between themselves and their members. We define labor's "logic of union-member relations" as the cognitive framework guiding union strategies for legitimizing the union to its members, securing the commitment of its members, and attracting new members to the union. We further argue that unions are organized around two logics of union-member relations: the servicing logic and the mutual-aid logic.

The servicing logic is organized around a utilitarian principle of legitimacy, which emphasizes the union's obligation to provide members with excellent benefits for a small cost. According to the servicing logic, members assume a *passive* role toward the union, relying on union leaders to provide them with a variety of services, which include contract bargaining for high wages, excellent benefits, and good working conditions as well as protecting members through the grievance process. Within this context, members do not expect the union to play a central role in their lives, especially outside of the workplace, and feel that their obligations to the union are met by paying dues, attending meetings occasionally, and voting on the contract. Union leaders and members regard these relationships as the legitimate way to organize a union; as long as the union leadership delivers these services, members are likely to regard the union as legitimate and fulfill their limited obligations.

In contrast, the mutual-aid logic is organized around a familial principle of legitimacy, which emphasizes that the union is like an extended family, a corporate entity whose members have multiple obligations to one another and share a collective responsibility for the well-being of one another. According to the mutual-aid logic, members assume an *active* role in the union, involving themselves in every facet of its activities. Distinctions between leaders and members are minimized because everyone is expected to be involved in the union, voluntarily helping to negotiate and enforce collectively bargained contracts as well as acting to protect one another. More important, however, members assume that the union plays a central role in their lives both on and off the job and that commitment is enhanced by their social involvement with one another. Within this context, members' obligations to one another and the union are more open-ended than they are in the servicing logic. To modern ears, the mutual-aid logic may appear to be an odd, even illegitimate, way to organize a union. In the nineteenth century, however, it was regarded as the legitimate way of organizing a union, and it enabled the nascent labor movement to survive in a hostile political and economic environment. Table 1.1 shown here illustrates the interplay between the two union logics and two member-commitment ideals.

Table 1.1 Mechanisms for Gaining Commitment

Individual Commitment	Servicing Logic	Mutual-Aid Logic
Segmented Commitment	Instrumental union legitimacy	Free-rider legitimacy dilemma
Core Commitment	Abandonment legitimacy dilemma	Normative union legitimacy

As we noted above, unions are currently organized around the servicing logic, which is based on a utilitarian principle of legitimacy. The servicing logic is very consistent with the instrumental orientation of members who have a segmented commitment to the union. As long as the union provides satisfactory benefits for a reasonable cost, they are likely to remain committed to the union and see its authority as instrumentally legitimate. A problem arises, however, when the union is unable to provide the services at a reasonable cost. In this instance, members driven by an instrumental attitude toward the union are likely to be less committed to it and perceive it as acting illegitimately.

In contrast, the mutual-aid logic, which is based on a familial principle of legitimacy, is very consistent with the normative orientation of members who have a core commitment to their unions. As long as the leadership acts as though the union is a family and involves members in its activities, individuals are likely to remain committed and regard its authority as normatively legitimate. Problems, however, may arise when the leadership does not act as though the union were a family. In this instance, members with a core commitment are likely to regard the leaders as illegitimate and work to replace them.

The servicing logic, however, is inconsistent with the normative orientation of members who have a core commitment to the union. These members are not necessarily motivated by economic benefits because they believe in the union as a fictive family. Within this context, they may believe that the servicing logic is not quite a legitimate way to organize the union and feel somewhat abandoned by the union. Because they value unionism, however, they are also unlikely to withdraw their commitment. Instead, they are likely to remain committed to their unions; in many instances, they may also work to redirect the union's emphasis away from a utilitarian one to a more familial one. Thus, the dilemma experienced by these members is that, while they feel ideologically abandoned by the union, they feel normatively committed to it as a fictive family.

In contrast, the mutual-aid logic is inconsistent with the instrumental orientation of members who have a segmented commitment to the union. These individuals are likely to regard the logic's multiple obligations as an unreasonable cost and thus act to minimize their involvement with members. Within this context, they may come to view the union as illegitimate. However, if they are able to have their instrumental expectations met for a reasonable expenditure, they are likely to remain instrumentally committed to the union and perceive it as legitimate. Thus these members present a dilemma for other members, who perceive them as free riders, shirking their familial obligations to the union as a collective.

As noted above, unions use logics of action to legitimize their authority and elicit members' commitment. In this book, we will argue that unions find themselves in the position of being organized around the servicing logic of action, have lost members' commitment because they are unable to provide the services expected of them, and consequently, have also lost their legitimacy. We further argue that this means simultaneously generating a new logic of action and increasing members' commitment. The mechanism for this exists, we argue, within the normative orientation of members who have a core commitment to the union. We define these members as constituting a community of memory (Irwin-Zarecka 1994; Zerubavel 1997). Communities of memory recall a group's past by retelling the same "constitutive narrative," by recalling the people who have embodied and exemplified its values, and by involving members in "practices of commitment"—rituals defining "the patterns of loyalty and obligation that keep the community alive" (Bellah et al. 1985, 152–155). These normatively oriented members remember when unions were organized around the mutual-aid logic. In particular, they remember when the terms "brothers and sisters" were more than a rhetorical flourish employed by union leaders. They recall when unions were fictive families, and they argue for the reconstruction of the mutual-aid logic in order to renew their unions. In doing so, they construct practices of commitment, which involve members in reconstructing feelings of family, brotherhood, and sisterhood. Through the process of involvement, members learn that the union is a family for which they share mutual obligations and a collective responsibility and become recommitted to the union.

Servicing Logic and Strategies for Labor Renewal

Unions are currently organized around the servicing logic. As membership has declined, therefore, unions have implemented a variety of practices to increase members' commitment and attract new members (Clawson and Clawson 1999; Masters and Atkin 1999). These strategies attempt to enhance members' commitment by influencing their perceptions of union instrumentality and, to a limited degree, by demonstrating the congruency between members' values and union objectives. Thus, they emphasize the benefits of membership and the union's role in securing those benefits. Regardless of the instrumental or normative orientation of these initiatives, there is an underlying assumption that members prefer a *passive* relationship with their union and, as a result, a tendency to ignore members' active involvement as a factor in building union commitment. This orientation is reflected in Masters and Atkin's review of labor's revitalization strategies when they discuss moving from a servicing union to a "value-added union." They write:

> Philosophically, the biggest difference between the business/servicing and valued-added conceptualizations of unionism is that while the former focused on promoting the immediate interests of union members, the latter emphasizes giving employees (union and nonunion alike) and employers a reason to support unions. The benefits are intended to be durable (competitively sustainable) and transferable across employment relations. Conceptually, unions become more appealing, which is a solution to their present difficulties (Masters and Atkin 1999, 309).

Here, valued-added does not refer to normative or ideological values. Rather, it refers to the utilitarian value of unions to both members and employers.

As a general rule, unions have relied on instrumental strategies, which emphasize a utilitarian relationship between members and the union. As in other exchange relationships, members are thought of as consumers who evaluate the costs and benefits of membership. Thus, unions have sought to attract new members and maintain the commitment of existing members by negotiating favorable collective bargaining agreements and protecting members' jobs. Nevertheless, as noted above, since the 1980s unions have been increasingly unsuccessful in making good on these promises (Kochan, Katz, and McKersie 1994; Bronfenbrenner et al. 1998). Indeed, since President Reagan's firing of the air-traffic controllers, the unions' power to strike has been increasingly eroded by management's ability to replace strikers with nonunion workers. Despite the Teamsters' widely reported successful 1997 strike against the United Parcel Service, unions generally perceive strikes as a dangerous tactic and, since the eighties, have conceded to management's demands to roll back wage increases and reduce benefits. Consequently, "union settlements, after decades of exceeding nonunion adjustments, have not kept pace with nonunion compensation adjustments" (McDonald 1992, 18). In addition, workers have witnessed their unions' inability to prevent plant closings and the loss of members' livelihoods.

Within this context, many unions have lost interest in the traditional collective-bargaining system and sought other mechanisms for protecting member's jobs and increasing workers' benefits. As a result, many have become involved in activities such as mutual gains bargaining, which emphasizes a cooperative rather than an adversarial relationship with management (Kochan and Osterman 1994; Cohen-Rosenthal and Burton 1993). According to the promoters of these activities, labor-management cooperation makes workers more productive, thus increasing American competitiveness and company profits and enabling members to command better wages and benefits. Thus mutual-gains bargaining involves labor and management in a variety of participation activities, such as quality circles, autonomous work teams, and gain-sharing plans. Despite the enthusiasm of some practitioners and academics for these activities, there is little evidence that they have either increased workers' wages or their sense of job security (Shostak 1995; Clawson and Clawson 1999). As Strauss (1995, 343) notes:

> Academicians (such as myself) argue that strong unions and cooperative relations are not only feasible but are good for companies, the economy, and society. Unfortunately, we have few examples of union management cooperation except where the union was already strong. . . . Even though it has been shown that mutual gain strategies can be successful, few companies are buying.

More important, while such activities provide labor with a mechanism by which to participate and become active in *management*, they do little to involve members in the affairs of their own union. Indeed, a number of researchers have noted labor's concern that these programs actually have a negative impact on union commitment because members associate any positive benefit with management (Eaton, Gordon, and Keefe 1992). In unionized plants, these employee-involvement programs have resulted in speed-up and increased stress, leading workers to conclude, "Management simply could not be trusted" (Milkman 1997, 174).

Still other researchers argue that for unions to survive, maintain the commitment of current members, and attract new members to the fold, they must become "full-service unions" (Strauss 1995). For instance, the AFL-CIO operates a program called "Union Privilege Benefits," which offers a variety of new services to its members (Hurd 1998; McDonald 1992). These services include inexpensive credit cards, life insurance, and legal services, and increasingly, they are also being offered to nonunion members, who are designated as non-voting, "associate members" of the union. Although it is hoped that these benefits will increase the commitment of current members and encourage associate members to organize their workplaces, there is little evidence they have done so.

Within the context of the servicing logic, unions have also implemented a variety of value or normative strategies for enhancing the commitment of current members and attracting new members. These strategies focus on creating positive union attitudes in workers; however, like instrumental strategies, they require little or no involvement on the part of members and are framed as another service offered by the union. Typically, they consist of activities designed to promote a positive image of unionism by highlighting its underlying values, especially its commitment to social justice. Unfortunately, many Americans have a negative image of unions, believing that union officials are corrupt, that bargaining agreements establish inefficient work rules and inhibit productivity, and that the wages and benefits received by union members are excessive (Puette 1992). According to Carver (1993, 61), "A positive image is the first step to increasing membership and enhancing union power vis-à-vis employers and Congress."

Since the mid-1980s, labor has conducted a number of media campaigns designed to enhance its public image. In 1988, the AFL-CIO launched a two-year, multimedia campaign, "America Works Best When We Say 'Union, Yes!'"(Shostak 1991; Puette 1992). The campaign's television ads featured prototypical union members thanking organized labor for its contributions to making America work. For instance, a black female clerical assistant in a library was shown thanking labor for providing four months of job-protected maternity leave and a Hispanic registered nurse was shown thanking labor for enabling her to focus on patient care. The ads closed with a shot of the AFL-CIO logo and the American flag. More recently, the American Federation of State, County, and Municipal Employees sponsored a number of ads showing the important functions performed by a variety of government workers (Carver 1993). In 1996, the New York City Central Labor Council launched a radio program, "New

York City at Work." Commenting on the program, Brian McLauglin, the council's president, stated:

> Our goal is to offer union and non-union workers information on those issues that impact the most their abilities to support their families. While we have great respect for the professionalism of the New York media, we feel that the viewpoint of working people is too often under represented in reports and analyses on the great issues of the day. (News Release, June 1996)

Labor has become more active politically, airing commercials and print ads that, while promoting a particular issue, highlight its basic values. For instance, in the mid-1980s, Plumbers and Steamfitters Local 33 in Des Moines, Iowa, ran an ad showing a worried young construction worker returning home from work with the following voiceover (Puette 1992, 149):

> Nine years ago Jack Ferris went to work for a nonunion company. They promised him job security, decent wages, and profit-sharing for his skills as a plumber. Today, Jack's dreams were shattered, so were the promises. He was laid off. Jack and his family have to start over . . . alone. Things might have been different. He could still have his rights if he'd belonged to a union.

During the 1996 presidential and congressional elections, the AFL-CIO ran a number of ads nationally. One ad, which could be altered for local conditions, highlighted the AFL-CIO's support for the minimum wage and targeted congressmen who had voted against such legislation. The ads stated that Congressman "X" voted against the minimum wage because America could not afford it and contrasted his congressional salary with what Americans would make under the minimum wage legislation. Finally, it urged viewers to vote in the upcoming elections by casting their vote for fairness and the dignity of working Americans and their families.

Unions have also sought to underscore their basic concern for improving the lives of all Americans by taking a leadership role in community activities. Since the 1940s, for instance, the AFL-CIO's Community Services Department has conducted thousands of community projects. These projects include operating retraining programs for displaced workers, running public education programs on substance abuse, AIDS, and other health issues, and teaching parenting skills to union and nonunion community members (Perlow 1979; Shostak 1991, 1995). In its partnership with the United Way, Community Services has also assisted in the solicitation and distribution of millions of charitable contributions, and working closely with the Red Cross, it has helped millions in need of disaster relief. Similarly, as part of a labor-community coalition, the Milwaukee Central Labor Council is working to implement an alternative economic plan for revitalizing the metropolitan region (Rogers 1995). Such services highlight labor's basic values, which are well articulated in the remarks of Leo Perlis, former director of AFL-CIO's Community Services, "We are, indeed, our brother's keeper. In our interdependent society, this, after all, is the bottom line."

Labor's media campaigns and community projects appear to be paying off. According to several studies, these efforts are improving labor's public image as a defender of social justice while providing its members with a sense of vigor, aggressiveness, and advocacy for change (S. Douglas 1986; Puette 1992). Americans also seem to be hearing the message that labor is a part of the community and can be relied on to improve the lives of all community members (Lester 1958; Rogers 1995). For instance, Cornfield (1999), reviewing data from the Gallup Poll, finds that, since the 1980s, public support for labor has been on the rise. Still, to date, these efforts, like the instrumental strategies described above, have neither stanched the decline in union membership nor won new adherents to the labor movement.

The Mutual-Aid Logic: An Emergent Labor Phenomenon

Some union activists and researchers have begun to recognize that organized labor's survival depends on a new kind of unionism.[3] Although the form of the new unionism remains elusive, there appears to be an emerging consensus that it will entail the *active* involvement of union members and will result in a high level of value congruency. Underlying this search for a new unionism is the mutual-aid logic of union-member relations, which is well articulated by a former local chairman of the Transportation Communications Union speaking about the need to revitalize unions:

> You want more people to take an active role. Personally, I believe unions should be more involved in people's daily lives, not just their work lives. . . . Union is "family," and I mean that from the bottom of my heart. (Plaganis 1995, 241)

3. See for example Johnston (1998); Heckscher (1998); Nissen (1998); Strauss (1995); Rogers (1995); Masters and Atkin (1999); and Clawson and Clawson (1999).

Strategies consistent with the mutual-aid logic emphasize both the normative and instrumental dimensions of commitment by involving members in union activities. Through their own actions, members learn the benefits of unionism while internalizing its core values of the labor movement.

The organizing model is consistent with the mutual-aid logic (Bronfenbrenner 1993; Muehlenkamp 1991; Johnson 1994). This model stresses the need for unions to "help workers to do for themselves, 'empowering' them rather than having them look to the union as an 'outside' organization providing services to its members" (Fiorito, Jarley, and Delaney 1995, 631). Similarly, Tetrick (1995) argues that union commitment does not occur as a result of a simple exchange between the union and its members. Instead, it occurs dynamically within the context of mutual obligations. The organizing model highlights the mutual obligations union members owe to one another by involving them in solving their collective problems. According to Grabelsky and Hurd (1994, 100):

> [P]roblems are seen as issues around which prospective or current members are organized, and workers learn the essence of unionism by participating in and experiencing collective action.

In 1995, John Sweeney, Richard Trumpka, and Linda Chavez-Thompson were elected to the top offices in the AFL-CIO promising to organize American workers on an unprecedented level. Since taking office, they have begun to restructure the AFL-CIO to reflect the organizing model, shifting its resources from servicing members to involving them in rebuilding the labor movement (Milkman 1998; Juravich 1998; Gapasin 1998). Taking their cue from activist unions such as the Teamsters (IBT), the Service Employees (SEIU), and the Electrical Workers (IBEW), they have established the "Union City Program," which, working through the AFL-CIO's Central Labor Councils, trains local rank-and-file volunteers in the lost art of organizing from the bottom-up (Kriesky 1998).

The key to programs based on the "organizing model" is rank-and-file involvement in reconstituting themselves as worker communities.[4] However, reconstituting community means more than teaching one another about the benefits of unionism and the tactics for winning National Labor Relations Board certification elections in order to obtain those bene-

---

4. For an excellent overview of the many projects that make up labor's current organizing model, see Bronfenbrenner et al. (1998); see especially Fletcher and Hurd (1998a and 1998b) for a typology of organizing models and their limitations.

fits. For instance, Markowitz (1998) compared two organizing strategies in order to assess their impact on workers after the unionizing campaigns ended. The two strategies varied in their levels of participation. She found that workers' participation in the organizing campaigns prefigured their involvement with one another after winning certification. When labor organizers did most of the organizing work, rank-and-file workers had a very low sense of community and were uninvolved with the union after winning its certification. In contrast, when workers were directly involved in organizing their co-workers, they had a high sense of community and remained heavily involved with the union after winning its certification.

Another strategy consistent with the mutual-aid logic is the development of member assistance programs (MAPs), which are peer programs designed to assist members and their families with a variety of personal problems (Bacharach, Bamberger, and Sonnenstuhl 1994). In these programs, union volunteers act as peer counselors, assisting their co-workers with substance abuse problems, psychological disorders, and family and marital difficulties. MAPs highlight that, in order to become a community, unions must do more than organize. As Cornfield et al. (1998, 256) remind us, "To become a community, a local union must become an arena in which workers befriend and help one another." This level of involvement is well expressed in the UAW's Chaplain Program, which is described as "caring people helping hurting people." One UAW member described how, after working his regular third shift, he volunteers as a chaplain:

> I spend a lot of evening and weekend hours visiting members or their loved ones in nearby hospitals. I go to funerals and funeral homes to do what I can to console people. I sit by the bedside of a sick and dying brother or sister.... But it gives me a lift because it means so much to the grieving people left behind. Many do not know how to thank me enough.... [B]eing a chaplain for the local is helping show we're family, that we do care in the UAW about one another. (Schmitt 1995, 49–50)

MAPs are an emergent phenomenon within the American labor movement. Currently, there are no studies that indicate the number of national or local MAPs (Bacharach, Bamberger, and Sonnenstuhl 1996). Nevertheless, we estimate that they are relatively numerous within American unions. For instance, the Labor Assistance Professionals, an occupational association of MAP directors and peer counselors, has grown from less than 100 members in 1994 to approximately 450 in 1998. Likewise, the Employee Assistance Professional Association has a labor division with approximately 500 members. In addition, based on prevalence studies of employee assistance programs, we believe there are currently between 3,000 and 5,000 labor-based MAPs in the United States (Department of Labor 1997; Hartwell et al. 1996).

Although an emergent phenomenon, MAPs are deeply rooted in the nineteenth-century labor movement's mutual-aid programs. MAPs emerged in the 1980s. During this period, employers under pressure from the federal government widely adopted drug testing, which often had the unfortunate consequence of undermining management-sponsored employee assistance programs. With drug testing in place, many substance abusers were summarily discharged rather than treated. At the same time, employer adoption of managed care began to limit workers' access to substance abuse and mental health treatment. Within this context, many unions began adopting MAPs as a strategy for assisting their members and ensuring them of quality health care. As one MAP director stated, "Managed care is forcing consumers and providers to develop different strategies. To do more with less . . . [members] are going to rely more on helping themselves" (Whitehead 1997, 30). Today, MAPs can be found in every geographic area of the country and in a wide variety of unionized settings, including education, retail, manufacturing, transportation, and construction.

While there is little evidence of the effectiveness of MAPs, one study suggests that members' involvement in MAPs is associated with an increase in union commitment. For instance, the director of the Tunnel Workers' MAP observed:

> Drunk sandhogs are hard workers and, when you sober them up, you get even more work out of them. . . . Guys that hadn't worked steady in three years, now they are foremen . . . a shop steward. . . . They didn't [just] stop drinking; they changed their personalities. . . . Now, they are assets to the union. (Sonnenstuhl 1996, 109)

"Community," "family," and "caring." These are the metaphors for the mutual-aid logic of union-member relations. The mutual-aid logic is not new; rather, it has reemerged within the American labor movement. During the nineteenth century, the mutual-aid logic was deeply embedded within American labor. In the twentieth century, it was replaced by the servicing logic. The mutual-aid logic's reemergence is reflected in veteran union members' comments on the dismal state of American unionism and their hopes for its renewal. For instance, a member of the International Brotherhood of Electrical Workers, commenting on his efforts to rebuild a sense of community in his union, stated:

> It hurts to know that in my local, which is like my home, the concept of brotherhood or solidarity is really gone. It's going to take time to rebuild. . . . Our members, my brothers and sisters, are not in the right space. They all should care that some of us are out of work—that some of us are out of health insurance. . . Those well-off members don't care. So I say, "Shame on us!" . . . There are a few of us speaking up . . . but we've a long way to go (Murphy 1995, 244).

The mutual-aid logic is also, as Hurd and Fletcher (forthcoming) remind us in their study of the organizing model, very fragile, subject to the labor movement's inertia. At both the local and national levels, labor remains organized around the servicing logic. Indeed, as the remark just quoted above suggests, both union leaders and members generally regard the servicing logic as the legitimate way of organizing their relationships and the mutual-aid logic as illegitimate. This presents a serious problem for the labor movement generally because, in the current hostile political and economic environment, unions are increasingly unable to deliver the wages and benefits that members have come to expect. As a result, unions are losing their instrumental legitimacy at the very moment when they need to mobilize their members to overcome the economic and political forces at work.

As will be suggested in this volume, some unions have responded to the crisis of instrumental legitimacy by reestablishing their normative legitimacy. In the last decade, at the height of its crisis of instrumental legitimacy, we have witnessed the expansion of the union's role in providing social, psychological, and emotional support to its members. Throughout the country, MAPs, which are founded on the sense of labor communalism, have been expanding. At the very point of labor history when questions have been raised about labor's ability to deliver on such instrumental bread-and-butter issues, many unions are returning to their historical communal function, developing programs that embody voluntarism, fraternalism, and sorority. The reemergence of the mutual-aid logic as the basis of normative union legitimacy may offer the labor movement a mechanism for reinvigorating its members' core commitment. It is the premise of this book that in examining the mechanisms by which MAPs involve members in caring for one another we will glean better insight into the cyclical history of the labor movement—more specifically, the cyclical history of union-member relationships as it varies from instrumentalism to communalism.

In the following chapters, we focus on the relationship between the mutual-aid logic and servicing logic within the labor movement and three local unions. Our purpose in this study is to discover how the two logics interact so that we might discern something of labor's future. Within this context, we focus on several guiding questions in order to construct a sociohistorical analysis of the two logics: (1) How did the early American labor movement come to perceive the mutual-aid logic as a legitimate way to organize unions? (2) How did the early mutual-aid logic loose its legitimacy? (3) How did the servicing logic emerge within the labor movement and come to be regarded as the legitimate way of organizing unions? (4) How is it that the mutual-aid logic is reemerging at this historical moment? Answers to these questions can help labor and social scientists understand how the reemergent mutual-aid logic might be used to enhance union commitment and the process by which it might gain legitimacy in the future.

This study grew out of a field investigation of MAPs in the transportation industry (Bacharach, Bamberger, and Sonnenstuhl 1994). In order to understand the MAP helping processes, we used a variety of ethnographic methods to gain analytical insight. In the course of our interviews with peer counselors, we discovered that many of the counselors thought of themselves as reconstructing a part of their union's past history. This was most evident in the remarks of one railroader:

> Hell, we aren't doing anything different than what people on the rails have always done to survive. We're just helping one another. The brotherhoods were all established as mutual-aid societies. Some of us may have forgotten that, but some of us haven't. We're just doing what our grandfathers did before us.

Peer counselors who were members of the Association of Flight Attendants and the Transport Workers Union expressed similar sentiments. Armed with these insights, we expanded our investigation into the development of these unions and generated the sociohistorical analyses of the mutual-aid logic and servicing logic, presented in chapters 3, 4, and 5.

On a more technical note, the data for the material presented in chapters 3, 4, and 5 were collected over a three-year period. We collected these data in three organizations: the CSX Railroad, the Association of Flight Attendants, and the Transport Workers Union under a grant from the National Institute on Drug Abuse (DA 06995–03). In each organization, we used a variety of data collection techniques, including in-depth interviews, participant observation, and archival materials. Within the Association of Flight Attendants, we interviewed sixty-six flight attendants, AFA union leaders, in-flight supervisors, and base managers. On the CSX Railroad, we conducted fifty-five interviews with railroaders, union leaders, and managers. Within the Transport Workers Union, we conducted interviews with thirty-six union members and officers. In each organization, we also collected a dozen interviews with union veterans, who were able to help us understand how their unions had changed over the years. Within each organization, we also participated in a variety of union events, including annual meetings, training programs, and social activities such as picnics, golf tournaments, and a concert at the Grand Old Opry. Our data collection left us with hundreds of taped interviews and reams of field notes. All of these data were eventually analyzed using the constant comparative method, a technique for the generation of analytical insight rather than the testing of theory (Glaser and Strauss 1967; Strauss 1987).

In chapters 3, 4, and 5, we present our analytical insights about the relationship between the mutual-aid logic and the servicing logic. These chapters are organized as case studies of each of the organizations. In each case, we discuss the role of the mutual-aid logic in the union's development and the subsequent replacement of that logic by the servicing logic as members became less dependent on one another and more dependent on the leadership to negotiate for employer-provided benefits. In each case, we also examine the development of the union's MAP. Specifically, we demonstrate how, in each union, the caring process comprising each MAP is helping to re-create the mutual-aid logic within the union. We conclude each case with a brief discussion of how members' involvement with their MAP is renewing their commitment and the factors constraining the mutual-aid logic's full emergence.

Although our analytical insights were generated from three case studies in the transportation industry, we believe that they can also be applied to other unionized sectors of the American labor market. As noted above, we estimate that there are between three thousand and five thousand MAPs in the United States. Our discussions with members of the Labor Assistance Professionals and the Employee Assistance Professional Association suggest that there is nothing unique about the emergence of MAPs within the transportation industry. For instance, MAPs exist in a wide range of unionized settings, including construction, manufacturing, service, and the public sector. In each of these settings, members initially built their unions around the mutual-aid logic, which atrophied as the servicing logic took hold. In many of these settings, we have discussed this shift with veteran union members and MAP advocates. Like the members of the three cases discussed here, many of them too lament the loss of mutual aid in their unions, remembering when things used to be different. Over and over, in these conversations MAP advocates say, "That is like us. We are returning to the old ways of members helping members." Within this context, we believe that our analytical insights appear to accurately reflect their experiences as well.

Still, our analytical insights should not be taken as definitive. We encourage other researchers to confirm, modify, or refute the idea that the insights from our three case studies can be applied generally to other unionized settings. Before presenting our three case studies, however, we first examine the relationship between the mutual-aid logic and servicing logic in the American labor movement.

2 Cycles of the Logics of Union-Member Relations

The study of institutions is deeply rooted in the history of the social sciences, where they are regarded as an antidote to rational-actor models. In contrast to these models, theorists emphasize that the ability of actors to act rationally is institutionally constrained.[1] The concept of institutions is one of the oldest in the social sciences and theorists have defined institutions in many different ways. Therefore, it is useful to begin our discussion with a simple observation made by Selznick (1957, 16–17), "The most significant meaning of [the term] 'to institutionalize' is to infuse with meaning beyond the technical requirements of the task at hand." That is, past practices become valued in their own right so that actors' future decisions are constrained by those valued past practices. Within this context, social scientists have studied a wide range of institutions whose accumulated practices constrain the rational behavior of actors. Within economics, for instance, Commons (1924) argued that the decisions of individuals and firms are constrained by "rules of conduct," imperfect and pragmatic solutions reconciling the past conflicts of actors and defining the limits within which they could pursue their self-interests. Similarly, within sociology, Durkheim ([1893] 1949; [1912] 1961) emphasized the collective normative framework that supplies the noncontractual elements of contract. According to Durkheim, society could not be based strictly on utilitarian exchange since any exchange agreement could

---

1. Space does not permit a detailed review of institutional theories within the social sciences. For useful discussions, see Powell and DiMaggio 1991; Scott 1995; Stinchcombe 1997; Brinton and Nee 1998; Edelman 1990, 1992; Sutton et al. 1994; Leblebici et al. 1991; Davis et al. 1994; Barley and Tolbert 1997; and Clemens and Cook 1999.

not be undertaken without some assurance that the parties would not violate the contract. Therefore, he argued that any contract requires pre-contractual solidarity, a basic feeling of trust between the parties involved, which is derived culturally from their collective beliefs, knowledge, and representations.

Within organizational theory, researchers disenchanted with theories portraying efficiency as the driving force behind decision-making have rediscovered institutional theory (Zucker 1977; DiMaggio and Powell 1983). In their work, the neoinstitutionalists emphasize the critical role of legitimacy in undermining actors' rational decision making, arguing that organizations sacrifice efficiency in order to maintain themselves in good standing with other actors in their organizational field. According to Meyer and Rowan (1977, 340),

> Institutionalized products, services, policies, and programs function as powerful myths, and many companies adopt them ceremonially. But conformity to institutionalized rules often conflicts sharply with efficiency criteria; conversely, to coordinate and control activity and promote efficiency undermines an organization's ceremonial conformity and sacrifices its support and legitimacy.

Within this context, neoinstitutionalists have examined the adoption and diffusion of a variety of institutionalized practices and programs. Organizations adopt them primarily because they value being seen by other actors in their organizational fields as reliable actors, utilizing the "most up-to-date" methods (Tolbert and Zucker 1983; Sutton and Dobbin 1996). Recently, institutional theorists have begun to turn their attention to understanding the processes of institutional change, asking how particular practices and programs are institutionalized and deinstitutionalized (Oliver 1992; Bacharach, Bamberger, and Sonnenstuhl 1996).

In this chapter, we use an institutional framework in order to understand the processes by which the logics of union-member relations have been institutionalized and deinstitutionalized within the American labor movement. We examine the historical significance of these logics in the emergence, coalescence, regulation, fragmentation, and renewal of the American labor movement. Specifically, we argue that the logics of union-member relations are cyclical and that the mutual-aid logic, as a mechanism for gaining member's commitment, was instrumental in the labor movement's emergence and coalescence. We also maintain that, since the thirties, a period characterized by regulation and fragmentation, labor has used the servicing logic to gain members' commitment. Finally, we maintain that the mutual-aid logic, which has been in abeyance, may be reemerging within the American labor movement, renewing the legitimacy of unions, and reinvigorating workers' commitment to unionism.

Following Scott (1995, 33), we define institutions as consisting of "cognitive, normative, and regulative structures and activities that provide stability and meaning to social behavior. Institutions are transported by various carriers—cultures, structures, and routines—and they operate at multiple levels of jurisdiction." By the cognitive component of an institution, we mean the way in which actors think about their world. Within this context, we agree with other cognitive theorists that "what a creature does is, in large part, a function of the creature's internal representation of its environment" (D'Andrade, 1984, 88). By the normative component of an institution, we mean those "rules that introduce a prescriptive, evaluative, and obligatory dimension into social life" (Scott 1995, 37). Normative considerations guide actors in deciding what one ought to value and how things ought to be done. By the regulative component of an institution, we mean those processes constraining and regularizing behavior: rule setting, monitoring, and sanctioning. Regulative components of an institution include informal mechanisms such as shaming as well as more formal mechanisms such as those established by the government to enforce compliance with the law. As Scott argued, these components (i.e., cognitive, normative, and regulative) are carried by the cultures, structures, and routines incorporated in those institutions.

Culture has a variety of meanings in the social sciences (Crane 1994; DiMaggio 1997). Its most basic definition is a system of meaning or symbolic framework, perceived by actors to be both objective and external, which provides orientation and guidance (Goffman 1974; Maines 1977; Geertz 1973). This system is composed of a variety of cultural elements from which actors construct reality; these cultural elements include beliefs, language, typifications, rituals, and stories. According to Swidler (1986), culture is a repertoire or "tool-kit" of habits, skills, and styles from which actors construct strategies of action. Culture constrains actors directly by limiting their perceptions of reality and indirectly by providing them with strategies of action, cultural competencies that often are not readily adaptable to other circumstances. On the other hand, culture, by providing a tool-kit for reconstructing perceptions and strategies of action, also empowers actors. Within this context, logics of union-member relations are symbolic frameworks guiding union members in their relationships with one another, and their meaning is encoded in the cultural forms members use to make sense of their world. For example, miners live in tightly knit occupational communities and use a variety of stories and rituals to reinforce the mutual obligations expected of one another, especially while working in dangerous circumstances (Sonnenstuhl 1996). However, union leaders may also use these forms to reframe union-member relationships (Voss 1996). For example, building on workers' Civil War experiences, some union leaders advocated developing unions around a military model of organizing rather than the more familiar fraternal model (Clemens, 1996).

While culture provides the crucible in which actors construct strategies of action, structure represents the more persistent aspect of behavior (Giddens 1984; Barley and Tolbert 1997). Following Scott (1995, 53), we define structure as "patterned expectations connected to networks of social positions: role systems," and we argue that the logics of union-member relations are embedded in the roles of union members. For instance, the servicing logic is embedded in the current structure of most unions by limiting members' participation to a small number of roles; consequently, members learn to depend on the leadership rather than themselves to take care of their needs (Barling et al. 1992). Structure also constrains and empowers actors. Roles constrain actors by defining members' obligations to one another; however, they also empower members by providing them with opportunities for constructing new strategies of action. For instance, union officers are elected by the rank and file to serve their needs. Within this context, presidents of unions whose members drink heavily, fearing that they will not be reelected, are often reluctant to implement alcoholism programs for workers (Trice and Beyer 1982). In these instances, alcoholism programs are likely to be implemented by rank-and-file members who are not similarly constrained and, therefore, feel freer to construct new beliefs about members' drinking behavior.

Logics of union-member relations are also embedded in workers' routines, which are "patterned actions that reflect the tacit knowledge of actors — deeply engrained habits and procedures based on inarticulated knowledge and beliefs" (Scott 1995, 54). A number of theorists have described repetitive performance programs as central ingredients in the reliability and stability of organizations (March and Simon 1958; Nelson and Winter 1982). Similarly, logics of union-member relations are embedded in the habits and work routines of workers. During the nineteenth century, for example, the mutual-aid logic was aptly expressed in members' everyday interactions as they built their lives within a workers' community (e.g., Ducker 1983). It is poignantly illustrated in the routine caring workers provided to injured co-workers, a sentiment aptly expressed in the poem, "My Partner," written by a member of the Western Federation of Miners, Joseph Rodgers, for his partner, Bill:

The southern heat, the arctic's chill
Have taxed the nature from our blood
For oft alarmed — sternly still,
We've at each other's sick bed stood.
Ah! When disease arranged a deadly war,
Bill acted nurse a dozen times more.
(Quoted in Derickson 1988, 71)

In this chapter we examine the institutional history of the logics of union-member relations, focusing on the manner in which the logics are embedded within the labor movement and on the factors that activate the logics of union-member relations. By embedded, we mean that the logics are carried within labor's culture, structure, and the routines of its members (Jepperson 1991; Scott 1995). As Friedland and Alford (1991, 248–249) suggest, logics are "symbolically grounded" in labor's culture and "organizationally structured" within its administrative apparatus and the routines of members' work lives. Such grounding and structuring gives the logic a sense of cognitive legitimacy, permitting members to take it for granted as the correct way to organize their activities.

More specifically, we argue that the logics of union-member relations are carried within the labor movement as illustrated in Table 2.1. During periods when the mutual-aid logic guides union-member relations, labor's culture will be highly communal; its structure will be participatory, and members' work routines will be characterized by intensive involvement with one another. During periods when the servicing logic guides union-member relations, however, labor's culture will be weakly communal, its structure will be oligarchical, and members' work routines will be characterized by their partial involvement with one another.

Table 2.1 Carriers and Logics of Union-Member Relations

Carriers	Mutual-Aid Logic	Servicing Logic
Culture	high communal	low communal
Structure	participatory	oligarchy
Work Routines	intensive involvement	partial involvement

As Commons maintained, institutions are working rules that the parties change in response to their shifting environment. In this context, if we consider changing logics of union-member relations as a key to understanding the labor movement as an institution, we need to consider at least three factors activating the shift from one logic to another: (1) the technical environment in which labor must operate, (2) management's philosophy about its relationship with labor, and (3) the legal environment for labor-management relations. By the technical environment, we mean the technology union members use to do their work as well as the economic and labor markets within which the union must operate. By management philosophy, we mean that, although labor-management relations may be characterized as adversarial, depending on circumstances, management may either reject working with labor entirely or seek to co-opt labor to its own ends. By legal environment, we mean the extent to which government supports unions as legitimate actors in the workplace. These activating factors suggest that labor's logic of union-member relations are shaped by its interactions with management, and as Friedland and Alford (1991, 248–249) suggest, logics are also "politically defined and technically and materially constrained." More specifically, we propose that the logics of union-member relations are activated as illustrated in Table 2.2. The mutual-aid logic is activated during periods when the technical environment is characterized by rapid changes in technology and markets, management is rejecting of labor, and the legal environment is hostile to unions. Conversely, the servicing logic is activated during periods when the technical environment is stable, management is able to co-opt labor, and the legal environment is supportive of unions. We further argue that, during periods when the legal environment is supportive of unions, labor, in addition to experiencing the cognitive legitimacy conferred by its institutional carriers, achieves the regulative legitimacy conferred by federal and state legislation.

Table 2.2 Activating Factors and Logics of Union-Member Relations

Activating Factors	Mutual-Aid Logic	Servicing Logic
Technical Environment	rapid change	stable
Management Philosophy	rejecting	co-opting
Legal Environment	hostile	supportive

In the remainder of this chapter, we examine the relationship between the mutual-aid logic and servicing logic within the American labor movement. First, we examine the origins of the mutual-aid logic in the emergent American labor movement, the factors shaping this logic, and its role in the federal government's legislative support for labor in the thirties. Then, we trace how, partially as a function of regulative legitimacy, labor began to adopt a servicing logic as a mechanism for gaining commitment and the mutual-aid logic atrophied into a state of abeyance or institutional "hibernation." We conclude the chapter with a brief discussion of the possible reemergence of the mutual-aid logic in the 1990s.

American Culture: Cycles of Communalism and Individualism

Although the United States is often glorified for its emphasis on individualism, this is an inaccurate depiction of American culture, which also values community. Throughout history, mutual aid has been a critical factor in the building and maintenance of all human groups (Katz 1993; Kropotkin[1903] 1989). During the Middle Ages, for instance, community members formed guilds, voluntary associations based on occupation, to provide for one another's mutual aid. According to guild statutes, members were required to demonstrate brotherly and sisterly feelings toward one another, to bring their quarrels to the guild's tribunal and abide by its decisions, and to support one another in times of adversity. Throughout Europe, during the eighteenth and nineteenth centuries, as a reaction to the process of industrialization, workers created friendly societies, multifunctional organizations that provided members with loans, medical insurance, and burial funds and that:

> joined the language of Christian charity and the slumbering imagery of "brotherhood" . . . with the social affirmations of Owenite socialism. . . . In times of emergency, unemployment, strikes, sickness, childbirth, then it was the poor "who helped everyone his neighbor." (Thompson 1963, 422–423)

Likewise, deeply rooted in American culture is an ethic of mutual aid. Commenting on his 1831 visit to America, Tocqueville observed:

> Americans of all ages, all conditions, and all dispositions constantly form associations. . . . Whenever at the head of some new undertaking you see the government in France, or a man of rank in England, in the United States you will be sure to find an association. . . . In the United States associations are established to promote the public safety, commerce, industry, morality, and religion. (Quoted in Schmidt 1980, 3)

Had Tocqueville visited America fifty years later, he would have been even more impressed with the number of fraternal organizations "sprouting all over the American landscape, like mushrooms after a spring rain, by the scores and hundreds" (Schmidt 1980, 3).

According to some social theorists, there is a dilemma at the heart of American culture, which values both individualism and communalism (Hewitt 1989; Erikson 1976). This dilemma may be glimpsed throughout history as Americans have struggled to balance these values. According to the Puritans, for instance, society was not based on a utilitarian contract but on a covenant of brotherhood, "defined by the common values and goals to which the members committed themselves and which gave to the individuals within it a 'common soul'" (McWilliams 1973, 123). Therefore, while encouraging members to be successful in their callings, the colonial Protestant churches also exhorted parishioners to be temperate and contribute to the common good (Conroy 1991). Similarly, republicanism saw the War of Independence as purifying Americans of their selfishness and making them into virtuous citizens who would pursue the public good (Lender and Martin 1987). During the early part of the nineteenth century, Americans participated in a number of social movements, including temperance, religious revivalism, and abolition, all of which were concerned with renewing the young republic's commitment to communalism in the face of the industrial revolution. Likewise, during the Progressive Era and the New Deal, Americans struggled to re-create bonds of mutual aid in order to counteract economic self-interest run amok.

The struggle to balance individualism and communalism continues today in Americans' quest for a sense of community, a place of warmth and support in a world seemingly driven by self-interest (Bellah et al. 1991; Wolfe 1998). Commenting on the small-group movement, Wuthnow (1994, 12) writes:

Small groups are a significant feature of what holds our society together. . . . Small groups draw people out of themselves, pull them out of their isolated lives, and put them in the presence of others where they can share their needs and concerns, make friends, and become linked to wider social networks. Small groups provide a way of transcending our most self-centered interests. . . . [They demonstrate] that we are a communal people who, even amidst the dislocating tendencies of our society, are capable of banding together in bonds of mutual support.

Writing about American politics, Schlesinger (1986, 40) argues that Americans' preoccupation with individualism and communalism is cyclical and reflects generational experiences. Periods of public purpose ultimately exhaust people who find they do not have time and energy "to save the nation and cherish one's family"; thus, periods of private interest arise as a reaction to the demands of public purpose. This retreat replenishes the self, family, and the private economy; nevertheless, it produces its own excesses of corruption in business and government as people pursue individual wealth at the expense of the commonwealth. Thus, the excesses of individualism call forth the communal spirit of public purpose as Americans struggle to bring their values back into balance. This cycle is neither automatic nor self-enforcing, rather, it takes people to make the cycle work.

> Those who believe in public purpose must interpret events, press issues and devise remedies. They must rise above those worthy special interests — labor, women, blacks, old folks and the rest — that have become their electoral refuge and regain a commanding national vision of the problems and prospects of the republic. (Schlesinger 1986, 45–46)

Just as American society cycles between the poles of communalism and individualism, the labor movement may be understood as being driven by a similar dilemma expressed in its movement from a mutual-aid logic to a servicing logic and back to a reemergent mutual-aid logic.

The Labor Movement and Its Cycle of Union-Member Relations

The American labor movement developed around the mutual-aid logic of union-member relations. Mutual aid was a common organizing frame in the nineteenth century, deeply embedded in the culture, structure, and routines of workers' lives; that is, much of American life was organized around workers' intensive involvement with one another on and off the job. Within this context, mutual aid provided a ready vocabulary for articulating workers' grievances against their employers and organizing themselves into unions (Clawson 1989). Early labor historians such as Commons and his students ([1916] 1966) focused on the development of "business unionism," conceiving of unions primarily as economic institutions designed to wrest fair pay from employers, who raised wages only when forced to by unions. Since the 1960s, however, labor historians have focused on the union as a cultural institution, highlighting workers' sense of themselves as communities of solidarity (Aronowitz 1992).[2] As Tannenbaum (1921, 60) observed, unions reflect "the moral identity and psychological unity men always discover when working together." In industries as diverse as mining, shoemaking, steelmaking, construction, railroading, printing, and clothing, the intense involvement of workers on and off the

2. See, for example, Thompson 1963; Gutman 1975; Montgomery 1979; Ducker 1983; Derickson 1988; Johnson 1978; Ducker 1983; Derickson 1988; and Lipset, Trow, and Coleman 1956.

job helped create and sustain workers' efforts to unionize (Cornfield and Hodson 1993; Klandermans 1986). The early unions, then, were cultural institutions because, in addition to providing such economic benefits as medical insurance and old-age pensions, they were centers of brotherhood and sisterhood offering entertainment, education, and moral uplift. They taught the value of unionism by involving members in activities such as visiting the sick, caring for deceased members' families, and organizing community events such as dances and picnics. Workers believed that mutual aid was "both integral to the union and desirable" and structured their relationships accordingly (Ducker 1983:168).

Prior to the American Revolution, workers structured their lives around their belief in mutual aid. At this time, the colonies were inhabited by farmers and shopkeepers, who as employers had specific obligations to care for their workers (Selznick 1969; Filippelli 1984). Under the apprenticeship system, for instance, parents apprenticed their sons to master craftsmen to learn a trade (Rorabaugh 1986). The craftsmen took the children into their homes and cared for them in good as well as hard times. In addition to learning the skills of the trade, apprentices within the context of the family learned the values and moral obligations associated with craftsmanship. The period of apprenticeship was usually for seven years, after which the new journeymen often remained in the employ and family of the master craftsmen. In larger communities such as Boston, Philadelphia, and New York, the trades established mutual-aid societies, often composed of both journeymen and masters, to provide sickness and death benefits and recreational activities for their members (Dulles and Dubofsky 1984).

Changes in the existing social system often precipitate the emergence of new social movements (Wuthnow 1987), and American unions developed as workers reacted to changing employment relationships. Shortly after the Revolutionary War, trade societies, as the first unions were called, began to emerge from craft mutual-aid societies (Commons et al. [1916] 1966). The unions emerged as master craftsmen, responding to improved economic conditions, absented themselves from the production process and increasingly took on the role of merchant capitalists. Until then, it had been accepted practice for the masters and journeymen to mutually set wages on the basis of their common knowledge about the cost of production. As merchant capitalists, the masters began to do so unilaterally. The journeymen responded by admonishing the masters to comply with the traditional practice and by striking when they did not comply. Within this context, the Philadelphia Typographical Society's 1786 strike against their employers, who refused to pay the six dollar weekly rate that had long been customary in printing, is regarded as the first trade union strike in America. Similarly, journeymen shoemakers, or as they were called at the time, "cordwainers," cited the arrogation of their right to set prices as one of the grievances that led them to form a separate mutual-aid society from their masters and to strike in 1792.

Although unions first emerged in reaction to the masters' new management philosophy, the labor movement developed slowly because the legal environment was hostile to unions. Courts regarded union actions such as the closed shop, strikes and picketing as conspiracies in restraint of trade (Orren 1991, 1992; Tomlins 1992). They argued that, under English common law, unions were conspiracies because they intimidated and coerced workers already under implied contracts to leave their places of employment. Therefore, siding with employers, the courts issued injunctions and fines against unions seeking to exert pressure on employers by picketing, striking, and distributing scab lists.

Another factor hindering the development of the labor movement was the economy. During periods of economic growth, workers organized to form unions and won concessions from their employers; however, during periods of economic downturn, union sympathizers lost their jobs and their organizations collapsed (Dulles and Dubofsky 1984; Sloane and Witney 1985). For instance, when depression engulfed the economy in 1819, most of those unions collapsed but when the economy improved in 1822, the labor movement's prospects improved as well. Between 1822 and 1837, new crafts were unionized, the first central labor unions were created, the Workingmen's party was formed, and the first national workers' organization was established. By 1836, approximately 300,000 workers were unionized, constituting 6.5 percent of the labor force. When depression hit in 1837, the movement collapsed again. This cycle of collapse and revival continued until the 1890s (Dulles and Dubofsky 1984).

Each time, as the labor movement reemerged, workers organized themselves around the mutual-aid logic, emphasizing their obligations to support one another. In most instances, like the printers and shoemakers, workers built their unions on the basis of their crafts. In other instances, workers used different mobilizing structures for recruiting members; nevertheless, they still used the mutual-aid logic to organize themselves. This phenomenon is well illustrated by women's efforts to unionize the Lowell textile mills, in which they organized all of the mill workers, regardless of their occupation.

Initially, the owners proposed to employ New England farm women from the surrounding area and turn the mills into a combination of private enterprise, finishing school, and moral reform society (Vogel 1977; Dublin 1992). While seeking to improve manufacturing conditions, the owners were also seeking a docile work force. As one employer observed, "Women are much more ready to follow good regulations . . . and do not clan together as the men do against the overseers" (quoted in Filippelli 1984, 44). In 1834, when the mill owners tightened work rules, cut wages, and fired workers for minor offenses, the women organized the Factory Girls Association and struck the mills. The Factory Girls Association emerged at Lowell because the women existed in a kinship and friendship network, which was reinforced by their communal working and living experiences at Lowell. According to Dublin (1992), employment had not recast women within a completely individualistic mold. Women continued to provide crucial support to one another, as neighbors and family members had done for years in the countryside. They recruited one another into the mills, secured jobs for each other, and helped newcomers make the numerous adjustments called for in a very new and different setting. Although the 1834 strike was short lived, the Factory Girls' strike of 1837 shut the mills down for several months; in the 1840s, the women formed the Female Labor Reform Association, which became Lowell's leading labor organization and a national center for the ten-hour movement.

The mutual-aid logic was also evident in craft workers' involvement in the early temperance movement (Blocker 1989). Within the crafts, temperance was one response to the emergence of large manufacturing establishments and the economic depression of 1837–1843. Many master craftsmen lost their shops. Unemployed, they were forced to work as journeymen or foremen in the new manufacturing establishments. As economic conditions turned harsher, many crafts added a temperance theme to the protective functions of their mutual-aid societies. This theme blamed the hard economic times on workers' intemperate habits and stressed that their mutual survival meant helping one another embrace sobriety and frugality.

The most successful workers' temperance organization was the Washington Temperance Society, which was established in 1840 and emphasized members' role in helping one another live sober lives (Tyrell 1979). The Washingtonians recruited members with spellbinding stories of their hardships from drinking, their inability to control their desires to drink, and their new found abstinence, which allowed them to live productive lives and care for their families. The Washingtonian program consisted of requiring members to sign a pledge of total abstinence and doing whatever was necessary to help one another maintain sobriety. The Washingtonians quickly became a mass movement; by March 1842, in New York City, there were at least thirty-eight Washingtonian organizations, many representing specific crafts.[3]

When prosperity returned in 1843, workers' experiences with the Washingtonians played a critical role in reviving the labor movement. Many of the movement's new leaders came out of the Washingtonians, where they learned how to speak publicly about their recovery experiences and the role of mutual aid in becoming sober. These oratorical skills were critical in attracting new members to the labor movement and the Washingtonian ideas about temperance and mutual aid became a reoccurring theme in the emergent labor movement (Blocker 1989). Instead of forsaking their drunken brethren, as their employers did, the unions chose to support them, arguing, "Never forsake a brother — if he fail once, twice, or even a third time [to become sober], receive him again" (quoted in Faler 1974, 393).

The early unionists did not invent the mutual-aid logic. Rather, the mutual-aid logic as the basis for member commitment was a common organizing frame for workers prior to the American Revolution, and unionists adapted it to their own organizing needs. Indeed, as the case of the Lowell textile workers illustrates, the logic was deeply embedded in the women's kinship and friendship networks, and they carried it over into the routines composing their work relationships, while also using it to construct the culture and structure of the Factory Girls Association. The mutual-aid logic developed as workers reacted to their changing environment. Increasingly, their environment was defined by new manufacturing technologies designed to undercut their skills, by a turbulent economy that undercut their employment, by hostile owners and managers who fought their attempts to organize, and by a court system that conceived of unions as conspiracies in constraint of trade. Within this context, the mutual-aid logic provided the early unions with normative legitimacy and workers with a continuing source of dignity and sense of community, while also enabling them to attract new workers to the early labor movement. During periods of economic hardship, co-worker mutual aid also provided a safety net for workers and their families, often making the difference between life and death.

3. Although the Washingtonians died out in the mid-1840s, this workers' movement was the model for many subsequent fraternal organizations dedicated to reforming drunkards, including the Good Samaritans; Sons of Temperance; the Rechabites; the Temple of Honor; the Red, Blue, and White Ribbon Clubs; Alcoholics Anonymous; and Secular Organization for Sobriety. The Washingtonians also were the model for the first asylums treating drunkards. For discussions of these fraternal organizations, see Blumberg 1991; Blocker 1989; Lender and Martin 1987.

Finally, our discussion suggests that neoinstitutionalists are correct when they argue that, in many instances, practices are diffused to new circumstances isomorphically, providing them with cognitive legitimacy, and the mechanism for this diffusion is analogy (DiMaggio and Powell 1983; DiMaggio 1997). The early unionists recognized that the unions were analogous to their fraternal craft relations and structured their relations accordingly. Framing the early unions within the familiar context of mutual aid facilitated the recruitment of new members by conferring a degree of cognitive and normative legitimacy on the early unions. However, as our discussion also suggests, isomorphism does not necessarily confer regulative legitimacy because the courts defined union activities as illegal.

Mutual Aid and Movement Coalescence

The mutual-aid logic was instrumental in the coalescence of the American labor movement. By coalescence, we mean that permanent unions were established to organize workers. The first permanent unions were developed in the latter half of the nineteenth century. The most successful permanent labor organization was the American Federation of Labor (AFL), which was established in 1881; for the next half century, it was the primary labor movement organization in the United States. Although the AFL was committed to organizing workers according to craft, it also organized many according to industry. For instance, the textile and mining unions organized all workers in an industry, regardless of skill level. According to Morris (1958), there were only a few pure craft unions in the AFL; the majority was composed of both skilled craftsmen and unskilled workers.

During the coalescence stage, the culture of both craft and industrial unions continued to emphasize informal forms of mutual aid within workers' communities (Derickson 1988; Cooper 1987). For instance, long after the Western Federation of Miners built hospitals to care for their members, workers continued to look after the families of sick members and nurse them when they returned home. Similarly, cigarmakers socialized with, and supported, one another on and off the job even though the union had an elaborate formal benefits program for members. However, under the guidance of the AFL, the structure of craft and industrial unions began to change when they developed formal mutual-aid programs for their members. These programs were intended as an added inducement for workers to join unions and retain their membership in hard times.

Samuel Gompers (1898, 1900), the AFL's first president, believed in the principle of voluntarism, the belief that labor and management should voluntarily reach agreement on how to manage their differences, free from government interference. He believed that voluntarism resonated with the traditional American emphasis on voluntary associations and that labor's provision of mutual-aid benefits cemented rank-and-file loyalty to unions that alone were responsible for protecting workers during periods of hardship:

> I saw clearly that we had to do something to make it worthwhile to maintain continuous membership, for a union that could hold members only during a strike could not be a permanent constructive and conserving force in industrial life. The union must develop within itself cohesive forces that would make for continuous effort. . . . An out-of-work benefit, provisions for sickness and death appealed to me. Participation in such beneficent undertakings would undoubtedly hold members even when payment of dues might be a hardship. (Gompers [1925] 1984, 54)

Unions gradually extended the scope of their mutual-aid programs; by 1928, unions were the primary providers of mutual-aid benefits to their members (Kennedy 1908; U.S. Bureau of Labor Statistics 1928; Sackman 1949). Among the mutual-aid benefits provided to members through union dues were: (1) health, disability, and unemployment insurance, (2) health and welfare programs such as old age homes, sanitariums, clinics, and hospitals, (3) pensions, (4) housing, and (5) recreational activities such as music and sport groups and vacation opportunities. Because the bulk of these benefits were based on member relations and interactions *outside* of the workplace, they were inherently instrumental in enhancing preexisting friendship networks, building a sense of community among workers, and enhancing the normative legitimacy of the unions.

Like the first half of the nineteenth century, the period of labor's coalescence was marked by a series of economic downturns. However, in contrast to the earlier period, many of the newly established unions were able to survive until economic conditions improved. For instance, the depression that swept the country between 1893 and 1896 did not deplete union membership. Both conservative unionists such as the Cigarmakers International Union and radical unionists such as the Western Federation of Miners attributed their survival to their strong traditions of mutual-aid (Cooper 1987; Kennedy 1908; Derickson 1988). Boasting about the success of his union's mutual-aid programs, George Perkins (1894, 168), president of the Cigarmakers International Union, claimed that, during the economic downturn of the 1890s, his union was able to retain its membership, attract new members, and "suffer no reductions of wages."

Labor's opportunities to organize, however, were affected only partly by economic conditions; they were also affected by the continuing alliance between employers and government, which continued to define unions as conspiracies. Employers enacted a variety of strategies for repressing and co-opting the labor movement. The decades between 1870 and 1900 were particularly violent (Dulles and Dubofsky 1984). Encouraged by the depressions of that era, employers undertook frontal attacks on the labor movement; they engaged in lockouts, hired spies to identify union sympathizers, summarily discharged sympathizers, black-listed union agitators, and employed strikebreakers on a widespread scale. In response, workers struck and rioted. Between 1880 and 1900, there were nearly 23,000 strikes affecting more than 117,000 establishments (Brandes 1970). In these conflicts, state and federal authorities remained allied with employers. The courts issued injunctions against the unions. State and federal troops were called out to break up strikes. Such acts of repression continued well into the first half of the twentieth century, even after the federal government softened its stance toward unions and called on labor and management to cooperate in order to win World War I.

Employers also sought to co-opt unions by providing welfare services to workers (Brandes, 1970). Included under the rubric of "welfare capitalism" were such activities as recreation and education programs as well as medical care, pension, stock ownership, and employee representation plans, which was an euphemism for company unions. Provision of such services were intended to undercut labor's mutual-aid logic and its ability to organize workers by making them more dependent on their employers and less dependent on unions for both their wages and services (Edwards 1979; Bernstein 1960; Derber 1970). Elbert H. Gray of U.S. Steel expressed this purpose directly, "We must make it certain that the men in our employ are treated as well as, if not a little better than, those who are working for people who deal and contract with unions" (quoted in Brandes 1970, 32). State and federal governments also encouraged companies to adopt welfare capitalism. For instance, President Roosevelt believed that International Harvester's support of welfare programs satisfied his criteria for a "good trust." Federal and state governments also participated in the co-optation process by passing progressive legislation on such labor issues as workmen's compensation, working conditions, and child labor, which helped undercut labor's claim to be the only institution that cared for workers and their families in hard times. Although some employers provided welfare services to workers as early as the eighteenth century, the biggest increase in employer adoption of welfare programs occurred after 1900 when employers tied it to their aggressive campaigns to promote the open shop.

During and immediately following World War I, AFL membership grew dramatically from 3,000,000 in 1917 to 5,100,000 in 1920 (Sloane and Witney 1985). This growth was due to the federal government's support for labor-management cooperation during the war. However, after the war, employers reacted to the growth of unions by pressing their most sweeping open-shop campaign, which was waged under the slogan of the "American Plan" and portrayed unions as alien to the individualistic spirit, restrictive of industrial efficiency, and dominated by radicals. A 1926 study of the 1,500 largest companies revealed that 80 percent had at least one form of welfarism and half had comprehensive welfare programs (Epstein 1926). Employers were particularly vigorous in promoting employee representation (i.e., company unions) as an alternative to trade unionism. In 1919, there were 225 welfare programs; in 1922, there were 725; and in 1924, there were 815 (Derber 1970; Brandes 1970). Between 1920 and 1923, union membership dwindled rapidly from the peak of 5,100,00 to 3,800,000 (Sloane and Witney 1985). S. B. Peck, chairman of the Open Shop Committee of the National Association of Manufacturers, stated:

> The assertion may be boldly made that the decreasing membership in most of the unions and the great difficulty they are experiencing in holding their members together is due to the fact that the employers — notably the so-called "soulless corporations" — are doing more for the welfare of the workers than the unions themselves. (Quoted in Dulles and Dubofsky 1984, 244)

Between 1925 and 1929, only a few companies adopted new welfare programs and many dropped them altogether. However, employers continued to support employee representation because they deemed company unions the most inexpensive and effective means of limiting unionization. At the end of the decade, union membership stood at a twelve-year low of 3,400,000.[4]

Welfare capitalism successfully challenged the labor movement's abil-

---

4. The American Plan and welfare capitalism were only partially responsible for this loss of membership; other factors contributing to the decline were the relatively prosperous times, unimaginative labor leadership, and renewed government hostility to unions.

ity to unionize workers, but it did not undermine the movement's reliance on the mutual-aid logic as a mechanism for gaining members' commitment. Throughout the twenties, unions served as the basis of their members' social lives and provided a wide range of mutual-aid benefits to their members. In 1928, the U.S. Bureau of Labor Statistics (1928, 2) concluded that the vast majority of unions provided mutual-aid services to their members and that:

> the more prosperous and progressive the union the greater its endeavors to extend the field of its services to the members. The advantages placed at the service of the workers redound to the benefit of the organization as such as well as the membership, for they serve as an added inducement toward joining the organization besides increasing the solidarity of the membership.

In sharp contrast to corporate welfarism, the Great Depression, which was set off by the stock market crash of 1929, presented a serious challenge to labor's mutual-aid logic. Between 1929 and 1933, union membership declined to a low of 2,973,000 workers (Sloane and Witney 1985). This loss of dues-paying members put a severe strain on the ability of unions to support striking workers faced with wage cuts and to provide mutual-aid benefits to employed and unemployed members. For instance, "one forlorn strike against a small mill had to be called off after the contents of the strikers' soup kitchen had been depleted by a group of hungry children" (Ulman 1961, 397; Ulman 1955).

The Great Depression also set off a wave of violent protests by unemployed workers. Initially, labor's reaction to the depression was comparatively mild. AFL's president, William Green, still adhering to Gompers' voluntarism, opposed federal unemployment insurance and urged the government to stabilize industry by supporting its program for a shorter work day and work week. Within the context of the mutual-aid logic, he also urged union members to help the unemployed. Other unionists, however, called for a socialist revolution; many joined the Communist party, which organized unemployment councils, protested tenant evictions, and advocated forming militant unions. Speaking before Congress in 1932, one AFL representative warned, "The leaders of our organization have preached patience. . . . If something is not done and starvation is going to continue, the doors of revolt in this country are going to be thrown open" (quoted in Filippelli 1984, 75). In the fall of 1932, a banker similarly warned

Congress, "There'll be a revolution for sure. The farmers will rise up. So will labor. The Reds will run the country — or maybe the Fascists. Unless of course Roosevelt does something" (quoted in Filippelli 1984, 177).

In this section, we illustrated that the mutual-aid logic was instrumental in the development of permanent labor organizations. During the economic depression of the 1890s, for example, the AFL attributed the survival of unions such as the Cigarmakers International Union and the Western Federation of Miners to their ability to provide mutual-aid benefits to their members. As in earlier times, many of these benefits were provided informally within the context of workers' occupational communities. Between the 1880s and 1920s, mutual aid was formally embedded into the structure of unions as they offered members an increasing variety of benefit programs, including health insurance, pensions, and recreational opportunities. Members directly financed those benefits from their dues. As the labor movement coalesced around the mutual-aid logic, management became increasingly resistant to workers' unionizing efforts. Indeed, the period is noted as one of the bloodiest in the history of labor-management relations. Violence served to heighten workers' sense of solidarity, uniting them in their opposition and forcing them to increasingly rely on one another for aid and assistance. Within this context, the mutual-aid logic continued to provide unions with the cognitive and normative legitimacy necessary to organize workers. During this period, however, management attempted to undercut labor's mutual-aid logic by providing workers with a variety of welfare programs, including the implementation of company unions, medical benefits, and stock ownership plans. These programs were provided for free to workers. According to some accounts, welfare capitalism was responsible for labor's inability to keep old members and attract new ones. In truth, labor's ability to organize workers during this period was also heavily influenced by governmental policies that, for the first time in American history, provided unions with a degree of regulative legitimacy. During World War I, for instance, the federal government encouraged labor-management cooperation, enabling union membership to grow dramatically. After the war, however, the federal government became less supportive of labor, making it increasingly difficult for them to keep and recruit members. The Great Depression also put a strain on unions, which were increasingly unable to provide members with the formal mutual-aid programs they had come to expect. At the same time, the Great Depression sparked violence among the growing legions of unemployed, finally prompting business and labor leaders to ask for governmental assistance.

Regulation and the Servicing Logic

In the 1930s, the Roosevelt administration passed legislation designed to assist the unemployed and regulate labor-management relations. While this legislation provided unions with the regulative legitimacy necessary to ensure massive recruitment of new members, the legislation was also instrumental in precipitating labor's move away from the mutual-aid logic to a servicing logic of union-member relations. In this section, we examine how, during the period of regulation (1935–1970), workers became less involved with one another and more dependent on union leadership to provide for their needs.

Prior to the 1930s, neither management nor government fully regarded unions as legitimate actors in the American workplace. When management found itself dependent on workers, it accommodated unions; when the dependency relationship changed, its accommodation turned into resistance (Bacharach and Shedd 1998). This situation changed when the federal government passed several laws, culminating in the National Labor Relations Act (NLRA) of 1935, guaranteeing workers the right to organize and bargain collectively through representatives of their own choosing, free from the interference, restraint, or coercion of employers (Selznick 1969; Gross 1974, 1995).[5] The law placed restrictions on what management could do to discourage workers from organizing, including a ban on company-dominated unions. It also established the wishes of the majority of workers as the basis for choosing a union to represent them and the use of secret ballots as a mechanism for determining the majority's wishes. Additionally, it created the National Labor Relations Board to oversee employers' compliance with the law, determine appropriate bargaining units, and conduct representative elections.

The regulative legitimacy conferred on unions by the government, however, did not lead immediately to peaceful relationships between labor and management. Employers initially resisted workers' efforts to organize, setting off a series of violent strikes. Nevertheless, the National Labor Relations Board's process for union recognition prevailed and, as a result, the labor movement experienced spectacular growth in union membership. In 1941, on the eve of World War II, it totaled 10,200,000; by the end of the war, it stood at 14,200,000. In 1954, it was 18,000,000, ap-

5. This legislation was modeled on the Railway Labor Act of 1926; both pieces of legislation legitimated practices already worked out by labor and management twenty years earlier (Bacharach and Shedd 1998). Neither was constructed by the federal government out of whole cloth and imposed on the parties.

proximately 35 percent of workers employed in the nonagricultural sector (Dulles and Dubofsky 1984).

Growth put a severe strain on the AFL, which continued to favor organizing workers along craft lines. In free elections, workers overwhelmingly chose to organize along industrial lines. Initially, the AFL tried to accommodate these workers and their unions within its structure; in 1938, however, the industrial unions broke with the AFL and organized the Congress of Industrial Organizations. The AFL and CIO competed with one another until their 1955 merger, which recognized that "both craft and industrial unions are equal and necessary as methods of trade union organization" (quoted in Sloane and Witney 1985, 83). A year later, in 1956, the AFL-CIO attained its largest membership of 15,500,000.

During the period of regulation, the labor movement also experienced a shift from its mutual-aid logic to its current servicing logic as a basis for gaining member commitment; that is, the servicing logic became embedded in labor's culture and structure and members' routines. The shift was particularly evident in how unions paid for member benefits. Prior to the NLRA, members paid for their own benefits out of union dues; by the 1960s, union dues paid only a small proportion of member's benefits. Most benefits were fully paid for by employers in both union and nonunion industries. In 1967, for example, unions paid a total of $96.8 million in welfare and pension benefits, which represented less than 1 percent of the $15.7 billion paid by all private employee-benefit plans (U.S Department of Labor 1970).

The shift from the mutual-aid to the servicing logic was precipitated by three, interrelated social processes. The first two shifted the responsibility for financing workers' benefits to their employers; the third restricted workers' participation within the life of their unions.

First, Roosevelt's New Deal administration implemented welfare legislation that undercut labor's mutual-aid logic by making government rather than unions the provider of workers' benefits in hard times. Thus, the New Deal implemented social security programs providing unemployment insurance and old-age pensions, two critical benefits previously provided by unions to their members. Also, during the Great Depression, a variety of federal and state programs were implemented to pay for the medical care of those on relief. Once these welfare programs were implemented, labor became an enthusiastic supporter vigorously lobbying for their expansion, and they grew enormously over the next three decades, providing both union and nonunion workers with a level of security previously unimaginable (Galenson 1985). During the two decades following

World War II, federal old age, survivors, disability, and health insurance expenditures increased fifty-fold, from $436.7 million in 1947 to $21.2 billion in 1967. In 1947, approximately 2 million people received old age, survivor's, and disability insurance; in 1967, more than 23 million people received such benefits (U.S Department of Labor 1970). Thus, the creation of the welfare state undermined Gompers's old argument that only the union would protect workers during hard times by shifting many of its mutual-aid functions to the state (Galenson 1985). In doing so, the federal government also weakened labor's mutual-aid culture and structure, as members came to rely on government services rather than themselves.

A second factor contributing to labor's shift to the servicing logic was the federal government's effort to stabilize the economy during World War II by switching the emphasis in collective bargaining from wages, hours, and working conditions to benefits. During the 1920s, a few unions began to shift the costs of benefits to employers; during World War II, Executive Order 9250 accelerated the shift by freezing workers' wages and encouraging unions to look elsewhere for an increase in workers' pay. Within this context, unions began negotiating for a number of fringe benefits, including vacations, overtime and night-shift bonuses, and health insurance. The National War Labor Board encouraged such bargaining as long as the costs of the benefits did not exceed 5 percent of wages, and the Treasury Department permitted employers to deduct those costs as a business expense. Thus, by the end of the war, collectively bargained health plans were established in many major industries; by the 1960s, collectively bargained health plans paid for by employers were the norm in unionized industries, and union members counted themselves among the middle class (Bok and Dunlop 1970; Sackman 1949). By the 1960s, more unionized workers than ever before received life, sickness, and accident insurance, survivors benefits, improved pensions, and supplementary unemployment benefits.

The third factor contributing to the shift was the growth in union membership. Such organizational growth frequently generates an increasingly complex and impersonal bureaucratic structure, which requires expert administrators to do for members what members were previously able to do for themselves. Moreover, according to the "iron law of oligarchy," democratic organizations degenerate into oligarchies as they increase in size (Michels [1911] 1949). Leadership perpetuates this distinction by controlling the means of communication with members, appointing staff members, and designating their successors. At the same time, members appear content to let the leaders and staff members handle the details of managing this increasingly complex bureaucratic structure. Although there has been a great deal of discussion about the iron law's inevitability within the labor movement (Lipset, Trow, and Coleman 1956; Edelstein and Warner 1979; Cook 1984; Benson 1985), there seems to be a growing consensus that oligarchization is most likely to occur during periods of stability when organizations are becalmed and the leadership has become complacent about its survival (Cornfield 1989; Zald and Ash 1966). Following World War II, unions experienced a relatively stable economic and political environment for two decades, allowing unions to make steady gains in membership growth and collectively bargained benefits. Having shifted responsibility for the provision of mutual-aid benefits to employers and the state, unions restructured themselves around collective bargaining, grievance handling, and arbitration (Cornfield, 1989). Several factors contributed to the bureaucratization of these functions, including a shift in managerial philosophy and practice and a growing body of legal decisions made by the National Labor Relations Board and arbitrators.

First, the growth in union membership demanded a shift in management philosophy and practice on the part of employers. Far from abandoning their preference for a nonunionized work force, employers were forced to accept the legitimacy of unions and sought to establish mechanisms by which to stabilize and standardize employee relations. A bureaucratized union served management interests in that it allowed for standardized personnel practices and consequently streamlined industrial relations processes. Furthermore, the procedures settled on by both labor and management as part of the collective agreement typically mandated that both parties adopt standard procedures for contract implementation. The adoption of such standard procedures encouraged the bureaucratization and professionalization of union administration.

Second, as NLRB and arbitrator decisions became manifest in an increasing body of rules and procedures, unions devoted more resources to these functions than the organizing of new workers. As these functions became increasingly specialized, the potential for unions to perform them necessitated the hiring of a cadre of professionals trained in areas such as law, economics, and public relations. One result of this process has been the declining involvement of members in their unions as they have come to view these activities as a service provided by the union (Grabelsky and Hurd 1994). In 1985, for instance, Benson (1985, 356), commenting on union democracy, stated, "If we add the numbers of unionists regularly active to one degree or another in committees, as stewards, etc., the total would range between 5 and 10 percent of the membership."

If the regulative legitimacy conferred by the government contributed to workers' declining involvement in their unions, it did have a positive effect on their feelings of security. By the 1960s, most union members felt that they had become securely middle class. In 1959, the Department of Labor reported that "the wage earners way of life is well-nigh indistinguishable from that of his salaried co-citizens" (quoted in Dulles and Dubofsky 1984, 378). A 1968 AFL-CIO poll reported that 45 percent of union families earned between $7,500 and $15,000, that nearly half lived in comfortable suburbs, and that most cited taxes and prices — typical middle-class worries — rather than jobs and wages as their primary political concern. Speaking to the *New York Times* on Labor Day 1969, George Meany, president of the AFL-CIO, agreed that labor had become middle class, "When you become a person who has a home and property to some extent you become conservative. . . . Labor has become conservative. I don't think there is any question of that."

Labor's conservatism is highlighted by its marginal involvement in the social movements of the sixties. Labor activists were involved in the temperance, abolition, and suffrage movements of the nineteenth century. In the sixties, however, union members remained on the margins of the civil rights, women's, and antiwar movements. For instance, the AFL-CIO strongly supported American involvement in Vietnam, and many union members beat antiwar protesters (Filippelli 1984; Morgan 1991).

During the period of regulation, the labor movement achieved its most spectacular growth in membership. This growth was fueled by the regulative legitimacy conferred on unions by the federal government and an expanding economy. Within this context, management came to recognize unions as legitimate actors within the American workplace; that is, management recognized those unions fairly chosen by employees in elections conducted by the National Labor Relations Board. Labor's success, however, transformed its logic of union-member relations. The mutual-aid logic was well suited to the earlier labor movement's hostile managerial, technical, and legal environment, allowing unions to survive in hard times. In an environment supportive of unions, however, it went into abeyance.

The servicing logic as a mechanism for gaining member commitment emerged to fit the labor movement's changed environment. This change in logic occurred over time as unions adjusted their structure and culture to fit the new environment. The growth in membership and collective bargaining agreements encouraged unions to become increasingly bureaucratized and dependent on experts. This structure made it increasingly unnecessary for members to participate in the day-to-day running of their unions. At the same time, the government and collective bargaining agreements guaranteed union members a growing array of benefits, which were provided by professionals rather than co-workers. In addition, the growing prosperity of union members encouraged them to move out of their old communities to the suburbs, where they were less and less likely to interact with their co-workers. All of these structural changes contributed to the breaking down of members' core participation in their unions and the mutual-aid logic, which had provided the earlier unions with normative legitimacy. In this sense, labor's shift to the servicing logic did not occur dramatically; indeed, the mutual-aid logic atrophied as members participated less and less with one another and became more and more dependent on experts to run the union.

Fragmentation and the Servicing Logic

An irony of a social movement's success is that it leads to fragmentation as some members perceive that things have gotten better and others perceive that the movement's goals still have not been achieved (Mauss 1975). As a result, the two sides often argue over tactics, precipitating a falling out which, if unchecked, may lead to the demise of the social movement. Since the 1970s, the labor movement has been experiencing a high degree of fragmentation that has sorely tested its servicing logic of union-member relations, particularly in an era when its managerial, technical, and legal environments have grown increasingly hostile to unionism.

The immediate issue precipitating fragmentation within the labor movement was its effort to consolidate the gains made during regulation, particularly its growth in membership and members' newly acquired middle-class status. Between the 1960s and the 1990s, the labor movement was unable to achieve these objectives. Union membership as a proportion of the national labor force plummeted to 21 percent in 1980 and continued to decline through the 1980s to less than 15 percent in 1995 (Bronfenbrenner et al. 1998). Similarly, union members have had to struggle to hold onto their middle-class status, seeing their wages and benefits decline during the recessions and era of concession bargaining that characterized the 1970s and 1980s (Carver 1993).

Fragmentation within the labor movement further weakened its mutual-aid culture by highlighting its lack of commitment to its espoused belief of bringing all workers into the union fold. During the period of fragmentation, this lack of commitment was most evident in the AFL-

CIO's efforts to organize nonunion workers. Toward the end of the 1950s, a dual labor market began to characterize the American economy. One labor market consisted of unionized workers, mostly white males who enjoyed good wages and worked at stable jobs. The other labor market consisted of nonunionized workers, mostly of women and nonwhites, who earned 50 to 60 percent of unionized workers and had little job security. Because the AFL-CIO was structured around servicing its members, it invested fewer resources in organizing and, at the time, was resistant to change. As late as 1972, George Meany remarked:

> Why should we worry about organizing groups of people who do not want to be organized? If they prefer to have others speak for them and make the decisions which affect their lives, without effective participation on their part, that is their right. . . . I used to worry about the size of the membership. But quite a few years ago, I just stopped worrying about it, because to me it doesn't make a difference.

Organizing nonunion workers, however, did matter to others, especially the nonwhites and females neglected by the AFL-CIO. In 1960, A. Philip Randolph organized the Negro American Labor Council in order to keep "the conscience of the AFL-CIO disturbed," and Herbert Hill, NAACP's labor adviser clashed with Meany at the AFL-CIO's 1962 annual meeting over its racial practices. After passage of the Civil Rights Act in 1964, this tension increased as black workers sought access to jobs previously denied to them. Similarly, in 1974, three thousand women from fifty-eight international unions met in Chicago to form the Coalition of Labor Union Women (CLUW). Working through their unions, the women pledged to organize women workers, to seek greater participation of women in union affairs, and take action against sex discrimination in pay, hiring, job classification, and promotion. Despite CLUW's efforts, 75 percent of union organizing budgets in the 1970s and 1980s went into campaigns in the manufacturing sector, even though 90 percent of all new jobs were created in the female-dominated service sector (Shostak 1991).

During the period of fragmentation, the labor movement did launch a number of organizing campaigns. The most successful of these were its efforts to organize public sector employees; prior to the 1960s, most of them were legally forbidden to join unions. Union membership among state and local governmental employees increased from 764,000 in 1968 to 2,205,000 in 1978, and another 2,400,000 public employees joined employee associations.

This spectacular growth, however, belied the movement's difficulties in other sectors of the economy. Between 1968 and 1978, employment in the nonmanufacturing sector increased 35 percent but union membership in that sector shrunk from 24.6 percent to 20.3 percent. Within its traditional stronghold of manufacturing, between 1974 and 1978, unions lost more than a million members, an 11 percent drop. This loss was due to a combination of factors: Increasingly automated work processes allowed manufacturers to produce more with fewer workers; government inflation-fighting put many union members out-of-work; employers renewed efforts to keep their companies union-free. Between 1980 and 1985, labor lost another 25 percent of its members.

The movement's failure to retain its members and attract new ones occurred as labor continued to invest most of its resources in servicing its members. According to Hurd (1998), labor's focus on servicing its members made sense in a period of prosperity but it became an increasingly untenable strategy in the 1980s as labor's economic and political environment worsened. In the 1980s, the American economy and unionized labor were rocked by recessions and global competition, which encouraged management to cut costs. These economic crises sorely strained labor's servicing logic by undercutting its ability to provide members with the job security and good wages they expected. Thus, American unions also precipitated the crisis in instrumental legitimacy discussed in chapter 1. The recessions of the early 1980s forced unions into a disastrous round of concession bargaining in which they gave back to management many of members' hard-won benefits. For example, approximately 45 percent of the 2,500,000 workers covered by contracts settled in 1982 did not receive a wage increase during the first year of their new contract. Global competition, which had been growing steadily throughout the seventies, increased under the Reagan and Bush administrations. This increased competition accelerated employers' decisions to close unionized plants and relocate to areas less sympathetic to unions, especially the southern United States and developing countries. Employer threats to relocate put increased pressure on unions to make even more concessions in order to save their plants.

Labor's use of the servicing logic as a mechanism for gaining members' commitment was also severely strained by an increasingly hostile political environment. The Reagan administration appointed lawyers sympathetic to management and hostile to unions to the National Labor Relations Board, and under their direction, the board reinterpreted many of the laws restraining employers' behavior toward unions (Gross 1995). For example, it is illegal for employers to intimidate workers who wish to unionize by threatening to close plants. The board reinterpreted the law to mean that it was acceptable for employers to discourage unionization by making predictions about plant closing based on economic conditions. It also became acceptable for employers to distribute articles on the closing of unionized plants and to show captive workers slides of their own plant padlocked (Hurd 1994). Similarly, the board reinterpreted employers' duty to bargain in good faith so that it now means merely to meet for the purpose of bargaining, an interpretation which has made it more difficult for workers to secure a first contract (Hurd 1996). Emboldened by such interpretations, employer violations of the law increased dramatically, so that by the end of the 1980s the firing of union sympathizers in order to deter organizing was commonplace (Carver 1993; Weiler 1991). In addition, the board's actions have facilitated employer's efforts to eliminate existing unions by making it easier for them to replace strikers with "permanent replacements" and by permitting them to openly encourage dissatisfied union members to conduct decertification campaigns.

A third factor undercutting labor's servicing logic was the evolution of new human resource management practices, originally implemented by employers in order to keep their organizations union-free. Like welfare capitalism, the new human resource management practices seek to secure workers' commitment to their employer by providing them with similar or better benefits than they might expect if they were unionized. Thus, employers reward nonunion workers with good wages, exceptional benefits, internal grievance and promotion procedures, and participatory programs for voicing their opinions. Secure from the threat of unionizing, employers experimented with more flexible, often semi-autonomous, team-based work structures that proved to be more profitable than comparable unionized settings during the 1970s (Kochan, Katz, and McKersie 1994). In the 1980s, some employers attempted to introduce such flexibility into their unionized settings. For example, many companies promoted a variety of labor-management experiments including quality of work life programs. Some unions went along with these programs; others resisted them, arguing that they were a violation of collective bargaining agreements and an attempt to return to the outlawed employee representation plans of the past (Parker 1985; Rundle 1998; Grenier 1987). Overall, employers' predominate strategy has been to co-opt established unions whenever possible and keep existing nonunion and all new facilities union-free.

During the period of fragmentation, unions continued to be structured around the servicing logic and their communal culture continued to atrophy as members became less and less involved with one another and increasingly committed to preserving their hard-won middle-class life-style. This cultural atrophy was driven by an increasingly fragmented labor movement, which highlighted workers' differences rather than their commonalties. As it became increasingly evident that labor was unable to protect members' jobs and their economic gains, the servicing logic has lost its instrumental legitimacy.

Summary

In this chapter, we presented an institutional history of the labor movement's logics of union-member relations, arguing that the labor movement cycles between the mutual-aid logic and the servicing logic and that the labor movement may be experiencing a renewal of its mutual-aid logic. We argued that the logics were embedded within the culture and structure of labor and the routines of its members and were activated by three factors: (1) the technical environment, (2) management's philosophy about unions, and (3) the legal environment. More specifically, we proposed that the mutual-aid logic was an appropriate mechanism for gaining commitment when the technical, managerial, and legal environment is hostile to unions. We also proposed that the servicing logic was an appropriate mechanism for gaining commitment when the technical, managerial, and legal environment is less hostile to unions.

Briefly, we found that mutual-aid was a common organizing frame in the eighteenth and nineteenth centuries. Early American craftsmen such as printers and shoemakers were organized as benevolent societies. When the master craftsmen became owner capitalists, the journeymen modeled the first unions after these organizations, emphasizing the values and benefits of mutual-aid in their work and family lives. Modeling unions on the familiar mutual-aid frame provided the emergent organizations with a degree of cognitive and normative legitimacy, at least in the eyes of their members. In this way, unions constituted themselves as workers' communities in which members felt obligated to care for one another in both good and hard times. Thus the mutual-aid logic was deeply embedded in the culture and structure of the first unions and the routines of their members, who took their intensive involvement with one another for granted. During the period of coalescence, the mutual-aid logic was even more deeply embedded into the labor movement as unions, under the leadership of the AFL, implemented a variety of benefit programs, which were paid for by members' dues.

For the first 150 years of its existence, the labor movement operated in a hostile environment. Employers, regarding labor organizations as illegitimate actors, refused to work with them and fired union sympathizers, and unions found their fortunes tied to an unstable economy fueled in part by new mass production technologies that made members' skills obsolete. In addition, the courts, siding with employers, declared union activities to be illegal constraints of trade. Within this environment, the early unionists such as the founders of the Western Federation of Miners, the Brotherhood of Locomotive Engineers, and the International Ladies' Garment Workers' Union believed that the labor movement's survival depended on the mutual-aid logic embedded in their workers' communities.

Between 1935 and the 1960s, the labor movement's environment and fortune shifted dramatically. As a consequence of worker unrest during the Great Depression, the Roosevelt administration passed the National Labor Relations Act, which conferred regulative legitimacy on unions. In addition, following World War II, the economy expanded steadily, enabling employers to accommodate unions. Within this context, workers were able to organize and collectively bargain with their employers, precipitating a dramatic growth in union membership, which peaked in the mid-1950s. The servicing logic of the labor movement developed within the framework of Roosevelt's New Deal social welfare programs and labor's success at the bargaining table. Labor's spectacular growth and its new ability to negotiate employer-paid benefits transformed the structure of unions from highly participatory organizations into oligarchies run by a relatively small group of elected officials and experts. By the 1950s, these leaders had fashioned for their members a secure middle-class life-style primarily paid for by the government and employers; as union members became economically secure, they left their workers' communities for middle-class homes in suburbia, which further disrupted their old communal routines. As the union structure and members' interaction patterns changed, the mutual-aid culture atrophied into its current servicing culture, which encourages members' sporadic involvement with one another and emphasizes their instrumental relationship to the union.

Labor's servicing logic, as embedded in its structure, its culture, and members' routines, was an appropriate mechanism for gaining commitment in the supportive environment it encountered through the mid-sixties. Within the context of the regulative legitimacy conferred by the government, unions were able to collectively bargain with employers and win economic security for their members. In turn, their success at the bargaining table conferred on them instrumental union legitimacy. Union leaders and members took the servicing logic as the appropriate way to organize their relationships.

In the 1970s and 1980s, however, labor's servicing logic became an ill-suited mechanism for gaining commitment in an increasingly hostile environment. During this period, the economy became more competitive and employers — who were antilabor even in the best of times — closed unionized facilities, vehemently resisted workers' efforts to organize new unions, and forced existing unions to give back many of their members' benefits. In addition, the National Labor Relations Board reinterpreted the law, making it easier for employers to resist workers' efforts to organize. It is within this context that labor is experiencing its current crisis. Unable to retain members' jobs and benefits, labor's servicing logic has lost its instrumental legitimacy and, with the board's reinterpretation of the law, unions have lost much of the regulative legitimacy conferred by the federal government.

Thus, the question facing labor is "How do unions regain their legitimacy in the current hostile environment?" One obvious strategy is for them to reestablish their normative legitimacy by increasing members' core commitment and, at a minimum, revitalizing the mutual-aid logic. How do institutions such as labor unions renew themselves? One possible mechanism is an abeyance structure (Taylor 1989). Abeyance structures are memories and practices that have become dormant. More specifically, abeyance structures are repositories for a group's collective memory; they are the enclaves within an institution where members retain old cultural beliefs and sustain a community of memory (Bellah et al. 1985; Schuman and Scott 1989.) Within the labor movement, a community of memory composed of older workers has kept the mutual-aid logic alive. Mutual assistance programs (MAPs) are a classic abeyance structure, which represent continuity with labor's historical mutual-aid practice of members helping members with alcohol and other personal problems. Like their predecessors in the Washingtonians and the White Ribbon Clubs, union members involved in MAPs believe that the most effective mechanism for helping co-workers with substance abuse and other personal problems is the emotional and social support of peers. As the founder of the Tunnel and Construction Workers' Program put it:

> If we brought in what they call a "professional" person . . . an outside social worker to run the program, you might as well not have a program . . . .

[The members] wouldn't consider it their program unless a sandhog [a tunnel worker] was running it. Remember, I talked about the sandhogs being very close with a lot of camaraderie. In a lot of areas, they only trust sandhogs. For them, . . . the best model is a guy from the union that they trust and know has had a recovery through the program. . . . You're not going to have that sense of trust and camaraderie unless you're a part of it. . . . You can't go out . . . and make believe, "Gee, I want to be one of you guys." They're not going to trust you. (Sonnenstuhl 1996, 93)

Until the early 1970s, recovering union members were very involved with their alcoholic and drug-addicted co-workers, twelve-stepping them on the road to recovery. Then, as employee assistance programs (EAPs) became increasingly professionalized and unions came to regard them as another service provided by their collective bargaining agreements, union members became less involved with their co-workers. In the late 1980s, some union members began advocating the development of peer-based MAPs. They were prompted into action by two developments. First, the federal government's war on drugs encouraged employers to adopt drug-testing procedures and to harshly discipline drug users (Staudenmeier 1989, Seeber and Lehman 1989; Jacobs and Zimmer 1991; Blum, Fields, Milne, and Spell 1992). Within this context, many union members were summarily discharged without being offered help from their employer-sponsored EAP. In addition, the explosion in managed care has made it increasingly difficult for union members to receive in-patient treatment (Zientek 1993; Popp 1993). In order to assure that their co-workers receive quality care, then, unions have begun to develop MAPs.

In calling for the wider adoption of MAPs, Edward Cleary (1992), former president of the New York State AFL-CIO, echoes their continuity with labor's old mutual-aid logic:

Let us not forget . . . as far back as the 1880s and 1890s, unions often did this [work] in association with the Women's Christian Temperance Union, which would set up white, blue, and red ribbon groups. These consisted of recovering people trying to maintain sobriety by helping one another. We need to remember where we came from, especially with escalating health care costs and the advent of managed care.

Because MAPs are constructed around the communal culture and structure of the mutual-aid logic, they teach workers the values of unionism by involving them in the provision of services to their fellow workers. At the same time, MAPs highlight members' critical involvement in rebuilding the workers' communities that were the essential building blocks of the labor movement and are critical to its renewal.

In the following chapters, we examine the logics of union-member relations within the railway brotherhoods, the Association of Flight Attendants, and the Transport Workers Union. Again, we examine, in each union, the cycle of mutual-aid and servicing logics as mechanisms for gaining member commitment. Within the context of our case studies, we illustrate how the unions are using MAPs to revitalize the abeyant mutual-aid logic as a response to a faltering servicing logic. In this way, we hope to illustrate how some unions are responding to their crisis of instrumental legitimacy by enhancing their normative legitimacy.

3 Reconstructing Brotherhood on the Rails

The railroad brotherhoods were among the earliest permanent unions in the United States.[1] Like other nineteenth-century labor organizations, the brotherhoods were organized around the mutual-aid logic of union-member relations, which was deeply embedded within their culture, structure, and routines. The mutual-aid logic within the brotherhoods was activated by the railroaders' rapidly changing technical environment, railroad management's rejection of unions, and an extremely hostile legal environment. The mutual-aid logic remained embedded within the brotherhoods well into the twentieth century. Railroaders' mutual logic is expressed in the stories retired workers tell about their feelings of camaraderie and fellowship, sentiments expressed in the following story told by a telegraph operator hired on the C&O Railroad in the 1930s:

> During my early years as a telegraph operator, I was given a short assignment at a small way-station. . . . When I went there, I had no idea where I was going to stay or get meals. . . . I was to relieve the third trick operator, a gentleman named Stinnett. I asked him where I might get room and board, and he said that the nearest was at Lyle. This would mean a three miles walk along the railroad tracks to relieve him, and a three mile walk back after getting off duty at 3:00 P.M. Mr. Stinnett rented a room in a house . . . and told me that I was welcome to use his bed. . . .

1. In this manuscript, we use the term *brotherhoods* as a cover term for all of the railroad unions. Officially, a number of the unions are known by their title as brotherhoods. These include the Brotherhood of Locomotive Engineers and the Brotherhood of Locomotive Firemen. Organizations such as the United Transportation Union, which are not officially titled brotherhoods, however, also acknowledge having roots in the fraternal model of union organizing.

I did so for the entire ten-day assignment. At no time was Mr. Stinnett willing to take compensation for use of his bed.

Although the brotherhoods preserved their mutual-aid logic longer than many other unions, they also eventually adopted the servicing logic of union-member relations. Within the brotherhoods, the servicing logic was activated during a relatively long period characterized by a stable technological environment, by railroad management's acceptance of unions, and a supportive legal environment. During this calm period when the servicing logic came into play, railroaders developed a segmented commitment to the brotherhoods, regarding them as instrumentally legitimate as long as they delivered at the bargaining table. The servicing logic served the brotherhoods and their members well. However, as their environment grew increasingly hostile, the servicing logic became an increasingly ineffective strategy for legitimating the brotherhoods' authority and for maintaining members' commitment. In the 1980s, the mutual-aid logic began to reemerge within the brotherhoods; this reemergence is manifest in its member assistance program (MAP), "Operation: Redblock," which is revitalizing members' core commitment to the brotherhoods and renewing the brotherhoods' normative legitimacy.

In this chapter, we deepen the theoretical insights presented in chapter 2 by examining the logics of union-member relations in the railroad brotherhoods. We examine the development of the brotherhoods' mutual-aid logic, the factors leading to its decline, and the conditions for its reemergence in the 1980s within the context of Operation: Redblock, a peer-based substance-abuse program. We also examine how the mutual-aid logic is being promoted by Operation: Redblock and the program's impact on railroaders' core commitment to the brotherhoods and perceptions of the brotherhoods' normative legitimacy. In order to understand the significance of Operation: Redblock within the brotherhoods, we begin our discussion with an examination of the railroaders' occupational culture and the role of drinking within it.

The Emergence of the Mutual-Aid Logic on the Railroads

Long before the brotherhoods developed, railroaders lived within vibrant workers' communities, whose mutual-aid ethic was well expressed in their drinking rituals. Drinking is a janus-faced symbol. Looked at one way, drinking promotes fellowship; looked at another way, it disrupts behavior (Johnson 1978; Clawson 1989; Staudenmeier 1985; Sonnenstuhl 1996). The first railroaders were drawn from agrarian and craft occupations where drinking on the job was common practice. Within the old craft workshops, for instance, drinking alcohol on the job was regarded as normal and the masters were expected to provide alcoholic beverages to the apprentices and journeymen. Everyone drank together, creating a sense of good cheer and camaraderie in the shop. When masters separated themselves from their workers and became merchant capitalists, they also stopped supplying alcohol to the shop and many became actively involved in the early temperance movement, arguing that drinking was responsible for creating most of America's social problems.[2] Just as the early unionists objected to the masters' setting wages unilaterally, the apprentices and journeymen protested the masters' enforcement of temperance. Consequently, the workers went to the bars and complained about the masters, transforming the old drinking ritual into a ritual symbolizing workers' resistance to the masters and the mutual aid workers owed one another (Johnson 1978).

The railroaders' occupational culture with its emphasis on mutual aid developed within the context of the temperance movement, the spectacular growth in railroading, employer efforts to discipline workers, and legal efforts to regulate the railroads. The railroads and temperance were both innovations of nineteenth-century America. Railroads grew at an astounding rate. In 1830, there were 40 miles of track; at the end of the Civil War, there were 35,000 miles of track; and on the eve of National Prohibition, there were 254,000 miles of track (Stover 1970). As a mass movement, temperance was an agrarian-based reaction to the social disruption of the industrial revolution, and the railroads with their abysmal safety records and violent labor disputes became a symbol of the dangers of that emergent social order (Staudenmeier 1985). Within the context of this growth, temperance played an important role in the efforts of railroads to discipline workers and to convince customers that the system was safe and reliable.

As a new enterprise, there was much to learn about the building and running of an efficient railroad, and the processes for doing so were not always intuitively obvious. First and foremost, there were no experienced workers to perform these tasks, and railroad owners lacked the knowledge for training them. Consequently, the pioneering years of railroading were

2. Temperance had several meanings in the nineteenth century. Initially, it meant abstaining from distilled alcoholic beverages; in the 1830s, it came to mean total abstinence from all alcoholic beverages. As applied to the workplace, the early reformers sought to prevent workers from drinking at work; later, some employers refused hire workers who drank outside of work as well. For useful discussions of the history of temperance, see Staudenmeier 1985 and Lender and Martin 1987.

characterized by trial and error. Eventually, what was learned would become routine according to what each craft (e.g., engineer, conductor, brakeman) needed to know and written down in the craft's "Rule Book" for each new recruit to learn. In the 1830s, however, such standards lay in the future and the railroads were faced with the immediate situation of disciplining an inexperienced labor force drawn from a variety of other occupations in which drinking on the job was customary.

Drinking was an integral part of the work culture of many pioneering railroaders (Staudenmeier 1985; Rorabaugh 1979; Lender & Martin 1987). One anonymous railway worker, writing in an 1869 edition of the *Locomotive Engineer's Journal,* described the railroaders' drinking in the following manner:

> During their trips, the fever of excitement was kept up by the influence of strong drink; and many a man had gained the reputation of being a swift runner and making impossible time when he was half drunk. . . . [Afterward] they would congregate in the grogshops and beer saloons to recount over their wonderful adventures on the road. . . . [They] would drink to soothe their grievances and demonstrate mutual support; drink evil and bad luck to some obnoxious and tyrannical official and drink long life and prosperity to themselves. (Quoted in Licht 1983, 238)

Because of such behavior, railroaders acquired a reputation for being intemperate and disorderly, and the public associated the railroads' dismal safety record with drinking by its employees (Ducker 1983; Reinhardt 1970; Staudenmeier 1985).

In order to convince the public that railroads were safe, railroad owners were among the first temperance reformers, vowing in the 1830s to hire only honest and sober workers of good moral character (Licht 1983; Staudenmeier 1985). After the Civil War, the railroads hired military officers as managers and such temperance qualifications were codified in railroad rulebooks. The railroads were also fervent supporters of such antisaloon innovations as reading rooms and YMCAs, which they regarded as a "necessary factor in railroad operations" (Rumbarger 1989, 141). They encouraged supervisors to strictly enforce the rules against intemperance and hired spies to ride the rails and report any misbehavior by the workers (Ducker 1983; Licht 1983). Offenders were disciplined harshly. Between 1877 and 1892, 2,300 employees (approximately 30 percent of the working railroader population) were dismissed on the Burlington system for using liquor; this was nearly twice the number dismissed for other offenses (Rumbarger 1989).

Eventually, the public outcry over the railroads' safety forced state legislatures to pass laws making negligence, carelessness, and drunkenness punishable crimes in cases involving accidents (Licht 1983). A series of state supreme court cases further established that corporations were responsible for hiring and retaining "fit" employees and therefore must assume responsibility for any accidents that occurred on their lines. As a consequence, the railroads were forced to show even greater care by not hiring drunkards, discharging workers who became drunkards, and preventing workers from becoming drunkards. Thus, at its convention of 1899, the industry adopted Rule G, prohibiting on-the-job drinking on all railroads:

> The use of intoxicants by employees while on duty is prohibited. Their habitual use or the frequenting of places where they are sold is sufficient cause for dismissal. (Quoted in Staudenmeier 1985, 140)

This standard, however, did not satisfy public concerns about railroad safety; in 1915, the industry adopted the more stringent version of Rule G, prohibiting workers from drinking alcohol both on and off the job.

Rule G was also ineffective at curbing workers' intemperance because the mobile nature of railroading and the stubborn nature of railroaders made it difficult for supervisors to enforce any rules, let alone those about drinking. Railroaders, believing that management " 'didn't know nothing'. . . wonder[ed] how the railroad survived under such densely incompetent management" and were contemptuous of their rules (Reinhardt 1970, 87). When not actually defying the rules, railroaders simply ignored them so that train crews often did as they pleased: Conductors let customers ride for free, firemen ran the locomotives, and drinking of "ardent spirits was pandemic" (Licht 1983, 100).

The early railroad unions also supported temperance as a means of organizing, promoting self-improvement among members, and creating positive impressions with the American public and railroad managers (Staudenmeier 1985; Blocker 1989). For instance, the Brotherhood of Locomotive Engineers (BLE), which was organized in 1863 and was the first permanent craft union organization of railway workers, underscored its support for temperance by making it the first element of its credo: "Sobriety, Truth, Justice, Morality" (Licht 1983). According to Charles Wilson, its president, such discipline was necessary in order to convince management that the union was a wholesome force with which it could safely negotiate. Intemperate engineers were often disciplined by the BLE; many were urged to join the Railroad Temperance Society.

Although the unions officially supported temperance, they rarely took action in order to keep alcohol off the railroads. Union leaders recognized that drinking continued to symbolize camaraderie to their members. They also realized that the saloons provided railroaders with a warm place to rest, eat, and socialize, and were consequently an important place to organize for collective action. More important, unions found it impossible to take action against intemperate workers at a time when management was doing all it could to reduce labors' ranks by firing union sympathizers.

Even during national prohibition, railroaders continued to drink on the railroads. For instance, Bell (Reinhardt 1970, 165–166) reported that, after passage of the Volstead Act:

> The railroad yard was the favorite gathering place of the town's sporting element. . . . The boomers got in the habit of doing their drinking at the yard. They would line up against the edge of the freight house platform, with a half-gallon jug for a wassail bowl, while the police hid in the adjoining lumber yard, hoping one of the celebrators would get drunk enough to stagger out of the neutral zone.

As one retiree summed up the railroad unions' early support of temperance, "While the unions may have wanted to keep their people sober, they wanted to save their jobs even more." Thus, drinking became a symbol of railroaders' resistance to managerial control and the railroaders' obligation to cover up one another's drinking became a potent symbol of the mutual aid they owed to one another.

The mutual-aid logic was also embedded in the structure and routine of railroaders' work and social lives. Railroading was dangerous and kept workers away a great deal of the time; when they were at home, they lived in railroad towns. These characteristics forced railroaders and their families to rely on one another. A retired switchman described growing up at the turn of the century in Olean, New York, a railroad town on the Allegheny Division of the Pennsylvania Railroad:

> We lived in an environment where most of the people that we associated with and the neighborhood in which we lived were all railroaders. . . . So that is why there was always a kind of family atmosphere amongst the neighbors. . . . Not only did we work together, we prayed together, we went on picnics together, outings together.

Before the brotherhoods were organized as beneficial societies, the railroaders were forced to depend on one another. This was particularly evident when workers were killed or injured on the job. Because their work was so dangerous, they were unable to buy insurance, which was prohibitively expensive. Their employers also felt little or no obligation to provide insurance, and when on-the-job accidents did occur, they could not be relied on to cover medical, disability, or burial expenses. Within this context, the railroaders customarily passed the hat for sick, disabled, or killed comrades. Employees of the Hudson River Railroad, for example, traditionally contributed more to Poughkeepsie's St. Barnabas Hospital than their employer, Cornelius Vanderbilt (Licht 1983).

Dangerous working conditions also compelled railroaders to look out for one another's safety, and this was the first thing that newcomers learned. As one retired brakeman explained:

> The first thing I always tried to impress upon the new hires was the fact that you don't handle pounds up there. You handle tons — hundreds of tons, thousands of tons. You don't get to make one mistake! So, don't make one! Number two is to take care of yourself and your fellow man!

The railroaders' work schedule also forced them to rely on one another (Licht 1983; Ducker 1983). Because railroaders were on call twenty-four hours a day, seven day a week, they spent more time with their co-workers on the rails and layovers than they did with their families. As a retired Union Pacific railroader aptly expressed it:

> You think the brotherhood didn't develop there? . . . We knew these men like brothers. We *were* brothers. When you share a bedroom and you share meals and you share your job, there is a bond that is built. And this went on for years. . . . Hell, I was spending more time with them than I was at home. Be out there for six days. Make a run for home. Had Sunday off. Get in the wee hours Sunday morning and have to leave Sunday evening.

Within the railroad communities the mutual-aid logic was still evident well into the first half of this century. For example, nearly all of the retirees whom we interviewed recalled that during the depression the railroad communities pulled together: Those families still having a member employed fed those families lacking any source of income. One retired maintenance-of-way worker recalled that in his hometown, the co-workers' sense of community led them to go beyond even that:

> In the Santa Fe shops, they were cutting back. Traffic was down. They were having to reduce the work force. Well, the men voluntarily surrendered the seniority system. Whereas in a reduction the younger men would usually

be the first to go, these men gave up on the seniority and divided themselves into two groups, each one working two days one week and three days the next. This way they could all have something to keep their families going.

Mutual Aid and the Establishment of the Brotherhoods

As we argued in chapter 2, permanent unions developed in the latter part of the nineteenth century and embedded mutual aid more deeply into their structures by implementing formal benefit programs. Similarly, by 1877, the three major railroad unions were organized along craft lines as beneficial societies: the Brotherhood of Locomotive Engineers, the Order of Railway Conductors, and the Brotherhood of Locomotive Firemen. During the 1880s and 1890s, a period of bloody labor-management conflict on the rails, railroaders began to organize more militant unions such as the American Railway Union and the United Brotherhood of Railway Employees, a process which would continue well into the first quarter of the twentieth century.

Although much has been made of the brotherhoods' economic contributions to members' welfare, railroaders joined them as much for the social opportunities as for benefits (Ducker 1983). All of the railroad unions offered members inexpensive insurance policies, which, for the first time, gave railroaders and their families a sense of financial security. However, the brotherhoods were also centers of good fellowship, offering entertainment, education, moral uplift, and assistance to traveling members.

In addition to providing insurance to their members, the brotherhoods assisted members directly. For instance, a member of the Brotherhood of Railroad Trainmen observed that if a union man was "overtaken by sickness or some other misfortune, . . . the brothers [would] come to his rescue and enable him to maintain himself and family until the clouds of adversity passed away" (quoted in Ducker 1983, 136). Such assistance was gratefully acknowledged in the brotherhoods' publications. For instance, Mrs. George Dice wrote to the Newton Mutual Aid Association that during her husband's illness "he never expressed a wish but what [the brothers] granted it; any and everything they thought he needed was bought at their own personal expense" (quoted in Ducker 1983, 136).

When members died, the brothers helped their families, raising money for burial expenses for those who were uninsured and giving emotional support to the grieving widow and children. One retiree recalled how the brothers honored their departed member:

We used to perform our own ceremonies at a grave. We used to wear all kinds of different paraphernalia. We used to have banners . . . [one] was made in the form of a railroad wheel with a piece of it cut out, which symbolized that a piece of us was missing. That was the brother who was missing.

The brotherhoods were also instrumental in assisting railroaders away from home. They pioneered the development of the Railroad Young Men's Christian Association, which was founded in Cleveland by George Myers, a station agent. The organization provided members with lodging, reading rooms, lectures, and study groups (Rumbarger 1989; Licht 1983). Brotherhood members also assisted traveling railroaders by permitting them to ride the trains for free, helping them to find employment, loaning them money, and providing them with lodging and food (Stromquist 1987; Ducker 1983).

In many communities, railroaders' wives formed ladies auxiliaries to relieve themselves of boredom while their husbands were away and to integrate newcomers into the community. For instance, in 1892 the wife of a Las Vegas brakeman wrote:

Those of us who have traveled around and lived in different railroad towns, know how lonely and desolate it seems to be a stranger in a strange place, not knowing whether there is anyone who would befriend us in sickness and sorrow. But now, as members of the Auxiliary, we know that, if we need assistance, we shall not have to look despairingly around us for doubtless sympathy. (Quoted in Ducker 1983, 130).

At their meetings, the women engaged in a variety of activities such as sewing, quilting, and card playing, but they also provided many services to the brotherhoods such as organizing suppers, dances, and parties. As one wife observed, these activities compelled the men to "spend an evening once in a while in a more profitable way than for them to go to town and get a little too much strong drink" (quoted in Ducker 1983, 131).

Commenting on the many social activities sponsored by the brotherhoods and auxiliaries, a retired switchman recalled how they welded members into workers' communities:

Unions used to set these things up in order to keep communications going. . . not just local meetings, but all these different kinds of functions. . . . So people who were part of the union in those early days were closely linked together within the framework of an organization that not only was designed to take care of their financial needs but also their physical and their social.

Reconstructing Brotherhood on the Rails   **63**

Economic and Legal Support for the Brotherhoods

In chapter 2, we also saw that a hostile technical and legal environment hindered development of permanent unions. In contrast, because of federal regulation of the railroads, the brotherhoods operated in a more stable economic environment and enjoyed a degree of regulative legitimacy withheld from other labor organizations until the 1930s.

Historically, the public both embraced and abhorred the railroads. On the one hand, Americans welcomed them because they opened up the country by facilitating the movement of people and products across vast spaces. On the other hand, in the laissez faire world of the nineteenth century, the railroads also achieved a reputation for corruption on a scale previously unknown in the United States. Critics complained about unfair rates, corruption of public officials, and monopolistic practices, and they referred to railroad owners as "robber barons." Responding to public outrage, the federal government created the Interstate Commerce Commission (ICC) in 1887, which was empowered to regulate railroad rates in order to protect customers from industry abuse (Kolko 1965; Orenstein 1990).

Under ICC regulation, the railroads had a difficult time responding to key changes in an environment characterized by increasing competition. In the process of restraining the "robber barons," the ICC eventually weakened the railroads to the point where they were unable to compete with the airline and trucking industries in the twentieth century. According to Orenstein (1990), this decline in railroad competitiveness, at least for the freight lines, lasted into the 1960s.

In contrast to the railroad companies, railroad workers fared rather well under ICC regulation. In order to ensure labor-management peace and keep the railroads operating for the public good, Congress enacted a series of legislative acts that provided railroaders with benefits that were unavailable to other workers at that time. Beginning with the Erdman Act of 1898 and culminating with the Rail Labor Act of 1926, these legislative acts initially provided for mediation in cases of labor-management disputes and eventually guaranteed railroaders the right to organize and bargain collectively. The Rail Labor Act has been remarkably effective in preventing strikes and keeping the railroads operating. According to Wilner (1991, 76), "Since World War II, there have been only 5 nationwide rail strikes, resulting in a total of but 10 lost working days." Under the Rail Labor Act, workers have also enjoyed steady wage increases. Between 1927 and 1987, wages for railroaders increased at a compound average rate of 5.27 percent — compared with 4.84 percent for manufacturing wages and 3.07 percent for the Consumer Price Index (Wilner, 1991). Reflecting on these wage increases, one executive commented:

> In a regulated environment there is nothing to be gained from resisting union demands since increased costs can be passed onto the consumer. The resistance that is displayed during negotiations is often ritualistic, done mostly to convince consumers that the resultant bargain was the best that could be achieved. (Quoted in Wilner 1991, 66).

Under the ICC, railroaders have also won a measure of income protection unavailable to other workers. When railroads merge with each other, sell lines to other railroads, abandon lines, lease lines to other railroads, and grant trackage rights to other railroads, adversely effected workers receive full income protection for six years.

Socialization and the Mutual-Aid Logic

Socialization is a critical variable in the development of union commitment and legitimacy (Barling et al. 1992; Zucker 1977; Berger and Luckmann 1967). Until recently, railroading was a father-son occupation, and the mutual-aid logic embodied within the brotherhoods was kept alive as it was passed along from one generation to the next. Within the context of their workers' community, fathers taught the brotherhoods' mutual-aid values to their sons by example. As a result, by the times the sons became railroaders, they also took the mutual-aid framework for granted, regarding it as cognitively and normatively legitimate. For example, all of the retirees recalled stories of their fathers or grandfathers fighting for the railroad unions. As young men they recalled their fathers telling them that a job with the railroad carried obligations to one's brothers, the primary one being to join the union. One retired engineer described joining the union as something one simply took for granted:

> It was just a bond. You were bonded together. You believed in the same thing. You knew you was doing something that was right for your family and for everybody. . . . You didn't only just feel like you was helping yourself, but you was helping your friends. You was helping everybody

else. You was standing together. . . . A belief that comes from your heart. Grass roots. You learn it and just grow up with it.

If joining the union was taken for granted, initiation into it was not. As a retired brakeman observed it was an important rite of passage, marking one's coming of age (Trice 1993; Trice and Beyer 1993):

> Up until World War II, a man got a job and the next thing he was looking for was to join a union. . . . They had an initiation fee and they would have a ceremony that they went through. They tried to get four or five or six men to join and they would put them all through at one time. Take three or four hours to do this. Everybody was happy about it. "Oh, my husband or my son was initiated into the engineers or was initiated into the fireman's union or the brakeman's or whatever last night." And it was a big deal, you know. It was a step up the social ladder.

All of the retirees observed that joining the union meant embracing the brotherhoods' mutual-aid logic. One of them aptly summed it up in the following manner:

> By joining, I saw myself getting fellowship — at the hall, the meetings. I felt that I had somebody that I could go to in time of need . . . I felt the sense of appreciation for what they had done for elderly workers who were maybe long gone from the railroad when I even started.

In this section, we have examined the brotherhoods' mutual-aid logic of union-member relations, which was embedded in their culture and structure and members' routines. Like other nineteenth-century workers, railroaders appropriated the common mutual-aid frame as the basis for organizing their relations with one another and formally incorporated it into the structure of the brotherhoods. Within the context of their intensive involvement at work and in the railroad towns, the brotherhoods were able to maintain the mutual-aid logic, which members regarded as cognitively and normatively legitimate, until the 1950s. Mutual aid enabled the railroaders to develop a strong community in the face of management hostility toward unionism. Fortunately for the brotherhoods, however, the regulated environment in which railroads operated also provided workers with a measure of economic security and regulative legitimacy unavailable to other workers. Within the framework of the mutual-aid logic, railroaders were intensively involved with one another and highly committed to the brotherhoods, which they regarded as cognitively and normatively legitimate.

The Brotherhoods and the Servicing Logic

In chapter 2, we argued that several conditions encourage the atrophy of the mutual-aid logic and its replacement by the servicing logic. These conditions are also evident in the brotherhoods' shift from its mutual-aid logic to its servicing logic. Owing to the success of the brotherhoods at the bargaining table, the railroad unions' mutual-aid logic began to decline in the 1950s. Within this context, railroaders developed a segmented commitment to the brotherhoods, which were seen as instrumentally legitimate as long as they provided for members' needs.

As a consequence of their bargaining strength, by 1987, railroaders were among the most highly paid workers in America (Wilner 1991; Martin 1992). But the railroaders' success at the bargaining table came with a price. The ability of the unions to win concessions from management eroded the unions' own involvement in providing mutual aid to their members (Ducker 1983). Unions no longer provided health care and insurance directly to their members. Rather, these now became bargaining issues over which the unions negotiated with management. As they had with wages, the unions managed to negotiate excellent health and insurance benefits for their members, which are paid from corporate profits rather than union dues.

By virtue of their bargaining power, the unions were also able to win significant concessions for union security and for improving working conditions on the road and layovers. Nearly all of the retirees that we interviewed mentioned these "victories" as playing a role in the decline of their unions' mutual-aid logic. For instance, in the 1950s, the unions won the right to a union shop — henceforth all of the railroaders in a particular location would be required to join the union. Although the retirees acknowledged that the union shop was an important accomplishment for the brotherhoods, they saw it as a "double-edged sword," undercutting members involvement with one another and their core commitment to the union. As one retired fireman told us:

> I hired on in forty-seven. The brotherhoods were fairly strong back then . . . we opted to close shop. That just about took the union out of the hands of the workingman. Union officers, they would do what they wanted. . . . I never did believe in forcing anybody to belong to the union. If you have to force somebody to belong to anything, you don't have a very good membership. They will stay a union member, but they won't care. . . . Then, you don't have many people that attend meetings. Therefore, you lose that interaction between union officers and the men and what their

wants and desires are. The men just ain't in no position to tell the officers, "No!"

Similarly, the retirees felt that these union gains at improving working conditions had "negative side effects." For instance, improvements in crew scheduling and improved housing conditions have translated into members spending less time together. Crews called to work prematurely no longer spend time in the yard hanging out and waiting for their trains; rather, they are sent home in a taxi. As one retiree remarked:

> The crews are down to where they don't spend the time together like they used to. They get on a train here and they go to wherever they are going to. They get off that train and get on to another one and come right back home. They only got a conductor and engineer on the crew. So you don't have the working relationship or the closeness that you had. You just sit up there.

Likewise, retirees believe that improved housing on layovers has also undercut members' core commitment because they no longer have to spend the night in a caboose, bunkhouse, or railroad YMCA. Instead, railroads were forced to provide each crewmember with a comfortable motel room. Consequently, fewer railroaders found themselves spending even their layover time with their brothers, preferring to take a hot shower, watch TV, and rest before making the trip home. One retired local union chairman remarked:

> They pulled off the cabooses, and they got them their own motel room. Now sure it was nicer. Who wouldn't want to come up into this, away from a caboose? But it broke up one thing — the bonding, the togetherness, the brotherhood. . . . It got us out of the caboose. . . . But in the process, and this I know now, we lost an important part of our brotherhood.

Nearly all of the retirees whom we interviewed saw the brotherhoods' victories as having altered the entire basis of railroad unionization. Instead of a fellowship and an organization grounded in the culture of mutual aid, members increasingly began to view the brotherhoods as service-providing organizations. Reacting to this change, the retirees feared that railroad unionism might not survive if members became "strictly into it for themselves." One retiree expressed it this way, "[We're in trouble] when the only time a brother goes [to a meeting] is when he needs something. . . like to adjudicate a management abuse or make a complaint against a brother."

Other factors also contributed to the decline of railroaders' mutual-aid logic, most notably the consolidation of railroads and railroad crafts, and the subsequent decrease in personnel, which began in the 1950s. By the 1960s, the number of railroaders had declined to the point that four of the brotherhoods — the firemen, trainmen, switchmen and conductors — joined together to form the United Transportation Union (UTU). Although they saw the merger as necessary in order to preserve their bargaining strength, many of the retirees felt that the elimination of craft-based systems of affiliation further undercut the brotherhoods' "raison d'être," fellowship. As a retired brakeman noted:

> Sure, we could all work together fine, but at the same time we didn't want to belong to the same union. It was kind of like a lot of us wanted to be part of the same group but also wanted to be separate. And the engineers is still separate. . . . So, when we finally did come together, there was just a defeatist attitude. No one really felt a part of anything anymore. They [the members] stopped attending meetings. The only thing they did, they paid their three or five dollars a month, whatever the dues were.

Consolidation of the railroads and creation of the UTU also undercut the mutual-aid logic by destroying several key elements of the social context originally responsible for the emergence and maintenance of that logic: the railroad towns, the union local, and the family linkages between generations of railroaders. In the old railroad towns, neighbors were a constant reminder of the railroader's identity and the fraternal values associated with that identity. Today, railroaders rarely live among fellow railroaders, and those old railroad towns still in existence tend to be populated by workers employed in other occupations. As one retiree put it, "The communalism of the old railroad town has been replaced by the cable television and four-by-fours of the suburbs." Lamenting the loss of the old railroad town, another commented:

> Most of them guys are dispersed all over the place. . . . So their neighbor is not necessarily a co-worker. He may be in the grocery business. He may be in any business. There is not that kind of local identity that existed in my time or in my father's time because of the simple fact there no longer exists that close association of railroaders — that tendency of all of the railroaders to live near the focal point of the railroad. Now some of them have got [to drive] a hundred miles to get to work.

Consolidation also forced the unions to close many of their locals, making it difficult for railroaders to attend union meetings. According to one former UTU official, at the time of the merger, there were 2,500 locals:

> We got seven hundred today. Back when I joined, oh hell, the union halls were right there in town. Today, some people have got a hundred miles to go in order to get to a meeting of their local. So me, I may be down in Miami, but my local may be in Jacksonville. . . . Nobody is going up to Jacksonville to a local meeting unless they've got one hell of a gripe.

The destruction of the old railroad towns also made it difficult for railroaders to pass their tradition of mutual aid from one generation to the next. By the 1960s, many fathers no longer encouraged their sons to become railroaders because they felt that railroading no longer offered the employment opportunity, and more important, the sense of fellowship, that it did in the past. As one retiree told us:

> I discouraged them. I told them . . . find yourself another occupation. The brotherhood was gone. We older men, we saw that it was fading. . . . Up 'til the fifties, we still had the brotherhood, the we-ness, the togetherness. I keep using that word, the compassion for one another. The reaching out and helping one another. But by the sixties, it was gone.

At the same time railroaders were discouraging their sons from entering the occupation, the federal government passed civil rights legislation, making their tradition of nepotism illegal. As a result the railroads were forced to hire workers who had no experience with railroading and the brotherhoods' mutual-aid logic. Consequently, for the first time since the birth of the railroads, there emerged on the rails a cohort of mostly first-generation railroaders. As one retiree told us:

> It was discrimination if the company started hiring the sons of the fathers that were employees of the company. . . . Here is what come. You had hippies . . . and along with them come that damn drug culture. Now we already had an alcohol culture. . . . Nobody knew what the hell to do with them. . . . We could understand the alcohol culture, but we didn't understand the so-called drug culture. We pulled back from it. We were afraid of it. We just didn't cotton to those kind of people and we didn't reach out to them because we didn't know what the hell we were reaching for.

The development of the brotherhoods' servicing logic could not have come at a worse time. In the 1970s and 1980s, their managerial, technical, and legal environments became increasingly hostile, making labor-management relations increasingly conflicted (Orenstein 1990). In 1980, Congress passed the Staggers Act, which partially deregulated the railroad industry by allowing the carriers to set their own rates without prior approval from the ICC and to act more freely in conducting railroad line-sale transactions. Between 1980 and 1988, more than eighteen thousand miles of track were sold to two hundred new, local and regional railroads. The majority of these "short-lines" employ nonunion labor (Wilner 1991). In 1988, annual wages of workers on the new railroads averaged $22,348, well below the $39,431 annual wages of workers on the major railroads. Also, during this period, under competitive pressures from the trucking and airline industries, rail executives seeking to increase profitability pressed the brotherhoods on a number of key labor issues. With the support of the National Mediation Board and several presidential emergency boards, rail executives have been very successful in wringing significant concessions from labor (Wilner 1991; Ornstein 1990). For instance, in 1985, the UTU and BLE agreed to accept certain changes: Increasing by 8 percent the number of miles a train must travel to constitute a day's pay; accepting lower rates of pay for new hires; and giving management greater flexibility in assignments. During this period, the ICC also began to put restrictions on railroaders' income protection; for example, it argued that income protection was not appropriate public policy when railroads sell tracks to nonrailroad companies. At the same time, management adopted a variety of new technologies, including computerized information systems, which made some railroaders' jobs obsolete and deskilled many others.

The shifts in managerial practice and work processes deepened the brotherhoods' reliance on their servicing logic by forcing the unions to focus their attention and resources on collective bargaining and political lobbying in order to preserve earlier bargaining gains. Because these efforts occurred at the national level, the focus of union activity increasingly turned away from the union local and toward the national union office, further distancing the union from its membership.

Although the brotherhoods resisted management, they found that the servicing logic was incongruent with the new environment, which precipitated their current crisis of instrumental legitimacy. Under intense pressure to deliver at the bargaining table, they lacked the means to do so. In the past, the mutual-aid logic provided union leadership with a powerful bargaining chip, namely the ability to mobilize a highly cohesive and loyal membership. However, the servicing logic failed to provide such a potential for collective power mobilization. Members increasingly looked to the union as an external agent providing services in return for membership dues, rather than as the embodiment of their community and collective interests. As one retired C&O engineer commented: "If our unions had stayed strong like the railroad company has done, we would be in much better shape today."

In this section, we examined the factors activating the brotherhoods' servicing logic. In part, this logic was encouraged by their success at the bargaining table, shifting responsibility for providing benefits from the unions to the railroads and the federal government. They also secured better living conditions while workers were away from home, which meant that railroaders spent less time interacting with one another. It was also encouraged by the increasing bureaucratization of the brotherhoods, which devoted the bulk of their resources to collective bargaining at the national level. The need to concentrate resources at the national level further encouraged the consolidation of union locals, which distanced members geographically from their locals and discouraged them from participating in the life of their unions. Management introduction of new technologies and work rules also weakened members' communal interactions on and off the job. In addition, government regulations prevented the brotherhoods from remaining father-son unions and broke up their old socialization practices. Within this context, the servicing logic developed as a consequence of the mutual-aid logic's atrophy; the servicing logic became embedded within the structure of brotherhoods as a consequence of its success at the bargaining table and shifts in its environment. These structural changes undercut members' communal interactions, which had sustained the brotherhoods' mutual-aid logic since the 1830s, and encouraged members' partial involvement with one another and their sporadic participation in the union. Consequently, railroaders developed a segmented commitment to the brotherhoods, regarding them as instrumentally legitimate as long as they delivered at the bargaining table. When the brotherhoods' managerial, technical, and legal environment became increasingly hostile in the 1980s and 1990s, the servicing logic proved to be incongruent with that environment. Unable to deliver at the bargaining table, the union leadership was increasingly seen by the railroaders as illegitimate. Thus the railroaders' commitment to the brotherhoods deteriorated, making it more difficult for the unions to win in future negotiations.

Reemergence of the Brotherhoods' Mutual-Aid Logic

In the 1980s, the mutual-aid logic began to reemerge within the brotherhoods. As many of the quotes above indicate, retired railroaders constitute a community of memory within the brotherhoods. Many veteran railroaders remember their old mutual-aid culture and have kept it alive in their stories. Not surprisingly, many veterans believe that the brotherhoods can solve their current problems by reestablishing their normative legitimacy by increasing members' core commitment. One program actively promoting a return to the mutual-aid logic is Operation: Redblock, the MAP supported by the brotherhoods. Its members also remember the old sense of community and are trying to restore it by involving railroaders and their families in changing their drinking culture. Although a great deal has changed in railroading, one thing has remained remarkably stable, railroaders' drinking culture. Operation: Redblock is a peer-based effort to transform that drinking culture and teach members the value of unionism in the process. In this section, we focus on how the unions on the CSX Railroad are re-creating the mutual-aid logic through Operation: Redblock.

CSX

CSX is a freight railroad serving the eastern United States from Chicago through Pennsylvania south to Miami, as well as a small area of Canada near Toronto. CSX is a megarailroad, which has been pieced together as a result of post-deregulation mergers. Nevertheless, over the last several years, integration of the various systems has progressed with relatively few problems. Its labor force has been reduced by a third and its safety record has gone from being the industry's seventh best to being first. CSX's competitors, business analysts, and customers now regard it as one of the best-run railroads in the country, and the company has seen its stock steadily rise on Wall Street.

The centralization of train dispatch and crew management functions in Jacksonville, Florida, reflects CSX's commitment to using advanced technologies in order to increase the company's productivity and profitability. For instance, train dispatch, which is the nerve center of the railroad, is a marvel of advanced technologies, referred to as "Star Wars." The dispatchers monitor the trains' movements on display panels and communicate directly with the engineers, telling them when to proceed, pull off to a siding, etc. The men and women who work at Star Wars describe their work as being "incredibly stressful" and state that they continually worry about making fatal mistakes in this high-tech world, which demands their constant attention.

Several unions represent CSX railroaders, and each has its own contract with the company. For instance, the contract in one division may require that trains operate with a four-man crew while the contract in another division may require that trains operate with a three-man crew. Likewise, different contracts may require that crew callers provide crew members with different periods of notification for reporting to work. Currently, there are thirty-four different labor contracts, which have become a "nightmare" for crew management who must know all of the contracts in order to perform their new jobs properly. For this reason, the crew management refers to its new headquarters as the "zoo." The railroaders simply call it, "crew mismanagement." Not surprisingly, then, one of the company's primary objectives has been to simplify its labor contracts by consolidating and renegotiating agreements to make them consistent with one another.

Although technology has had a significant impact on railroading, some aspects of railroaders' lives, particularly on the freight lines, have not changed significantly in the last century: Railroading remains hard physical labor and still requires workers to spend long periods of time away from home. Railroads run seven days per week, twenty-four hours a day, and freight lines such as CSX do not always have a fixed schedule. Train and engine crews do not always know when they will be called into service. When crew management notifies them that they have been called into service, they are expected to show up fit for duty within a few hours. Once in service, crewmembers may still spend up to twelve hours operating the train and, in some cases, several days on layovers, waiting for the train to be reloaded so that they can make the return trip to their home terminal.

The Drinking Culture at CSX

There is little dispute by either labor or management that until a few years ago railroaders still possessed a deeply embedded drinking culture at CSX. However, in discussing the culture, both labor and management are quick to point out that does not mean that everyone who worked on the railroad drank on the job or was a drunk. Rather, the distinguishing feature of the drinking culture was the requirement for railroaders to cover up one another's drinking behavior in order to protect one another's jobs. A former BLE local chairman explains:

Because of the camaraderie of the brotherhood, there was an unwritten rule that you don't snitch on your fellow worker. In cases where you knew about somebody who was drinking or came to work that way [drunk], or asked you to get them something [alcohol], you just didn't say anything about it. You did everything you could to cover up for them. You just did not snitch on anybody. You just did not associate with anybody who talked with the officials, and you did not allow anybody to get into trouble regardless of what it took to cover up for them. And that not only involved drinking but other rule violations.

When newcomers first began working within the old culture, the first thing they learned was their responsibilities about drinking. For instance, they were often told that it was their responsibility "to keep a bottle under a particular switch in the yard or to hop off the train at a particular crossing to pick up a six pack or bottle." In addition, they learned that "in order to be accepted, you had to drink." A former local UTU chairman recounted how, as a newcomer, he was taught to cover up for drunken crewmembers:

As a new hire, . . . we [the brakemen] were doing some industrial switching and the conductor went to the liquor store. . . . We got the job done, and the conductor gets back on the engine [and gives the engineer a fifth]. As we were leaving for our next location, the engineer reaches in his bag, pulls the fifth up, puts it on the control stand, and says, "Its time for a drink." . . . I reached for one of the three-ounce water glasses. . . . [The engineer] says, "What's wrong with you, Boy? Can't you drink it like a man?" . . . I turned that fifth up and, when I finished, there might have been two inches in the bottom. . . . By the time I got there [the switching location], I was completely out of my mind. When I got to the next place, the conductor locked me in the caboose to keep me from getting hurt. When we got to the final terminal, the conductor locked me on the caboose while they put the train away and, after that, they took me and put me to bed.

In this way, the new men were encouraged to break Rule G and learned that they were responsible for covering up for their fellow crewmembers.

Again, it is important to underscore that everyone on a crew did not participate in drinking episodes but did feel compelled to cover-up, even when it was against their best judgment. This sentiment is graphically illustrated by the following story recounted by a former BLE chairman who told us that he felt conflicted over his responsibility as an engineer to operate his locomotive safely and his obligation as a union member to cover up members' drinking behavior:

I let it be known right quick that I would do something if anybody came out with me on a job either drinking or having something with them. . . . I didn't know what I would do, but I knew I would do something. I did stop a train one night. A guy set up a bar on the train, . . . a suitcase with a plywood top . . . glasses full of ice . . . I asked him to put the bottle up and he refused. . . . I told him, "I'll just get another brakeman!". . . [I forced him to throw] a brand new bottle of whiskey out the window into a brick yard. . . . He hasn't spoken to me to this day.

More often, through the mid-1980s, when crewmembers tried to enforce Rule G, they were typically excluded from the drinking crews and forced to interact with the other "rule readers":

There were a few of those around our railroad and everybody knew that you just don't work with them. He's a no good SOB; don't work with him. He won't drink. He's a hard ass. He's one of those "rule readers"! Let's just not work with him. So what happened was those people grouped together [the nondrinkers] and then those who would use, party, and have a good time grouped together.

According to another local UTU leader, Rule G was never much of a deterrent even though "everyone knew, if you got caught, you got fired." He attributed the lack of deterrence to the lack of supervision on the road. Other railroaders actively involved in the affairs of their local attributed the lack of deterrence to management's selective enforcement of Rule G:

We even had officers who participated in it. They knew we were doing it. . . . They'd use the incidents to puppetize [those whom they knew were drinking]. They would play their strings and use those people to tell them what was going on out there. They'd have something hanging over their heads so they'd say, "I need to know about so-and-so." Those people who were responsible for a Rule G every day would literally spill their guts to protect their own jobs.

CSX managers admit that, in the past, they selectively enforced Rule G. Managers' explanations for selective enforcement, however, are more benign than the explanations offered by railroaders. Often, these explanations had to do with the fact that these managers lived in a small railroad town and found it difficult to "hurt" a neighbor. Often they were themselves sons of railroaders. For example, one top management executive stated:

As an officer, I fired some and hid some — "You go over there and sleep it off. No use you losing your family and everything.". . . When I lived in all these small, little towns, the guy who got drunk was my neighbor. His kids played with my kids and went to school together. Even though I was his boss, it could have been a tough relationship.

Operation: Redblock and Mutual Aid

Within the railroad industry, the term *redblock* refers to the signal light telling locomotive engineers to stop their trains because of potential dangers ahead. Operation: Redblock is designed to deal with the dangers of alcohol and other drugs by keeping those who abuse these substances off the railroad, and it accomplishes this goal by providing union members with a constructive alternative to covering up for co-workers who are in violation of Rule G. The roots of Operation: Redblock, then, are grounded in the brotherhoods' mutual-aid logic and in management's inability to keep alcohol and drugs off the railroad.

The railroads were early adopters of employee assistance programs (Hitchcock and Sanders 1976). According to a study of railroad employee assistance programs, the *REAP Report*, the programs were effective at helping workers who sought assistance from them. The employee assistance programs, however, failed to keep alcohol and other drugs off the railroads because they did not reach those chemically dependent workers for whom co-workers continued to cover up (Mannello and Seaman 1979). The report concluded that, in spite of the existence of the twenty-year-old management-based programs, 23 percent of railroad operating personnel were "problem drinkers" and 5 percent reported to work "very drunk" or became "very drunk" on duty at least once in the study year, in direct violation of Rule G. In addition, they concluded that, because substance abusers feared dismissal, most Rule G violations went unreported and few problem drinkers ever received the assistance they needed from the railroad employee assistance programs.

Both management and labor perceived the *REAP* report as stigmatizing to the industry. Management worried that the report would further discourage potential travelers and companies with freight to haul from using the trains. Likewise, many railroaders were fed up with risking their lives and jobs to protect co-workers who drank and used drugs. They felt that something had to be done to save their reputations as decent, hardworking railroaders while protecting co-workers' lives and jobs. Consequently, both labor and management sought changes in the employee assistance programs, with the general goal of enhancing safety on the rails and promoting a more positive image of the industry and its workers.

In 1980, a Union Pacific Railroad brakeman proposed the idea for Operation: Redblock. His idea was simple. Since management had failed to change the railroaders' drinking and drug-using culture, the unions would have to change that culture themselves. To do so effectively required guarantees from management that workers who violated Rule G would be treated rather than discharged summarily. Working with the BLE and the UTU, the Union Pacific was the first railroad to agree to adopt Operation: Redblock. Since then, Operation: Redblock has spread to a number of other railroads, including Amtrak, Burlington Northern, Conrail, Metro-North, and CSX.[3]

In developing Operation: Redblock, labor and management have constructed several mechanisms for helping workers in violation of Rule G. These are the Rule G By-Pass Agreement, the companion agreement, and procedures for "marking off" Redblock. According to the Rule G By-Pass Agreement, an employee in violation of Rule G can seek treatment from the railroad's employee assistance program rather than face discharge. In lieu of being disciplined, the employee can go to an employee assistance counselor, comply with his or her advice, and return to active duty when the counselor certifies the employee is able to do so. Workers who have been drinking or drugging may also mark off Redblock. The mark-off is a set of procedures for keeping employees under the influence of alcohol and other drugs off the railroad. Mark-offs are of two types. First, workers who have been drinking or drugging and are called to duty may mark themselves off duty that day without any penalty. This is treated as an excused absence. Alternatively, an employee may report to work and be under the influence. In this case, he or she may also mark him- or herself off duty and be excused. In addition, if the worker who is under the influence does not mark himself off, his co-workers may mark him off and send him home. After being marked off, the Operation: Redblock committee, which is composed of union volunteers, determines whether the worker needs treatment. If he needs treatment, the committee members refer him to the company's employee assistance program. If the committee determines that the worker does not have a problem and was called to duty unexpectedly, they will praise him for marking off and not endangering his co-workers.

In 1984, the UTU and the BLE successfully negotiated for the adoption

3. Although results from two studies (Eichler et al. 1988; Bacharach, Bamberger, and Sonnenstuhl 1994) suggest Operation: Redblock has been highly successful at changing the railroaders' drinking culture, the list of railroads adopting programs is surprisingly short.

of Operation: Redblock on CSX's Chessie System, which had been a participant in the REAP study. As the vice president of operations on the Chessie explained to us:

> The EAP just wasn't reaching a lot of these guys. . . .We were intrigued by what was going on in the UP [Union Pacific] because they were addressing the peer-pressure issue. I became absolutely convinced that we would never solve the problem, unless we got the employees involved in the process. . . . Until we could reverse it [the peer pressure], we were just swatting at gnats. . . . The UP model held some hope. . . . I listened to two or three union officers. . . . They convinced me that the unions really were as interested in solving this problem as management was and that they would take certain risks and go to the mat themselves to accomplish it. . . . It was an act of faith we were cultivating that both sides would do their part.

Today, Operation: Redblock exists throughout CSX, and both sides still recognize that mutual trust is the key to the program's success. According to one Redblock coordinator:

> This whole process hinges on one word: Trust! To get people empowered with the ability to effect change, they have to be able to trust that the people responsible for our railroad are going to support them, are going to be receptive to their ideas, their thoughts, their philosophies. They are building trust daily within those committees and the activities they do.

Whereas CSX railroaders are suspicious of employee assistance and regard it as a management program, they regard Redblock as a union program whose mission is to save workers' lives. Indeed, prior to Operation: Redblock, many railroaders felt uncomfortable seeking help from the company program, and their co-workers felt unable to provide them with the help which they needed. The following comments from a UTU member, who was a local union chairman at the time, reflect his initial skepticism on first hearing about Operation: Redblock, "At first, I thought it was a snitch program. After attending the initial session, I realized that Redblock was an extension of what we had been doing forever, protecting our members."

Management supports Operation: Redblock financially, but the unions run the program. A local chairman summed up this sentiment:

> Redblock is supported by CSX, and the support we get is that Redblock has the final say. We have a right to say, "Yes, this man has finished treatment. Yes, this man is going to his aftercare program. And, yes, this

man is going back to work." We don't have that fear of someone slamming down the gavel and saying, "No, he's not!" We have to keep that upper hand in that situation.

The primary jobs of the two Redblock coordinators have been to establish Operation: Redblock teams at every CSX terminal and to teach team members how to train their co-workers in the program's mark-off procedures. The following remarks from one BLE team member illustrate how such training transforms members' thinking about helping co-workers with drinking problems:

It's just an accepted thing [to cover up]. When a man's having a problem, everybody just bands together and takes care of him and helps him. Gradually, we had to realize that we couldn't do that anymore. We weren't helping the man, we were hurting him and that's what Redblock education has got across to people. You're not helping a fellow taking care of him and helping him along in his [drinking] problem. You need to help him overcome his problem.

The Redblock team at each terminal is composed of a captain and several volunteers. According to the program's coordinators, the ideal committee includes recovering alcoholics and addicts as well as social drinkers and abstainers. All team members, however, are unpaid volunteers who are committed to creating a safe working environment by keeping alcohol and other drugs off the railroads and helping their co-workers deal with substance abuse problems.

The overall thrust of Operation: Redblock has been to develop a close working relationship with CSX's employee assistance program. That is, the Operation: Redblock teams have generally sought to identify chemically dependent co-workers and work with employee assistance to ensure that they receive appropriate treatment and long-term support for maintaining their sobriety. This relationship, however, is predicated on the belief that the employee assistance counselors, who are employed by management, can be trusted to help their union members and not act as management's allies in ridding the railroad of troublesome individuals. A Redblock coordinator explained how the program tested the employee assistance counselors:

We tested [the EAP counselors] by giving them information that they had the opportunity to pass on [to management], and they didn't do it. That established a belief with us that we can trust these guys. We can depend upon them to do what they need to do. . . . Employee assistance counselors deal with the problem. We deal with getting the [individual with a] problem off the railroad and identifying [an individual] early enough so that the EAP counselor can do something about it. I think that is the main key to our success.

What is remarkable in this statement is not so much that management passed labor's test, but rather the way in which labor chose to test management. Labor chose to "test" management in the same way that they had traditionally "tested" new hires. Indeed, many of the helping processes incorporated in Operation: Redblock are deeply rooted in the brotherhood's traditions of mutual aid.

Helping Processes within Operation: Redblock

In principle, Operation: Redblock programs are built on an occupational variation of the constructive confrontation model espoused by employee assistance programs (Trice and Roman 1972). Within this framework, supervisors are taught to use progressive discipline to motivate alcoholic and other troubled employees to accept treatment from the employee assistance program. Similarly, the occupational version of the constructive confrontation model employed by Operation: Redblock requires team members to confront their co-workers with the realities of their situation and encourage them to seek help from CSX's employee assistance program.

In practice, however, Operation: Redblock programs are built on the brotherhoods' mutual-aid tradition. Just as, years earlier, co-workers in the caboose helped one another by discussing their personal experiences rather than by telling their buddy what to do, today's team members, many of whom are AA members, are likely to offer solutions more by acting as a personal example than by giving advice. Furthermore, even when more than just subtle "suggestion-by-example" is needed in order to save a co-worker's job, team members always present themselves as the suspected alcoholics' or addicts' allies. They vouch for the trustworthiness of the employee assistance counselors and urge members to seek help from the program in order to save themselves from being charged with Rule G and summarily discharged. The following remarks, which come from an Operation: Redblock captain, illustrate the critical importance of being a peer who can vouch for the program's trustworthiness:

With the inception of Redblock, we found that no one could help a person except his own [union] brother. The peer pressure of alcoholism is when you drink with your brother; in order to get sober, you have to walk with your brother as well. . . . It's the security that an employee can give his fellow workers by being there when he needs him.

When confronting their co-workers, Redblock team members, like supervisors who refer employees to an employee assistance program, make a pragmatic distinction between problem drinkers and alcoholics. This distinction is based on the different ways in which both groups respond to their offers of help (Trice and Roman 1972). Workers who are warned about the adverse consequences of their drinking and subsequently drink without suffering such consequences are defined as problem drinkers. The majority of workers marking off on Redblock fall into this category. After Redblock team members have given these workers information on responsible drinking, they can drink within the limits of these guidelines. In contrast, workers who are repeatedly warned about their behavior, who continue to drink, and who still suffer adverse consequences are assumed to be unable to control their drinking and are defined as alcoholic. An Operation: Redblock coordinator summarized how he expects team members to respond to problem drinkers and alcoholics:

First time, give the man the benefit of the doubt, just tell him not to do it again, give him some information, education about Redblock. . . . Second time, a pretty strong insistence that he see the EAP, realizing full well we don't have a hammer over his head but an insistence that we're not going to put up with this. Tell him, "This is the second time . . . [that] you've marked off Redblock." [Tell him that he] may not have a problem but [he's] becoming a problem for us because we had to deal with [him] a second time. Then, the third time, we simply invoke co-worker bypass and insist he go to the EAP, because if he comes out a third time, in any normal length of time, he probably has a problem. . . . That's where we get to the point of dealing with early-stage alcoholism and drug addiction as opposed to late chronic-stage alcoholism [or drug addiction].

In most cases, workers who mark off "Redblock" have a legitimate reason — they had been drinking and were called by crew management unexpectedly. Nevertheless, the team follows up every mark-off in order to ensure that those who need help receive assistance. A Redblock team member describes a typical committee confrontation with someone who was caught short and how the committee used the opportunity to reinforce the program's message:

He was drinking, called up, and marked off "Redblock." We [the Redblock committee] were notified. . . . We just told him that he had done the right thing by marking off Redblock. By doing that he helped preserve his job. He preserved his safety and the safety of his family. . . . We asked him next time to be a little more responsible when he drinks: "If you think you are going to work or if you know you are going to work, don't do it."

Another Redblock member described how his committee confronted an employee, who marked off and was known to have a drug problem:

I took two other guys with me. I told the employee that I wanted to talk to him. We met and talked about his situation. Talked about the use of drugs. . . . We told him that we didn't want any drug use. . . . Told him he had better get his act straightened out, that if he wanted to do drugs, he better plan on quitting the railroad. If he wanted to work for the railroad, he better plan on quitting drugs. . . . He was very defensive, "Well, I only use occasionally. You can't tell me what to do." . . . I said, "You're right . . . but we can refuse to work with you if we think you are under the influence. You are the one who is going to have to prove that you are not."

In contrast to committee confrontations, individual Redblock team members — or any other union member — may confront a co-worker who is in violation of Rule G. When performed by inexperienced Redblock members these confrontations may be fraught with a great deal of anxiety because the individual does not know how the co-worker will react. A Redblock member describes his first confrontation:

It was terrifying because we were still experimenting with the program. . . . The first person we marked off was my best friend. . . . We didn't know who [in management] was keeping records, although we [the unions] insisted that there be no records. . . . It was nasty. My best friend called me everything but a milk cow. . . . He challenged our friendship; he challenged my right to breathe. . . . It was tough that a friend could be so abusive, but it was because he was afraid for his job. If it had happened three months before, he would have been charged with a Rule G and fired. . . . Shortly after that mark-off, he admitted that he was wrong; he admitted that he was abusive. Our friendship continues today.

The role of Operation: Redblock members is formally completed once they have confronted co-workers and motivated them to accept help from CSX's employee assistance program; however, some teams have become involved in following up these referrals. Follow-up consists of asking whether co-workers are receiving appropriate treatment and the necessary support to maintain their sobriety. This interest in follow-up, however, comes from the field and has only recently begun to flow upward to those involved in administering the program. For instance, one coordinator noted:

> We advise people on Redblock committees, "You take care of prevention; you take care of marking this guy off; you confront him. You find out if he does have a problem, kick him into the counselor and then get out of it." Now all of our committees, once this guy comes back, will take a little special interest in that guy. . . . They'll take a little extra time to maybe not pat him on the back but to stroke him a little bit. Tell him, "We're glad you're back and what can we do for you? Are you okay?" . . . That's sort of the informal monitoring of recovery. It's done informally without anyone saying, "We're watching you."

Still, Redblock members who have been influential in helping a co-worker seek treatment are inclined to follow through by visiting the co-worker and by looking out for his family while he is in treatment.

Many Redblock team members told us that they thought extensive follow-up is critical if alcoholics are to have successful long-term outcomes and that the Redblock needed to be a part of the alcoholics' long-term support group. One member of an Operation: Redblock team commented:

> It's great to do prevention; it's great to do early identification for addiction; it's great to have an EAP there to treat them. But there is another step. The next step is helping them to maintain their sobriety after they get back into the work force. . . . A lot of times the circumstances of the job are so burdensome, so stringent, that they cause a person to find reasons to relapse. So this is just a natural process . . . to take care of that person who is returning to work.

Our research suggests that many team members, especially those who are in recovery, find it impossible to promote prevention without also helping their co-workers avoid a relapse. For instance, recovering members told us that they regarded doing follow up with co-workers as being part of their own recovery process. As one recovering alcoholic put it:

> When I got sober, I promised I'd help anybody any way I could, any time of day or night. . . . I just use my own experience, telling them how people have helped me. Since I have been sober, there have been thirty-two fellow employees found help the same way I did across my table. It is a brother helping brother situation. We are our brothers' keeper, and that is the

strongest point that I can make about Operation: Redblock. It does make you your brother's keeper.

In some locations, Redblock teams dominated by recovering members have formally incorporated follow-up into their Redblock role. According to the coordinator quoted above:

Some territories have formalized support groups. They say, "When you come back [to work], this group of people will be here to help you through the rough times of maintaining your abstinence." Then there are groups who say, "We're here. Call us if you need us." That's part of the growth that we're talking about: Where we start taking Redblock a little beyond the workplace and start giving the support.

Cultural Change, Union Commitment, and Legitimacy

Operation: Redblock has been well implemented on CSX. Through extensive training and education programs, union members and their families are involved in Operation Redblock intervention and fund-raising activities. Virtually all of the railroaders are knowledgeable about Redblock, its mark-off provisions, and the use of those provisions for keeping alcohol and other drugs off of the railroad and helping co-workers who are chemically dependent. In our interviews and field observations, we noticed several social consequences related to the program, including, of course, the transformation of the railroaders' drinking culture, the primary objective of the program. Most important, however, we found a renewal of railroaders' core commitment to each other, their unions, and the labor movement as a whole.

Although policymakers such as the National Institute on Alcohol Abuse and Alcoholism have increasingly emphasized changing cultural beliefs as a mechanism for prevention, only a small number of studies have looked at such activities within the workplace (Sonnenstuhl 1996). Our data suggest that Operation: Redblock has succeeded in changing the railroaders' drinking culture by directly challenging its norms of cover-up. As discussed above, both crewmembers and Operation: Redblock team members challenge such norms every day by educating their co-workers about the bypass agreement's mark-off provisions, by confronting co-workers who come onto the property in violation of Rule G, and by assisting those who suffer from substance abuse. Members of Operation: Redblock teams, for instance, described this cultural transformation to us:

You don't see [the drinking] anymore. You don't see it, period. Like every day, eighteen years ago, you would come to work and then drink. You don't see it, period. It's not there anywhere. I knew an old switchman one time that laid in the shanty for three months drunk. They put his name on the ticket and he got paid every day. They just wouldn't bother him. They just left him back there. . . . That can't happen today.

Similarly, a BLE chair observed that because of Redblock, crewmembers no longer felt obligated to cover up for co-workers who were in violation of Rule G:

The attitudes of workers have changed. . . . The people have seen a better life out there, not having to worry about meeting someone who might be under the influence or . . . protecting an individual and risking their own life or job to take care of that individual.

A UTU local chairman also noted Redblock's effectiveness in keeping workers who had been drinking off the property and its economic value to the union:

I know what this program is worth to the people I represent. It means I have to spend less time and [union] resources defending them [Rule G violators]. . . . I know those crews are physically in good shape — not under the influence . . . [because] there's no way with a two-hour call a man is going to get drunk, especially if he knows there are enough of us out there who aren't going to work with him. So the peer pressure aspect works. Peer pressure is free — doesn't cost the railroad anything and it doesn't cost the union anything.

Such glowing remarks, however, are not confined to labor officials. Many CSX officials also praised Operation: Redblock. The following statement from one division manager was typical:

Use of alcohol and drugs is no longer being tolerated by working people out there. They are regulating themselves and I see a definite decline in the use of these types of substances. . . . [My division's random drug test] had the lowest positivity rate of any of the divisions. . . . We attribute that directly to the Redblock program.

In addition to transforming the railroaders' drinking culture, Operation: Redblock has reinvigorated members' core commitment to their unions and the labor movement. For instance, many team members, particularly those who were also local officers, told us that they were involved in Redblock because it represented the best of unionism — "members helping one another." Others said they were involved with Redblock because the program had helped them and, in turn, they wished to help their co-workers. A brakeman who had been helped by the program expressed this sentiment:

[When I got caught,] I didn't know whether I had a job. . . . The head of the Operation: Redblock committee is also my union man. All he told me was, "Don't worry about it. You're going to have your job. It's being turned over to Operation: Redblock. But the company doesn't hold this against you. You're now in somebody else's hands." That was kind of reassuring but I had family and bills. . . . That's why I'm involved in Operation: Redblock [as a committee person] . . . to reassure the employee that this is for you. That you are going to have a job.

The commitment of Redblock members is highlighted by their refusal to accept pay for their work in the program. Indeed, members argue that Redblock is not like working on company safety committees, which pay them for attending meetings. Rather, they claim that they are doing Redblock work for themselves. They attribute the program's overwhelming success to members' voluntarism:

The only truly volunteer program is Operation: Redblock, and that is what made it fly. That's what gave the people the ability to sell it or give it away to their peers. We're not doing this because the company is paying us. We're doing this because we care about our workplace; we care about our brothers and sisters. We have a right to effect change. . . . It gives [members] a sense of ownership and a greater sense of pride in what they are doing.

Indeed, the program coordinators believe that Redblock's long-term survival depends on members' sense of voluntarism. One coordinator put it this way:

The members are going to continue this program with or without us because they have seen the benefit of what it has done. . . . Institutionalization comes from doing it so long that it changes the culture. . . . You change the culture by changing one mind at a time; one attitude at a time. . . . In Cincinnati . . . the local chair was so adamantly opposed to this program that he would fight you. I left there with him as a supporter. One person at a time. . . . The members have seen what this program has done and they're not going back to the old days.

Instead of returning to the old days, Redblock team members are extending their involvement in the program in a variety of ways. Some, as we noted above, rather than remain dependent upon CSX's employee assistance program, have begun to develop their own assessment and referral skills so that they can act as peer counselors for their members. Some have begun to apply the peer assistance model to help co-workers with problems other than those involving substance abuse. At a recent conference celebrating the ten-year anniversary of Operation: Redblock on CSX, team members discussed how they could help co-workers who had family problems or were involved in such critical incidents as derailments and collisions. Others have extended the program by taking its message into their communities. Many of the Operation: Redblock team members conduct alcohol and drug education programs in schools, churches, other unions, businesses, and shopping malls.

Most significantly, however, nearly all of those involved in Operation: Redblock see the program as returning the brotherhoods to their mutual-aid "roots" and becoming a model for the rest of the labor movement. One Operation: Redblock activist told us:

> I see this program growing into a labor movement. . . . We have a group of people that have realized they have an effect on the workplace; they have an effect on people's lives. A lot of people get a lot of strokes out of helping people. Probably the best eulogy you could ever get is, "In life, the guy helped somebody along the way!" So I see this as something more than a program; it's a process of getting people reinvolved in labor . . . an opportunity to make people understand that being a union member gives you some responsibilities as well as a right to work on this railroad.

By involving railroaders in Operation: Redblock, the brotherhoods have begun to reconstruct their mutual-aid logic, strengthen members' core commitment, and reestablish their normative legitimacy. Through their involvement in Operation: Redblock, younger union members are learning the values of unionism while also providing a valuable service to their co-workers. Members may still be unable to attend distant union meetings, but Operation: Redblock allows them to become active in their locals. The program also brings railroaders' families together. Through Operation: Redblock teams, union locals are once again organizing family events: barbecues, raffle-drawings, outings to zoos and parks, and golfing tournaments. Regionally, Operation: Redblock teams sponsor events such as steam-train excursions and concerts at the Grand Ole Opry. These events raise funds for Operation: Redblock and promote community awareness of alcohol and other drug problems; on a deeper level, like the picnics, dances, and ladies auxiliaries sponsored by the early brotherhoods, they involve families in the affairs of the union, binding union members and their families closer together.

Through Operation: Redblock, railroaders and their families are once again beginning to experience core commitment to the brotherhoods, regarding them as normatively legitimate. As a retired New York Central switchman told us:

> It is not easy to instill a sense of brotherhood among individuals that didn't have it ingrained in them at an early age, but it is something that the unions must begin to do. For an individual who comes in without that kind of experience, it has to be a learning process. . . . He has to learn that from somebody. That goes back to the absolute need for unions to turn their acts around and begin to emphasize the role of fraternalism. Especially for those people coming in who didn't have the privilege of gaining parts of this knowledge from their families, this movement back to our roots is probably the most important thing that we could do now at this juncture in our history. To get back to where we came from and to begin to bring together railroaders by acquainting them with that simple fact that the future belongs to those who are better prepared to accept the role of fraternalism and mutual aid. . . . But I am also of the belief that it won't work if we just tell them this . . . they have to feel that they are involved in it. As the saying goes, "Tell me something and I will listen. Teach me something and I will remember. But if you involve me I will understand." That is exactly what it is all about.

Concluding Remarks

In this chapter, we examined the logics of union-member relations within the brotherhoods. Generally our findings are consistent with the model presented in chapter 2. During the nineteenth century, the railroaders' hostile managerial, technical, and legal environments activated the mutual-aid logic. Until the 1950s, the mutual-aid logic was deeply embedded within the culture, structure, and routines of railroaders. Culturally, mutual aid was a common organizing frame for workers in the nineteenth century. The early railroaders organized their lives around this communal frame of action; they lived in workers' communities characterized by intensive interaction with other railroaders and their families. When the brotherhoods were organized, railroaders' mutual-aid logic was formally embedded into their structure in a wide variety of benefit programs. These benefit programs did not replace the members' informal interactions; rather, they reinforced them by highlighting members' basic obligations to help one another, especially in times of hardship. Members took the mutual-aid logic for granted, regarding it as cognitively and normatively legitimate — the appropriate way to organize their relationships. According to the brotherhoods, the mutual-aid logic enabled the railroad unions to survive and prosper well into the twentieth century.

In the 1950s, shifts in the brotherhoods' managerial, technical, and legal environments activated their servicing logic and their mutual-aid logic atrophied. Paralleling our discussion in chapter 2, the brotherhoods were victims of their own successes. Operating within a highly regulated environment, they secured excellent benefits for their members, which were paid for by their employers and the government. Through collective bargaining, they also secured improved working conditions, which undercut members' old patterns of interaction on and off the job. Meanwhile, because of the consolidation of locals and centralization of collective bargaining at the national levels, the brotherhoods' structure became more oligarchical. These changes made it more and more difficult for members to participate in the lives of their locals. Within this context, the servicing logic developed because members no longer intensively interacted with one another and because there were fewer mechanisms that allowed them to participate in their unions. Consequently, members developed segmented commitment to the brotherhoods, regarding them as instrumentally legitimate as long as it delivered at the bargaining table.

In the 1980s, the brotherhood's mutual-aid logic began to reemerge. It reemerged because the servicing logic was incongruent with the brotherhoods' increasingly hostile managerial, technical, and legal environments; however, it would not have reemerged without those veterans, who remembered the old ways and argued that a return to them was necessary in order for railroaders to prosper once again. Operation: Redblock members are actively promoting the mutual-aid logic by involving members and their families in the transformation of the railroaders' drinking culture.

Operation: Redblock members are a diverse group comprised of recovering alcoholics and drug addicts, social drinkers, and non-drinkers. Through their active involvement in the program, they have helped many co-workers become sober and transformed the railroaders' drinking culture. More important, however, involvement in Operation: Redblock has also deepened members' core commitment to the brotherhoods and refurbished their perception of the brotherhoods' normative legitimacy.

Those helped by the Operation: Redblock have become team members, working to advance its prevention and treatment goals. Members' involvement with Operation: Redblock has also encouraged them to broaden its original objectives by reaching out to co-workers with other personal problems, by developing their skills as peer counselors, and by implementing a peer-based follow-up component for the program. At the same time, Operation: Redblock members have become involved in other union activities, including labor-management efforts to improve working conditions, community education programs for the prevention of substance abuse, and family-oriented events to bring members closer together. Within this context, Operation: Redblock is helping to re-create the mutual-aid logic by involving members in the lives of their co-workers and the brotherhoods. As they reconstruct their workers' community, members learn that "being a union member gives you some responsibilities as well as a right to work."

While our analysis of the brotherhoods is consistent with our model, it also provides some additional insights. It again highlights the importance of regulative legitimacy for the development of a strong union; however, conferral of such legitimacy need not signal an immediate shift to a servicing logic. The brotherhoods' mutual-aid logic remained intact long after the federal government recognized their legitimate role on the railroad. Rather, it was the brotherhoods' increasingly oligarchical structure and the changes in member's interaction patterns that signaled the servicing logic's emergence and the mutual-aid logic's atrophy.

Our analysis of the brotherhoods also highlights several crucial factors for the reemergence of the mutual-aid logic. While the community of memory plays an important role in bringing the logic out of abeyance, our analysis suggests that union members will do so around issues deemed critical for the union's survival and for which the servicing logic has proven inadequate. It also suggests that the community of memory must be deeply committed to its actions, because the change in logic is likely to be resisted by union leaders and members, who view the servicing logic as the legitimate way to organize union-member relationships. The founders of Operation: Redblock regarded substance abuse as a real problem on the railroads and believed that something had to be done about it, particularly in light of the failure of railroad employee assistance programs to prevent drinking on the job. Within this context, the community of memory had a difficult time convincing union leaders and members to accept their proposal for Operation: Redblock and an even more difficult time overcoming the objections of railroad executives.

Since its inception, Operation: Redblock has required a great deal of time and energy from its volunteers. Nevertheless, their efforts have begun to pay off in members' heightened awareness of the brotherhoods as workers' communities.

Finally, it is also critical to state that the mutual-aid logic is a long way from being institutionalized within the brotherhoods. Operation: Redblock is one mechanism that the community of memory is using to reconstruct it. In order for the logic to become institutionalized, it must become embedded within the culture, structure, and routines of the brotherhoods. Still, within the context of Operation: Redblock, the mutual-aid logic has attained some normative legitimacy, at least among those railroaders involved with the program. Nevertheless, the bulk of railroaders still regard the servicing logic as the legitimate way to organize a union. Therefore, the culture, structure, and routines of the brotherhoods will probably continue to reflect that logic for some time to come. It remains an empirical question for future research whether the mutual-aid logic will eventually become fully institutionalized, reestablishing member's core commitment and the brotherhoods' normative legitimacy.

4 Renewing Sisterhood in the Air

Like the brotherhoods, the Association of Flight Attendants (AFA) is a craft union; unlike the brotherhoods, however, it is a predominately female union, which developed around the mutual-aid logic of sisterhood. As in the brotherhoods, the mutual-aid logic was activated by the flight attendants' hostile environment. Rapid technological change and both management's and labor's rejection of an independent union of flight attendants led by women characterized this hostile environment. Indeed, the airline industry has been characterized by a deep strain of paternalism, the tendency for management and union leaders to treat flight attendants as dependent children requiring a father's care and guidance. Unlike the brotherhoods, the AFA's mutual-aid logic developed in a supportive legal environment. Despite this regulative legitimacy, the AFA was not organized as a permanent independent union until the 1970s because of the airlines industry's paternalism. As a countermeasure to this paternalism, the mutual-aid logic enabled the flight attendants to survive and eventually organize themselves as an independent union. In this chapter, we examine the flight attendants' mutual-aid logic, tracing its development within their workers' community, its decline after a long campaign to win independent union recognition, and its reemergence within the context of the AFA's member assistance program (MAP).

Like the brotherhoods' Operation: Redblock, AFA's MAP is organized around a group of peer counselors who care for their co-workers. However, in contrast to Operation: Redblock team members, the AFA peer counselors are involved in all stages of the helping process, assisting flight attendants with a wide range of personal problems, including substance abuse, emotional distress, eating disorders, and family problems. Like the brotherhoods, the AFA recognizes that its MAP is an important mechanism for renewing flight attendants' core commitment and AFA's normative legitimacy.

The Community of Flight Attendants and the Emergence of the Mutual-Aid Logic

AFA's mutual-aid logic developed within the cohesive workers' community constructed by the first flight attendants. As we argued in the previous chapter, new occupations often form around new technologies (Gritzer and Arluke 1985 ; Trice 1993). The development of airline transportation gave birth to a number of new occupations, including pilots, mechanics, and flight attendants. The flight attendant occupation was born in 1930 when Boeing Air Transport,[1] in order to promote an image of airline safety and comfort, hired women trained as nurses to provide in-flight service to passengers.

From its inception, the flight attendant occupation developed within a supportive environment. Air transportation was a regulated industry, covered by the Railway Labor Act of 1926. In 1931, pilots organized the Air Line Pilots Association (ALPA); in 1936, the Railway Labor Act was explicitly extended to other airline workers. Thus, from its earliest beginnings, the flight attendants' efforts to unionize enjoyed a high degree of regulative legitimacy. The flight attendants' occupation also developed within a growing market for airline travel. For example, in 1934, American added flight attendants to its crews; in 1935, TWA followed suit in response to a post-crash investigation suggesting that, if there had been a cabin attendant on board, more passengers might have survived. As the airlines adopted larger planes such as the DC-3 for their fleets, the demand for flight attendants increased. By 1941, a thousand women were employed as stewardesses.

Like Lowell's textile owners discussed in chapter 2, airline management was also favorably disposed toward working women, whom they perceived to be docile, short-term employees and treated paternalistically. According to Cook (1982 xvii), during the first decades of the occupation, management treated the flight attendants "like daughters of Victorian, middle class families, girls who needed protection during the few months they would work." Management promoted the work as a glamorous job and expected the women to quit when they married. Boeing's original job description required candidates to be less than twenty-five years of age, less than five feet five inches tall, and weigh less than 115 pounds. These

1. Boeing Air Transport was a forerunner of United Airlines.

standards reflected management's image of the glamorous woman; in 1934, Boeing also added a "no-marriage rule," explicitly requiring that flight attendants be unmarried and forfeit their jobs when they did marry. The glamour image was prevalent throughout the industry. For instance, a lawyer for United remarked:

> The stewardess was an important part of our culture. This was not a working woman; this was a glamorous job. (Quoted in Nielsen 1982, 30)

Within the industry, this glamorous sky girl image persisted well in to the 1970s. At the height of the women's movement, for example, airline management continued to regard them as "vestal virgins," short-term employees from upper-class and middle-class families who were looking for husbands (Nielsen 1982, 20) and marketed the flight attendants' sex appeal. National Airlines advertised, "I'm Cheryl, fly me!" In 1975, Continental management used Playboy bunnies as stewardesses.

Viewed from within the occupation, however, flight attending is unglamorous, hard, often demeaning work (Nielsen 1982; Hochschild 1983). In the early days, flight attending was particularly difficult. The planes, which flew at a height of two thousand feet, were not heated, pressurized, or air-conditioned, and they were particularly hard on attendants' ears. In addition to serving passengers refreshments, reassuring them about the plane's safety, and answering their questions, the flight attendants also assisted with other tasks. They helped refuel the plane, rolled it into the hangar for repairs, stowed luggage on board, and made last-minute arrangements for passengers whose flights were delayed or canceled. When all of the passenger seats were occupied, the attendants sat on a mailbag or suitcase at the back of the plane. Jessie Carter, one of the original "sky girls," likened the experience to "going cross-country on the stage coach" (quoted in Nielsen 1982, 11). Flight cancellations and delays often put great strains on the attendants, who were never certain when they might return from a trip and who therefore learned to depend on one another for assistance when necessary. The following story recounted by one early flight attendant highlights the strain that the women had to endure because of scheduling difficulties:

> I reported for work on the twenty-fourth of December on a DC-3. We went to Seattle, Portland, Midel, Pendleton, Boise, and Twin Falls. We were supposed to land in Salt Lake. Salt Lake was socked in. . . . After striking out in Salt Lake, we landed in Ogden for fuel. Then we went over to Cheyenne, Laramie, and then to Denver. There was supposed to be

somebody in Denver to relieve me but there wasn't. So I ended up going on to Cheyenne, Laramie, and Lincoln, and Omaha. There the guy told me I could go to the hotel and go to bed. So I went to the hotel and took a shower. . . . The phone rang. He said, "Get back out to the airport." . . . We went back the same route we came. He said somebody will relieve you in Denver. Well, there was still nobody to relieve me in Denver, so I went back to Laramie, Cheyenne, Ogden, and Salt Lake. No one was there either, so I had to stay on the airplane as we hippety-hopped back to Seattle. But we made it only as far as Portland. When we got up there, Seattle was fogged in. At four o'clock in the afternoon they decided we would take a bus. But before we could put them on a bus, I had to take them out first for dinner. . . . We finally got up to Seattle about six o'clock in the morning. . . . At that point I didn't think the job was so hot.

Despite management's paternalism, the flight attendants felt dependent on one another for their survival. Their mutual-aid beliefs developed as a practical strategy for managing their work and were deeply embedded within the culture, structure, and routines of the flight attendant community. Several job characteristics contributed to the flight attendants' mutual-aid logic.

First, as a result of management's no-marriage rule, flight attendants rarely stayed on the job more than eighteen months. As one veteran observed, "[The] average was eleven months. . . . I mean there were always some that flew two years, or maybe three. My word, but that was really unusual." Consequently, flight attendants came to depend on one another, particularly those with a few months' more experience, in order to learn the ropes. Several of the older retirees told us they were "in awe" of those more senior to them; one noted that she and her roommates referred to the senior flight attendant in their apartment as the "Mother Superior" and turned to her as their primary source of job-related information. Another recalled:

We respected the more senior flight attendants. You felt sort of a camaraderie and you were kind of flattered when they'd take an interest in you. They could pass on to you their knowledge. Give you work clues on how to simplify the job and how to do a better job. You enjoyed the ability to meet some of these older, twenty-five-year-olds.

Flight attendants also developed a strong sense of mutual aid because their work and living arrangements melded these two spheres of their lives. Until the demise of the no-marriage rule, flight attendants, unable to afford their own apartments and unable to marry, lived in "stew zoos." Typically, roommates contributed to a household budget, divided up housekeeping chores, and acted as a surrogate family by giving advice to, and sharing their work exploits with, one another. Because of their brief careers, roommates came and went frequently; nevertheless, all of the retirees observed that their relationships with roommates were intense and long lasting. One American veteran described it in the following way:

You'd transfer into a base when you graduated and you knew no one. . . . The first thing you do is find someone to live with. The degree with which they accept you with open arms and bring you into their fraternity, well that is terribly important to you. You share the food. You cook. You go through all of those things of living together. . . . You borrow somebody's blouse because yours is dirty . . . or you borrow hose . . . I mean it is intimate living, and terribly exciting. . . . When it is your turn to take in a new roommate, which happened constantly, then you do for them what someone did for you. That is how it works, and that is endlessly ongoing.

Within the "stew zoos," then, the flight attendants relied on one another for a wide variety of help, including such routine activities as switching trips to enable someone to visit family members and boyfriends and such nonroutine events as covering up someone's secret marriage or an unwanted pregnancy. As one retiree noted:

We relied on each other a lot, like to change trips. That was a big one because we all did that. If you were dating somebody in a different city and you could only get together on a certain day, you could call up another girl and ask her to take your trip. If she had just gotten in from her trip, she'd probably still do the trip. We just did that for each other. [We also] loaned each other money. Conditions simply demanded that kind of thing.

As a consequence of their mutual-aid beliefs and practices, the flight attendants developed a tightly bonded, workers' community, which they continue to feel is largely unintelligible to outsiders. For instance, the flight attendants whom we interviewed felt that outsiders did not understand what it means to cope with the dangers of flying. A retiree explained:

[Our world] was like a world of its own. . . . I don't think we would have had the ability to explain it to anyone outside of the business. That is why airline people stayed with airline people. . . . When you came home from a bad trip, you knew there was somebody there who understood what you were talking about. In the first couple of months that I was in Newark, there were three bad crashes. . . . I landed just a few minutes after one of them and had to drive by the crash scene to go home. It was just one of those things you never ever get over. . . . You understood the risks that were there. You didn't think or talk about them too much because, well, you just kind of understood that part of each other's lives. I think that was the main reason for our bonding.

Feelings of sorority were not confined to one's immediate co-workers; rather, these feelings extended to all flight attendants in the industry. According to one TWA retiree:

There was a certain feeling of a sorority because even when you met another girl, another stewardess from another airline, you almost felt that you could walk up and say, "Hi!" Whether you want to call that sorority or a kind of sisters of the sky, [we found] that just because we are wearing a different uniform doesn't mean we are different. . . . In fact, it was always fun to get together with them. . . . For example, in Paris, I remember the whole crew was going out for dinner, and there was an American Airline stewardess sitting there. She couldn't find her crew. We said, "Well, you don't need them, go with us!"

Mutual Aid and the Struggle for an Independent Union: From Workers' Community to the AFA

The flight attendant community's mutual-aid beliefs and practices were instrumental in the struggle to organize a permanent independent union, the AFA. In this section, we examine how the mutual-aid logic sustained this struggle and was embedded within the union culture and structure of flight attendants. As mentioned earlier, the flight attendants' unionizing efforts enjoyed a supportive legal environment. However, because of paternalism and a rapidly changing technological environment, they were unable to develop a permanent independent union until 1973.

In their efforts to unionize, the flight attendants were not taken seriously either by airline executives, who saw them as short-term employees, or by the Air Line Pilots Association (ALPA), which felt that it should represent all workers within the industry. These sentiments were evident in the organizing activities at United, which in 1946 created the first independent flight attendants union, the Air Line Stewardesses Association (ALSA). The flight attendants faced little opposition from management. According to a United executive:

There was no anti-union campaign at UAL because we believed it better to deal with a recognized agent. The stewardesses, as short-term employees, especially would be easier to deal with as a union. (Quoted in Nielsen 1982, 32)

However, they were opposed by ALPA, which directly challenged ALSA's authority to represent flight attendants by forming the Air Line Stewards and Stewardesses Association (ALSSA) to compete with it for members. They also faced formidable opposition from within their own community. Many of the flight attendants saw little incentive to unionize because, like management, they too perceived their work as short-term and a stepping-stone to marriage and the business of running a family. Some believed that a union was unnecessary because the company treated them well; others felt that they could not afford the dues. One veteran remarked:

> Well, my friends and I, we just didn't have the likes of sixty dollars to join, so we never did. And besides we weren't going to fly that long. . . . I wasn't expecting anyone to have to fight for me. It was probably very young thinking; I wasn't worried about anything.

The mutual-aid logic inherent in flight attending was instrumental in overcoming the women's reluctance to organize. Ada Brown, ALSA's first president, was well known to, and trusted by, United's flight attendants. She had worked as a stewardess for three years, as an assistant stewardess in San Francisco, as a chief stewardess in Portland, and as an instructor of new hires in Chicago before returning to the rank and file to organize a union. She and a group of inexperienced volunteers signed up 75 percent of the United flight attendants in two months. Recalling this event, Ada Brown said:

> No outsider could have organized our group. Even within our ranks we had difficulty, although we had the confidence and personal acquaintance of most of the girls. They just did not like the idea of unions. (Quoted in Nielsen 1982, 32)

The veterans whom we interviewed confirmed that they signed up for the union because of their confidence in these "older women." One commented:

> These women had the foresight to recognize that there were those [among us] that were going to be around a lot longer than 18 months. They also recognized the control the company had over us; the fact that, because we were primarily women, our salary levels were very, very low. And [they

realized] that the company could do this because they felt that nobody was going to be around long enough. . . . You would fly with one of these women. They wouldn't really try to force their opinions on you, but they would just tell you that you have got to fight these things.

The organizers also utilized the flight attendants' sense of sorority to begin campaigns at other airlines, including Braniff, Continental, Western, American, Mid-Continent, and Inland airlines.

In its first negotiations with United, ALSA was relatively successful. Since 1930, stewardesses' beginning salary had been $125 per month; under the contract, the salary was increased to $155 per month. Among the other concessions wrung from management were a commitment to pay one-half the costs of uniforms, a guaranteed rest period, and restrictions on flying time. Actual flight hours were limited to 85 a month with no more than 255 hours within any consecutive three-month period. In addition, ALSA negotiated provisions for grievance procedures and dismissals, which were written into the agreement. The 1946 contract also formed the basis for successful agreements negotiated in 1947, 1948, and 1949.

ALSA's success, however, was short lived. Although it had won recognition as an independent union, ALSA did not have the financial resources to provide many basic services such as holding conventions to elect officers, publishing and distributing information, and representing members in grievances. Handicapped by high turnover and the lack of a union shop, the flight attendants found themselves chronically strapped for funds to support their activities. In addition, ALSA found itself competing against other unions, including the Transport Workers Union, the Teamsters, and ALPA for flight attendant membership.

As a result of its financial difficulties and an increasingly competitive organizing environment, ALSA voted in 1949 to affiliate with ALSSA and become part of ALPA. Irene Eastin, ALSA's president, remarked, "Those of us who understood ALSA's financial situation knew we could not remain independent and perform the necessary functions of a union" (Nielsen 1982, 48). By affiliating with ALPA, the flight attendants saw a rapid growth in union membership. By 1951, ALSSA's membership had grown to 3,300 attendants on eighteen airlines. However, the flight attendants' twenty-three-year tenure as a division of ALPA was a turbulent period marked by enormous growth and change within the airline industry and continuous conflict with the pilots, especially the union's officers. Within this context, the flight attendants' mutual-aid logic was critical to the division's survival and members' spirit of independence.

After World War II, air travel exploded in the United States, and the industry underwent a number of important changes that set the context for the pilots' and flight attendants' long-running conflict. Between the end of the war and the early seventies, the airlines introduced bigger and faster planes, which required more flight attendants to service more passengers, often in less time. In the early fifties, the airlines introduced large propeller planes such as the DC-6; in the late fifties, they added jets such as the DC-8; in the seventies, they added jumbo jets such as Boeing's 747. As a result, more flight attendants were hired to service a steadily growing number of passengers. However, because the number of flight attendants on a crew did not keep pace with the increase in passengers, each flight attendant had to service more and more passengers as the flying time between destinations became shorter and shorter.

ALPA, as the representative of both the pilots and attendants, negotiated with the airlines in order to improve working conditions. However, from the beginning, it was clear that the pilots' and attendants' interests were opposed to one another. This opposition was evident at ALSSA's first convention in 1951, during which three contentious issues arose. First, the attendants were for certification of the occupation; the pilots opposed it, fearing that it would challenge the captain's authority on the plane. Second, ALSSA wanted a union shop, which would have required all flight attendants on a carrier to become dues-paying members; the pilots opposed it arguing that, if unions made themselves attractive, members would join voluntarily. Third, the flight attendants wanted their own charter from the American Federation of Labor.

For the next two decades, the pilots and flight attendants were deeply divided over the charter issue. In 1960, the schism became a crisis when negotiation between the two sides broke down. Half of the flight attendants left ALPA to join the Transport Workers Union, where they continued to use the title Air Line Stewards and Stewardesses Association. The remaining half organized as the Steward and Stewardess Division of ALPA. Still, the schism persisted within ALPA until the Association of Flight Attendants was established in 1973.

Behind the struggle over authority were two interrelated issues: gender and economic self-interest. The pilots saw the "girls" as short-term employees whose economic interests were opposed to their own. This conflict was brought into sharp relief by the airlines' introduction of jets. The pilots saw jets, which were fast and large, as offering desirable working conditions because, traditionally, they negotiated their salary on increments that were tied to a base salary, mileage, night flying, and capacity.

With their added seating capacity and faster flight times, jets meant higher salaries to pilots. In contrast, the flight attendants had negotiated their contracts on the basis of the hours per month they were allowed to fly. Consequently, they saw the faster flying times and added seating capacity of jets as doubling their work load; they had to fly more flights and service more passengers. Within this context, they wanted to negotiate fewer hours in the air. This conflict was further exacerbated because the bigger jets also meant that more attendants were being hired. Within this context the pilots feared that the flight attendants would eventually outnumber them and that a flight attendant might even lead their union. A pilot assigned to evaluate the "stewardess problem" stated that the evaluation committee was concerned about "who could determine who their president was going to be" (quoted in Nielsen 1982, 112).

As the Steward and Stewardess Division of ALPA struggled to maintain the flight attendants' independent identity within ALPA, it also confronted a losing battle with the airlines. Handicapped by high turnover and the lack of a union shop, the Steward and Stewardess Division was chronically strapped for funds. For instance, one retiree recalled:

> We were in the hole all the time. If a flight attendant got in trouble, they would say, "Well, I'll pay my dues if you will take care of me." . . . There were times when we had only thirty percent or forty percent of flight attendants paying dues. I know one year I was in negotiations — I think this was in the late fifties — and the union didn't have enough money to pay our hotel bill. My father sent me $500.00 for Father's Day. That was the only way the four of us could stay and keep negotiating. There was one girl who would steal food off the airplane. She would steal the airplane food in order to feed us.

The Steward and Stewardess Division of ALPA was also handicapped by the airlines' paternalism, which was regarded by management "as normal and natural" (Nielsen 1982, 82). During the forties and fifties, the flight attendants were unsuccessful in their early attempts to do away with the no-marriage rule because arbitrators were unwilling to rule on issues that were not part of the written agreement. Commenting on stewardess tenure and turnover in 1965, a United vice president remarked, "If it got up to thirty-five months, I'd know we were getting the wrong kind of girl. She's not getting married" (quoted in Nielsen 1982, 83). In addition, the airlines concluded that the stewardesses were immature and needed constant supervision. As a result, management downgraded the job of chief stewardess and charged male supervisors with supervising the women, who regarded the men as petty and incompetent. Although the flight attendants had been successful in negotiating discipline and grievance procedures, they were unable to prevent management's arbitrary enforcement of its grooming regulations. Girdles were to be worn; hair could not extend over the uniform blouse collar; nail polish and lip stick were required; stockings were to be free of runs and blouses were to be pressed and free of sweat stains at all times. Commenting on her experiences during the fifties and sixties, one retiree observed:

> We started getting people into the flight attendant upper management echelon that didn't have any background in the job. They started managing in ways that were inappropriate because they didn't understand the complexities of the job. . . . You began to hear about girls that perhaps were being pursued by the company for infractions. An infraction could be as simple as not wearing heels, removing your hat in flight, not wearing the proper style of shoe, [or] not having your nails manicured. Little teeny things like that.

In addition to using harassment as a mode of workplace control, the male supervisors oversaw the speed-up that resulted from the airlines' adoption of faster and larger planes. The flight attendants were forced to serve more passengers in less time on longer trips and with fewer and shorter breaks.

Within the context of its conflicts with ALPA and the airlines, the flight attendants continued to rely on one another "to retain their sanity" in the face of increasing work pressures. A veteran attendant observed:

> The loneliness, the irregularity of the hours — if you are keeping a stiff upper lip and the smile on the face under all of these circumstances, then you need someone to beef to. Right? Like the army, your buddy keeps you going. That is solidarity.

During the fifties and sixties, several factors facilitated the flight attendants' continued reliance on their mutual-aid logic. First, because the industry continued to apply the no-marriage rule to flight attendants, the women continued to live in "stew zoos" so that their work and leisure continued to be closely intertwined. Second, although the industry was expanding, airline bases remained small and scattered around the country so that all of the flight attendants at a base knew one another. For instance, a TWA veteran explained to us:

> We knew everybody at our own base back then. I was based in Kansas City. Most of the bases were smaller. Detroit was a very, very small base, maybe

twenty hostesses . . . whereas Kansas City was one of the larger bases, . . . maybe three hundred hostesses on the schedule at the time. So, some of our bases were smaller, and they were even more congenial. . . . But the people that I flew with are still my very best friends.

Third, with the introduction of the larger planes, the flight attendants began to work in crews of two or more. When not serving passengers, the flight attendants customarily sit on the jump seats and talk about work and their personal lives. Flight attendants refer to this ritual as "jump seat counseling":

> When you go away, you are with other flight attendants who become your family. . . . Flight attendants will sit on the jump seat and tell each other anything and everything. It's not done so much to get immediate advice, as it is to kind of bond. But it's done by comparing situations and giving each other advice. . . . During the trip, these strangers are expected to become your family. Opening up to them on the jump seat or during the layover — telling them something personal for everything personal that they tell you — does that. They then become people that you can depend on during the layover.

When on layover, the airlines housed the flight attendants two to a room so that the women often spent all of their waking and sleeping hours together. Another TWA veteran noted:

> We formed very close friendships because we bid the same flight, and we were together all month. . . . We usually had layovers that were at least twenty-four hours; sometimes [there were] three-day layovers. We did form fast friendships.

Fourth, the flight attendants' reliance on mutual aid was enhanced by their informal communications network, which linked members together across the country. The veteran flight attendants referred to this network as their "wireless" and used it to gather information from around the system as well as solicit help from one another. A retiree described its use in helping a flight attendant in need of an abortion:

> You never went to the company, because they could not know. . . . You would tell them that you had a sick mother. . . . When the problem was resolved, your mother got well and you came back to work. Meantime, your friends — other flight attendants — would have gotten their friends in a different city to help you find a doctor and then give you a place to stay or something like that. We would use the grapevine because it all had to be very quiet. It wouldn't be a local thing. If something like that

happened in Denver, you would have to rely on someone's sister in Milwaukee, something like that. . . . Everyone would help you just drop out of sight, and then they would be sworn to secrecy.

Although the mutual-aid logic enabled the flight attendants to cope with their work and personal problems, they became increasingly dissatisfied with their second-class status, which was exemplified by ALPA's continuing to view them as short-term employees and giving their interests short shrift in negotiations. A split with ALPA was inevitable; it was precipitated by changes in the legal environment, challenging the paternalism of the airlines and ALPA. In the sixties, as the women's movement gained momentum, the Stewards and Stewardesses Division of ALPA found itself in the forefront of many legal challenges to sex discrimination. For instance, under Title VII of the Civil Rights Act of 1964, they mounted a series of challenges to the no-marriage rule, wage differentials between stewards and stewardesses, and the airlines' arbitrary use of grooming and weight regulations. At the same time the flight attendants were militantly challenging the airlines in court, the government and the AFL-CIO were putting pressure on ALPA to revise its bylaws so that flight attendants could be elected president of the union. ALPA steadfastly refused to change its bylaws because the pilots would not accept a flight attendant or a woman as president. Instead, ALPA agreed to recognize the Stewards and Stewardesses Division as an independent union, AFA, albeit one affiliated with the pilots. According to the affiliation agreement between ALPA and AFA, each union governs its own affairs, establishes and implements its own policies, and remains administratively and fiscally independent.

Throughout the fifties and sixties, the flight attendants' mutual-aid logic was embedded within the Stewards and Stewardesses Division's culture and structure as well as members' routines. The division's culture was highly communal, its structure was highly participatory, and its members were intensively involved with one another on and off the job. Through the mutual-aid logic, flight attendants sustained their core commitment to an independent union, which they regarded as normatively legitimate. The mutual-aid logic enabled the flight attendants to cope with the work-related problems that, as a division of ALPA, their union was unable to resolve through negotiations. The mutual-aid logic also sustained the flight attendants in their long struggle to overcome the deep strains of paternalism in the airline industry and ALPA. Indeed, the regulative legitimacy conferred on their unionizing efforts, while necessary, was not a sufficient condition for a permanent independent union to develop. From the occupation's inception until 1973, airline executives' and union leaders' paternalistic beliefs effectively prevented them from taking the "girls" seriously, even when the flight attendants demonstrated their ability to take care of themselves by negotiating excellent contracts on their own behalf. However, a second piece of federal legislation, the Civil Rights Act, established the appropriate conditions for the AFA to develop in 1973. By recognizing that women and men were equals, this legislation provided the flight attendants with a degree of regulative legitimacy sufficient for them to assert their independence from ALPA.

AFA's Servicing Logic

As we have seen in chapters 2 and 3, labor's success may precipitate an unintended shift from the mutual aid to the servicing logic. Activated by a relatively supportive environment, this transformation occurs when the technical environment is relatively stable, management adopts a strategy of co-optation rather than rejection, and the legal environment is supportive of labor. This was the context in which AFA emerged from ALPA, a stronger union than its predecessors were. As an independent union, it represented twenty thousand dues-paying flight attendants and saw many of its legal challenges to the airlines' discrimination practices begin to pay off. The no-marriage rule was overturned so that the average length of service increased from eighteen months to six years and wages increased from five thousand dollars a year to ten thousand dollars. AFA also demonstrated its strength by negotiating an excellent agreement with United, which included increased base pay, restrictions on the numbers of flying-hours, and the provision of single-occupancy hotel rooms on layovers. As in the brotherhoods, these negotiating successes had the unintended consequence of undermining the communal interaction patterns on which the flight attendants' mutual-aid logic was constructed. Within a very brief period, flight attendants' core commitment to AFA was transformed into segmented commitment.

For instance, overturning the no-marriage rule provided flight attendants with economic stability; it meant that the flight attendants were able to think of their work as a career. However, as flight attendants married and began to live apart from one another, it also undercut their communal life in the "stew zoo." As one United retiree told us:

> When the marriage rule changed, you were getting flight attendants with families. The job was no longer their primary interest. The job was a

means to an end. . . . Now you have got kids and husbands. . . . So the focus was on their *real* family, not on the job or their flight attendant family.

Another remarked:

There is probably far less involvement [in one another's affairs] today than there was in the old days. I think they are so busy in their own lives. I mean, you are talking about women who are married, with children, and that puts them in a totally different place. . . . Back then, most of us had a similar life-style off of the airplane.

Similarly, the agreement to provide single-room occupancy on layovers meant flight attendants spent less time interacting with, and confiding in, one another.

Unfortunately, the stable environment in which AFA first emerged was short-lived. Shortly after it was established as an independent union, its technical and managerial environments turned hostile, undercutting AFA's mutual-aid logic and making it more dependent on its servicing logic. Indeed, shifts in AFA's technical and managerial environments also transformed members' patterns of interaction. In the 1970s, state and federal governments deregulated the airline industry, creating a more competitive environment. Under deregulation, the airlines were free to establish their own routes and charge their own fares (Cappelli 1985, 1987; Walsh 1988). Deregulation set off a wave of mergers and acquisitions within the industry and encouraged the start-up of new nonunion airlines. In order to keep ticket prices low, the airlines sought to compete by keeping labor and other operating costs low. Within this context, the airlines created a hub-and-spoke system, which makes flying more cost efficient by concentrating major operations within the hub. Larger planes fly passengers between hubs and smaller planes move them outward along the spokes to their destinations. As a result, the airlines closed their old, scattered bases and moved the flight attendants into the hubs.

Airline mergers and the creation of the hub system also disrupted the flight attendants communal interactions by contributing to the closing of the "stew zoos." The hub-and-spoke system turned the majority of flight attendants into commuters, often living hundreds of miles from their home base. Airline mergers also undercut the occupation's mutual-aid norms by breaking up the old carriers and bringing together attendants who did not know one another. Attendants who were already feeling isolated within the merged airlines experienced the break up of their old cultures as "a traumatic thing for all of us to have to go through." Some attendants continued to wear their old carrier's wings underneath their new uniforms to remind them of those earlier experiences.

The airlines also sought to keep costs down by lowering workers' salaries. Although initially reluctant to negotiate a two-tier wage system, all of the unions, including AFA, eventually accepted it (Walsh 1988). AFA acceptance of the two-tier wage system further disrupted the old communal patterns by differentiating between two classes of workers.

Finally, management sought to lower costs by speeding up operations in the air (Hochschild 1983). Management first sped up operations by changing trip schedules, extending the number of duty-hours in a trip, and minimizing the time spent on layovers (Puchala 1980). According to one flight attendant:

> You get off the airplane. You've barely got enough time to go to the hotel and sleep, maybe get a quick bite to eat before you get on the airplane again in the morning.... We used to get done at 3:00 o'clock in the afternoon and not have to go until the next morning.

Speedup has also been accomplished by reducing staffing levels to one attendant for fifty passengers, the minimum allowed under FAA safety regulations. Within the context of the airlines' mass marketing of lower fares and the growing number of passengers, flight attendants have found it difficult to keep up. As one attendant explained:

> The company then got away from expressing the desire for us to make public contact. The meal service became the primary function of your job.... You became like a robot. You didn't have the flexibility that you previously did because you were dealing with far more passengers and half the amount of time.... Meal services were so time consuming, you didn't have time to do anything else. If you did have time, you were too tired and you didn't make an effort.

Prior to deregulation, flight attendants were able to cope with work problems such as speedup by falling back on their mutual-aid logic. However, management's cost cutting strategies undercut the flight attendants' old communal interactions, making it difficult for them to befriend and support one another either in the air or on the ground. Consequently, many flight attendants felt alienated within an occupation previously promoted as a model of sociability. As one flight attendant aptly put it:

A flight attendant's job is very lonely at times. Different cities. Different crews. They only work with people 30 days at a time and then they change crews. So somebody who is not well adjusted, not having a confident personality, will find this an extremely lonely situation to be placed in. They will need to find some way to cope with the situation.

Like the brotherhoods, AFA's mutual-aid logic atrophied because of members' changed interaction patterns. Instead of depending on themselves, the flight attendants, encouraged by AFA's bargaining successes, came to depend on the union, particularly the national office, to service their needs. Consequently, they looked to national headquarters to solve their problems. Within the context of the servicing logic, members developed a segmented commitment to the AFA, regarding it as instrumentally legitimate. When AFA failed to deliver, members instrumentally oriented to AFA withdrew their commitment and questioned its instrumental legitimacy. Within this context, several locals withdrew from the union. National Airlines' flight attendants voted to join the Transit Workers because AFA failed to support the local's call for a strike. Northwestern's flight attendants, dissatisfied with their contract, struck and voted to affiliate with the Teamsters. Continental flight attendants, feeling undercut by AFA during its national negotiations, voted to establish its own union, the Union of Flight Attendants.

The Reemergence of Mutual Aid: AFA's MAP

As we argued in chapter 3, as the union's environment becomes increasingly hostile and the servicing logic becomes an ineffective mechanism for gaining members' commitment, it becomes more likely that the union will seek to revitalize members' core commitment and strengthen its normative legitimacy by reconstructing its mutual-aid logic. The mutual-aid logic's reemergence, however, will be predicated on a community of memory responding to a problem that the union regards as critical to its survival and for which the old servicing logic has proven inadequate. Within AFA, the community of memory behind the reemergence of its mutual-aid logic was a group of veteran flight attendants who were recovering alcoholics and were responding to co-workers' increasing levels of work stress and the union's inability to curb management's abusive practices via collective bargaining and grievance handling. It is not surprising that the idea for a peer-based MAP came from veteran flight attendants who had experience with the union's old mutual-aid logic; it also is not unusual that they were recovering alcoholics experienced in AA twelve-step work. Their experience with the old mutual-aid logic was kept alive in their remembrances of these earlier communal experiences, and their twelve-step activities reinforced the old logic's emphasis on helping co-workers. According to one of the veterans:

> We finally just hit our limits in terms of how much we could be pushed around and in terms of how much stress we could live with and deny. When the eighties came along, we realized that if anybody's got these problems, it's us. Conditions got to the point where our people just started saying "NO! We're in pain and, if you, management, aren't going to recognize it and deal with it, we will!"

AFA's Board of Directors supported implementing the MAP for flight attendants. Within the context of the servicing logic, they sought government funding for the program. In 1978, the group of veterans submitted a proposal to the federal government to support a peer-based MAP within AFA. The proposal was promoted as the first effort to implement a peer program within a predominately female union. The proposal was approved as a joint labor-management initiative, but the airline executives refused to support a program administered and staffed by flight attendants. Like the railway executives discussed in chapter 3, they preferred to implement a more traditional employee assistance program (EAP) model, which would be staffed by treatment professionals, emphasize the role of supervisors in the identification of troubled workers, and encourage troubled workers to voluntarily seek help from the program. Like the railroads, the airline executives would also encourage co-workers to inform the EAP about troubled flight attendants. Asserting its independence, AFA decided to implement the MAP on its own; when the government withdrew its funding, it also decided to pay for the program from members' dues. In these actions, AFA's officers, wittingly or unwittingly, supported the veterans' advocacy to reconstruct AFA's mutual-aid logic.

The Structure of AFA's MAP

Having accepted the veterans' admonitions to return to their communal roots, it was also necessary for AFA to embed those beliefs in the structure of the MAP. AFA embedded the mutual-aid logic in the MAP by structuring it for flight attendants with a wide range of personal problems, including chemical dependency, marital and family difficulties, stress, and eating disorders. AFA also constructed the MAP around a peer network composed of working flight attendants, who perform their peer counseling role as uncompensated work. In addition, the philosophy of AFA's MAP explicitly recognizes its concerns with building a cohesive community. Although the program was initiated by a group of recovering flight attendants, its philosophy is more reflective of the community mental health movement's support of lay professionals than Alcoholics Anonymous' belief in twelve-step work (Caplan 1964). In the 1960s, community mental health centers faced two problems. First, there were too few professionals to treat Americans' mental health problems; second, due to the activism of that era, many groups such as African-Americans, Latinos, students, and women distrusted professionals. Within this context, psychiatrists advocated hiring and training indigenous community members to help treat members of their community. These lay professionals were trained to use facilitative counseling skills to establish a relationship with their clients, help them solve their problems, and become highly functional community members. [2]

Facilitative counseling highlights members' obligations to care for one another by emphasizing six skills characteristic of highly functional helpers (Carkhuff, 1969): (1) empathy is the ability to understand what the client is experiencing, (2) respect is the ability to let clients know that they are worthy of being respected, (3) concreteness is the ability to suggest specific solutions appropriate to clients' conditions, (4) genuineness is the ability of the helper to be himself or herself in the helping relationship, (5) confrontation is the ability to provide clients with an undistorted picture of their real world, and (6) immediacy is the ability to help clients understand what they are really trying to say. In the long-term development of effective helping relationships, empathy, respect, and confrontation are particularly important in assisting clients to become highly functional. Empathy is necessary in order to establish and maintain a helping relationship; and confrontation is necessary for clients to resolve their problems and become highly functional. The display of respect for clients moves them from one stage of the helping relationship to another. Initially, the helper respects them unconditionally; however, as clients learn to manage their problems, the helper's respect becomes increasingly conditional: "Given your developmental stage, I will respect you only *if* you function at your highest level" (Carkhuff 1969, 87).

2. Comparative research suggests that lay professionals are at least as effective, and in many instances more effective, than professional counselors (Hattie, Sharpley, and Rogers 1984, 540). After the Reagan administration cut back on social welfare spending in the early eighties, the professional treatment community lost interest in the training of lay professionals.

In community mental health centers, professionals supervise the lay professionals. In a similar fashion, the MAP's structure consists of a national office, staffed by the director and her staff, all of whom are professionals, and local member assistance committees at each of the airlines' domiciles, or home bases. The national office is responsible for providing training and consultation to the peer counselors. The local committees are embedded in AFA's local union structure; they are responsible for publicizing the program, counseling troubled attendants, referring co-workers to community resources for help, and providing follow-up to those whom they have helped. In addition, the committees also are responsible for coordinating their activities with other local committees such as those that deal with arbitration, grievance, and professional standards.

Reflecting the nature of AFA locals, the MAP committees vary in size and orientation (Bamberger and Sonnenstuhl 1995, 1996). Smaller domiciles typically have smaller committees; larger domiciles have larger committees, which often have a greater division of labor. Some peer counselors become expert in substance abuse; others become expert on mental health issues such as eating disorders and depression; still others may specialize in working with gay or lesbian flight attendants. Committees also vary as to whether they focus primarily on substance abuse or mental health issues, and their orientation is generally dependent on the peer counselors' perceptions of their co-workers' problems. For instance, a peer counselor who did not have an alcohol or drug problem told us:

> Maybe I have blinders on, but I just don't see alcohol and drugs as that big a problem. Like in Charlotte, the committee is dominated by recovering people and they're checking in three or four people a week for drug rehabilitation and alcohol. I think we have only checked in one the whole time I have been here — since 1989. . . . In any case, I think I have my specialties and I think other people have theirs.

The president of the AFA local appoints the chair of the local member assistance committee, who has a variety of responsibilities. These duties include maintaining the committee's relations with local base management, coordinating committee activities with the program's national office, and ensuring that the committee complies with the program's policies on record keeping and confidentiality. The chair's most important responsibility, however, is the recruitment, training, and supervision of peer counselors.

Flight attendants recovering from alcoholism and other addictions make ideal peer counselors because they have experiential knowledge of the problems for which they are often providing help. The majority of the peer counselors, however, are not recovering from alcoholism or other addictions. Rather, they are simply union members committed to helping other flight attendants solve their problems. Many become peer counselors because they have been helped by the program. Some become counselors as a way of becoming involved in the union; others become counselors because they are interested in mental health as a second career.

Peer counselors receive training from the national office, which offers two one-week training programs, a basic skills course for new members and an advanced course for experienced peer counselors. These courses are taught by a variety of staff, including the director, experienced AFA peer counselors, and outside consultants. The basic course emphasizes facilitative counseling skills. Through intensive role playing, for example, the counselors learn how to empathize with troubled co-workers, show them positive regard in order to build up their sense of self, use confrontation to breakdown their defenses, and concreteness to help them solve their problems. In addition, the peers learn such basic knowledge as how to identify troubled co-workers, to construct a network of community treatment resources, and to refer their co-workers to those resources. The advanced course focuses on the management of specific kinds of cases including alcoholism and other addictions, stress, psychiatric disorders, and family problems. In addition to role playing and lectures, peers learn by sharing their own experiences with one another. Flight attendants are encouraged to share their own experiences in overcoming such problems as alcoholism and eating disorders, and the experienced peer counselors share their joys and frustrations with helping their troubled co-workers. Through such storytelling, the newcomers learn the importance of relying on one another and mutual aid's role in preserving the occupation.

Both courses also caution peer counselors to know their limits when helping troubled co-workers and to protect themselves from burning out by supporting one another. Within this context, local committees provide peer counselors with ongoing training activities for polishing their facilitative counseling skills and using them to prevent burnout. In order to prevent burnout, the peer counselors also rely on one another for advice and encouragement, particularly when dealing with difficult cases. For example, one committee chair explained how she called and received support from another peer counselor whom she had met at training:

Well, I usually call [her] if I need a little mini-supervision or if I have a question about a case. . . . You know, like, these are some of my ideas I have. What do you think is the best way to do it?

The following remarks by one peer counselor highlight the program's caution to know one's limits and its admonition to set clear boundaries in order to prevent burnout:

> You have to learn not to get so involved. My big thing is trying to help people that have a drug and alcohol problem. I really want to help them and I want them to see how my life has been turned around since I stopped. But, I have to let it go. Like I say, "It's like the fish. I let the line out and I dangle the bait. If they want to take it, they can."

Peer-Based Helping Processes

The mutual-aid logic is also embedded in the routines by which the peer counselors help their co-workers. The helping process engages the peer counselors and AFA members in an intensive relationship that bridges their work and social lives. In that sense, the AFA MAP partially re-creates the old communal patterns and core commitment members' experienced in the stew zoos.

The helping process in the AFA MAP is similar to, but different from, the brotherhoods' Operation: Redblock Program. Like their counterparts in the railroad program, all of the peer counselors are volunteers who interact with their co-workers while performing their normal occupational duties. In contrast to the Operation: Redblock team members, however, AFA peer counselors are involved in all stages of the helping process, from intervention through follow-up. In each stage, AFA peer counselors enact their roles both passively and actively. In their passive role, the peer counselors help troubled co-workers who ask for their assistance; in their active role, peer counselors seek out their troubled colleagues, providing them with assistance even when they have not asked for it. In either case, the peer counselor's objective remains the same: to help the flight attendants solve their problems and become highly functional individuals on and off the job.

In the intervention stage, the peer counselors are concerned with motivating troubled flight attendants to accept help. Some flight attendants, recognizing that they are troubled, seek help from the peer counselors voluntarily. When flight attendants fail to recognize their troubles, AFA's peer counselors offer to assist them by providing them with unsolicited information about their problems and offer to help them solve those problems. In each of these circumstances, the peers' facilitative counseling skills play a crucial role in their co-workers' decisions to seek and accept help.

Studies generally find that women are more likely than men to seek help voluntarily (Horwitz 1977, 1990; Sonnenstuhl 1986). Likewise, most troubled flight attendants seek help from AFA's peer counselors voluntarily because, after either self-reflection or discussions with friends, they recognize they have problems and decide to seek help. One peer counselor explained how co-workers seek help from her:

> While we're out there on the ride, people know who we are and tend to come forward and tell us things. . . . We don't really go out there and pound the pavement to find people that are in need of help. But, we do let them know by being amongst them.

According to the flight attendants, they voluntarily seek help because they trust the program. For instance, one recovering attendant commented:

> This program has a lot of credibility with flight attendants. There's very little hesitation among them to use it. But, I think when people start to feel that the MAP is going after people . . . especially if it's seen as being for these *other* people's own good, I think that's a very touchy, iffy area. . . . It might start to undermine credibility and the trust that people have in the MAP.

The flight attendants' trust in the program is based on their perceptions of the peer counselors' qualities: The flight attendants perceive that, as their co-workers, the peer counselors are able to empathize with, and genuinely care about, them. For instance, one flight attendant told us why she sought help from AFA's MAP rather than her carrier's EAP:

> [The peer counselors] seemed different to me, in that the company EAP [had] somebody paid to do that and the flight attendants were volunteers. The flight attendant volunteers that helped me had both been in treatment themselves and shared that with me. I was just real impressed with them. For one thing, they both had something that I wanted. There was a lot of serenity there. They were caring but they weren't pushy. They say it's a program of attraction rather than promotion. That's what I like about it.

Peer counselors expressed similar beliefs about flight attendants' motivations for seeking her help. One explained:

> I think people came to me because they knew I'd been through the pit of Hell. A lot of people knew about what had happened to me and felt comfortable talking to me for that reason. . . . When people know you've

been in the pit of Hell, chances are you're not going to be real judgmental. . . . You're going to listen. . . understand. . . have some empathy. People started telling me their stories. Sitting on the jump seat, I heard stories of child abuse . . . drug and alcohol problems and eating disorders.

Many flight attendants are reluctant to seek help voluntarily either because they do not recognize their problems or because they deny having them. With such co-workers, the peer counselors use their facilitative skills to build a caring relationship with the troubled flight attendants. This is an interactive process in which the flight attendants are empathetic toward the troubled flight attendants, initially show them unconditional respect, and gradually become more confrontational as they attempt to overcome the attendants' resistance to recognizing their problems and accepting help.

Typically, peer counselors become aware of their co-workers' problems because they have directly observed a flight attendant's difficulties or heard about them from other flight attendants. In these cases, peer counselors speak to the troubled flight attendant, letting them know that, if she has a problem, they are empathetic and available to help. One explained her initial intervention with someone whom she observed:

> Her eyes were red, and she was in the bathroom trying to fix herself up. . . . I was trying to be nonchalant without saying I work for the MAP. . . . She said she had a few drinks. She was up 'til two or three in the morning. She had broken up with her boyfriend. . . . "I said, God, I know how it is. It will be all right. I use to come to work with a hangover and, God, isn't it the worst thing?" . . . Telling her I knew what it was like. If she ever needed to call me through MAP, she could. . . . I gave her my card, and she thanked me.

Another peer counselor described her initial phone call to a flight attendant whom crew members suspected of having a drinking problem:

> I said, "Your friends are concerned and even some people who are not your friends are concerned. People have called me and voiced concern. It's only because they care about you. I care about you too." She said, "I'm okay. I've been under a lot of stress." I said, "If things change in the future, you know that I am always available."

In some instances, the flight attendants are relieved at the peer counselors' overtures and accept their offers of help because, as one attendant put it, "There was a compassion in her voice and there was a certain tone that made me feel comfortable talking to her." In many instances, however, flight attendants do not accept help when it is first offered. Nevertheless, even in these cases, it is the flight attendant's perception of the peer counselor as being empathetic and respectful that creates the possibility of the attendant accepting help in the future. For instance, one flight attendant, who was treated for alcoholism, described her initial reactions to a peer counselor who called and offered her help:

I bluffed my way out of it saying, "Who wouldn't be [upset]? You would be in pretty bad shape too if your marriage of thirteen years had just ended." . . . [The peer counselor] said, "Okay!" . . . I thought to myself, "Well, I took care of that." . . . I [also] thought, "When was the last time I flew with anyone who had shown the least bit of concern about me or said, . . . 'Gee, How are you doing? Anything wrong?'"

Typically, peer counselors will make several overtures to the reluctant flight attendants. In subsequent interactions, peer counselors continue to be empathetic and respectful while gathering more information about the attendants and formulating their strategy for future interventions. For example, one peer told us:

There are two types of women alcoholics. There are women who drink and become loud, abusive, and irrational. . . . With those, I think, probably you need "tough love." . . . The shrinking violet. . . . Those you can't scream at. If you do, they'll shrink even more. . . . You have to bring them out with a sense you love them. You find them of worth. You give them hope. . . . All this takes much more time.

However, as they gather more information about a flight attendant's problems, they will also be more confrontational, pointing out that their problems are not going away and continue to create difficulties for them. As one troubled flight attendant noted about the peer counselor who eventually assisted her:

She kept pushing me. I'd keep saying that I'd get back to her — that I was leaving on a trip. . . . I pretty much was trying to dodge her.

Eventually, flight attendants reluctant to accept help are likely to develop more serious difficulties such as performance problems. These may first become apparent to the counselors when other crewmembers ask them for help; later they may become apparent when supervisors bring them to the attention of the peer counselors. In these interventions, the peer counselors, acting in response to information from supervisors and/or co-workers, confront their troubled co-workers with evidence of performance problems and offer to help them before they become enmeshed in the disciplinary process. An AFA peer counselor described her intervention with a bulimic flight attendant:

> I got a call from some crew members about her. I called her and said, "We are getting reports that you are eating half the crew meals and going into the bathroom and throwing up. Your color is also bad. We know that you've had a problem in the past. You need to see your doctor." . . . She thanked me for my concern . . . but she never called until her supervisor got on her back. Then, she wanted us to get him off her back.

As this example suggests, reluctant flight attendants are often motivated to seek help in order to escape from their supervisors. In some instances, such as the following case, supervisors will contact the peer counselors about troubled flight attendants prior to taking disciplinary action. An AFA peer counselor explained how she intervened to circumvent supervisory action:

> I have a pretty good relationship with some of the supervisors. . . . Once the supervisors have given them an oral warning . . . some [of the supervisors] will put a note in my box saying so and so needs help. . . . Then, I tell them [the co-workers], "I have gotten a note saying something is wrong. You are having some problems with your work, dependability, or whatever. We can help you. We can get the supervisor off your back."

Still other peer counselors have taken more direct action to assist co-workers in job jeopardy. One peer counselor intervened with an attendant who was about to be fired. According to the flight attendant, who is now a recovering alcoholic:

> I was hung over. . . . I walked into the hanger. This is when [the peer counselor] stopped me and said, "I need to talk to you. We need to talk, right now." I looked at her like, "Who the hell are you?" . . . She then said that she was recovering. I can remember all of a sudden the fear was so overwhelming to me. . . . She said that she needed to talk to me and [told me] not to go over to the terminal to see my supervisor.

All of the above interventions bring increasing pressure to bear upon the flight attendant to accept help. From them, troubled flight attendants learn that they are not fulfilling their work responsibilities, that they are troubled, and that the peer counselors are committed to helping them solve their troubles and keep their jobs. Underlying all of these increasingly confrontational interventions, however, is the peer counselors' empathy and respect for their co-workers, and in the end, it is the troubled flight attendants' perceptions of these qualities that enable them to accept help. As one recovering attendant stated it:

[My peer counselor] had a lot of compassion. . . . Suggested that I go in that day. I did. . . . I didn't even have time to bring any clothes or any toiletries. . . . The next day, she showed up with everything I could ever need.

In the AFA program the boundaries between treatment and follow up are fuzzy because the peer counselors are not the flight attendants' primary treatment agents; rather, the peer counselors refer most flight attendants to community treatment agencies for treatment. Thus, the treatment and follow up meld together as peer counselors, on referring troubled flight attendants to a community resource, begin to follow up with them to ensure that they are receiving appropriate help and are complying with their treatment plan. In these interactions, the peer counselors continue to be empathetic, genuine, concrete, and confrontational; however, because the emphasis in these stages is on complying with treatment recommendations, the peer counselors make their respect for the flight attendants conditional on their steady progress toward becoming highly functional.

When peer counselors refer flight attendants for alcoholism treatment, for instance, follow up begins as soon as they enter treatment and continues until they are living sober lives. As one peer counselor explained:

If I have somebody in treatment, I always make one visit. I like it if I can talk with the counselor. . . . I like to be a part of that aftercare recommendation. I like to explain to the therapist or the counselor what it's like to be a flight attendant, what is reasonable to expect.

On their return to work, the peer counselors continue to interact with the flight attendants, reinforcing what they have learned in treatment by letting them know they understand and giving them concrete advice for coping with alcohol on and off the job. For instance, one peer counselor tells returning flight attendants that their fears are normal but, if they follow the AA program, they will soon feel okay. She tells them:

You come back feeling like a billboard's been put somewhere around the airport and everybody knows. Really, no one knows. . . . Because [alcohol has] become such a stigma in your life . . . you can never have it ever, ever again, there's a certain amount of resentment that everyone else is having a good time and you can't. . . . The first thing you want to do is isolate [yourself] with your secret. You got to be real careful you don't put yourself out there with the things that you find threatening. . . . You venture out little bit by little bit and test the waters. You find out sometimes that it's not the world that you remembered. . . . Slowly you become more comfortable and you start functioning like everyone else. Socializing, doing things, talking about yourself. It takes a while. I say to people, "Don't expect to feel any better for eight months. And [meanwhile] you're going to feel like hell."

Others advise returning attendants to attend AA meetings on layovers, have hotels remove alcohol from their rooms, and, if they need it, ask for help. For instance, one peer counselor suggests that flight attendants who are having a weak moment on the plane:

Ask for friends of Bill W. [the founder of AA] to come into the galley in the back of the airplane for some support. That's been done before. . . . Eight or ten people will show up. So, that's a real positive thing that they can do at a weak moment.

In addition to providing returning flight attendants with advice, some peer counselors talk with them on a regular basis. For example, one peer counselor recounted that she spoke with a returning attendant:

Almost every day for a while in the beginning. . . . Those conversations were just like conversations of two friends, someone that is supporting her. . . . She would tell me about her breakthroughs, about the things that she was discovering about herself. Mainly she talked about her progress, where she was, how she felt, where she was today.

Others provide more direct support by flying with newly recovering attendants.

I have gone with people who have come out of treatment. . . . I specifically selected those trips to fly [with them]. People have [also] asked me to fly with them. And when I do, . . . they talk to me, and I can talk recovery. I'm not in recovery myself, but I can talk recovery. If somebody is a little bit fearful of being back at work, at least they have somebody that they trust that they can talk to.

Ideally, most attendants return to work and learn to live sober lives, with the help of their peer counselors. However, some flight attendants refuse to follow their treatment plan. In these cases, the peer counselors confront them, emphasizing that continuing support is contingent on their following their treatment plan. Such confrontations are designed to reinforce those behaviors expected of recovering attendants and highlight that the peer counselors' respect is conditional on their becoming all that they can be. For instance, one peer counselor, recounting her frustrations with a resistant attendant, told us:

I was just tired of the bull shit, the whining. She had done the same thing over and over and over. She knew the program, she just didn't want to do it. I would say, "Well, when you decide when you want to help yourself, call me. But I can't do this for you. . . . What is this doing to your child?" . . . But if she didn't want to hear anymore of that logic what more can I do.

Likewise, another peer counselor told another flight attendant:

There are a large number of people that need help, that want help. I think you really do, but you've shown me no indication of that. I only have so much time. I'll work with you, but if you're not going to follow the suggestions, then you better look for help elsewhere. I don't have the time to make suggestions unless you follow through. When you're ready to do that, you call me.

Typically, the peer counselors follow up their alcoholism cases for a year. However, even after closing cases, they are watchful for potential relapses and willing to assist those who relapse and want help. One peer counselor recounted:

A flight attendant wrote a letter to the committee saying [she] smelled alcohol on the breath of someone we had gotten into treatment [a year earlier]. I flew with some friends of this person's — a friend of her's told me that she had started drinking again. . . . I knew I was going to be flying with her the next week. . . . After the flight, we went to her room. She said, "Yeah, well, this is what's happened. My boyfriend and I have had a problem. We were going to split up except we bought this house together. So we have to live together." [She then told me about] all the problems that have come up. But [she said] that she had started going back to [AA] meetings and that she was going to get back on the track and everything. I talked to her again about a week later because she called me to thank me for being concerned and talking to her. . . . But she still has a problem. I'm going to call her again.

In this section, we have seen that, through the MAP, AFA is reconstructing its mutual-aid logic by revitalizing members' core commitment and its normative legitimacy. AFA is reembedding the mutual-aid logic within the flight attendants' culture, structure, and routines. Culturally, as in the railroad brotherhoods, veterans remembered the logic and argued that AFA's current problems could be resolved by involving members in taking care of themselves. Structurally, the role of peer counselor involves members in helping one another with a wide range of personal problems. In addition, because MAP committees are closely linked to professional standards and grievance activities, they are also deeply embedded in their union locals. The counseling role is also deeply embedded in the normal routines of the flight attendants' lives. Peer counselors are working flight attendants and, therefore, readily available to their co-workers, performing jump seat counseling, referral to community resources, and following up with troubled attendants to ensure their recovery. In this way, the MAP is reembedding the mutual-aid logic in the AFA, renewing members' core commitment, and strengthening its normative legitimacy.

The MAP's Impact on Members' Commitment and AFA's Legitimacy

As in Operation: Redblock, we observed that members' involvement with AFA's MAP has a number of important social consequences. First, the membership generally holds the MAP in high regard because of its success in helping troubled flight attendants. According to one recovering flight attendant, "Ten years after its establishment, nearly all AFA members know of at least one co-worker that has gone through the program." Still, some flight attendants remain reluctant to use the program. Nevertheless, they too are learning that AFA's MAP is trustworthy and are using it. According to a union leader who is actively involved with the program:

> A lot of people are afraid of the union. How many calls do we get a day where someone says, "I've never called the union before, and I'm really not sure if I should tell you about this." But then, in any case, they come right out with the problem.

Clearly, one important consequence is that the MAP provides flight attendants with another mechanism for becoming involved in the union. Indeed, many members do not want to become involved with what they regard as "union politics"; however, they do want to do something for their co-workers. As one local union official expressed it:

> A lot of flight attendants don't care about their union all that much, even if they do care about their co-workers. All they want to do is their job and go home. They certainly don't want to get involved in political aspects of the union. . . . The MAP allows them to help their co-workers and the union without having to deal with union politics.

Second, the program has helped to renew the flight attendants' mutual-aid logic, making them feel less dependent on paternalistic management and more dependent on one another. As one union officer explained:

> For many years I did the union orientation for all the new flight attendants. . . . Tell the ten best things of your union in an hour. I always made it a point of delving into the program. It was there and, if these are the kind of problems that you're having, let's use that before it comes to work and the attention of management.

Likewise, an attendant, who had been helped by the program, told us that peer assistance "increased our ability and willingness to depend on ourselves," and another union officer acknowledged, "I think it lends solidarity because we're all working together."

Third, the MAP has enhanced AFA's normative legitimacy by changing flight attendants' perceptions of the union. Many no longer see AFA as an amorphous entity with little meaning in their lives; now they believe that AFA is a legitimate actor in their personal lives. According to a recovering flight attendant, having the program sets AFA apart from the "typical union, concerned only with its own institutional interests and distant from its membership . . . [because AFA] takes an interest in members' personal concerns." For many, the union's interest in them is personified in the peer counselors. As one flight attendant observed about the peer counselor who had helped her:

> She was very reassuring and was clearly taking my side. I had no idea what my rights were, what I should have been doing. I felt like she was very educated in that area and that she was looking out for my best interest.

Another recovering flight attendant aptly summed up her appreciation observing, "[The peer counselor's follow up] makes me feel wonderful — that they [the union] give a darn." Thus the peer-based network and its incorporation into the local union structure is succeeding in building closer personal ties between AFA and its membership.

Fourth, by helping flight attendants solve their problems, the program has also helped renew their core commitment to AFA. For instance, attendants who have been helped by the program feel a great deal of gratitude to the union and, therefore, are more willing to support it. As one recovering flight attendant told us:

> Well, I didn't have this inherent ill-will against the union or anything like that. When I was drinking and using, I just thought they were another political body doing what they thought best for the betterment of the employees. I didn't give it any thought outside of that. There were just more things that were more important to me at that time. But after, because the union did have the MAP and the way that those [peer counselors] responded to me, I thought these people were like saints. I still can't thank them enough for being there for me. They just gave me a real good feeling about life and the power of the human spirit to help others.

Many of those helped by the program demonstrate their renewed commitment to AFA by becoming peer counselors or taking on other union responsibilities. For many, becoming a peer counselor is a way of "giving something back to the union that helped me."

Fifth, AFA has begun to use the program as an important competitive advantage in its organizing drives. Union organizers have found that the reputation of the AFA MAP often precedes the AFA into unorganized workplaces and they are using it in their organizing drives. For example, in an organizing drive at Northwest Airlines, the AFA distributed a six-page pamphlet on the advantages of AFA representation. A relatively large portion of the brochure is dedicated to a description of the MAP. In other organizing drives, AFA's peer counselors have provided help to the targeted flight attendants as a way of highlighting that AFA understands their problems and cares about them.

By involving flight attendants in the MAP, AFA, like the brotherhoods, is reconstructing its mutual-aid logic, renewing members' core commitment, and strengthening its normative legitimacy. Through their involvement as peer counselors, a new generation of flight attendants is learning the values of mutual aid while also providing a valuable service to their co-workers. Similarly, those flight attendants helped by the peer counselors have learned the meaning of mutual aid; as a result, they are volunteering as peer counselors to care for others and are taking on other union responsibilities such as organizing other airlines and serving on local committees. Through AFA's MAP, the flight attendants are experiencing and rebuilding their occupational community.

Concluding Remarks

In this chapter, we have attempted to deepen our understanding of the logics of union-member relations by focusing on them within AFA. As with the railroad brotherhoods, our analysis generally supports the theoretical framework presented in chapter 2. AFA's mutual-aid logic was critical in the flight attendants' survival and eventual development as a permanent independent union. The mutual-aid logic was activated by its hostile environment, which was characterized by rapid technological change and paternalism. It emerged out of the working and living conditions encountered by workers in this newly created occupation. During the occupation's formation, flight attendants were highly dependent on one another to learn and perform their jobs. At the same time, living in the "stew zoos" created a highly emotional experience in which flight attendants learned to rely on one another rather than management. These experiences developed the flight attendants' core commitment, which was critical for organizing the first flight attendants' union at United, and they continued to be a crucial factor in the flight attendants' ability to survive during their twenty-three years as a division of ALPA.

However, after AFA was organized as an independent union, the mutual-aid logic atrophied due to changes in members' communal interaction patterns and members developed segmented commitment to the union, regarding it as instrumentally legitimate. For instance, several factors contributed to the disintegration of the "stew zoos," including civil rights legislation, which enabled the flight attendants to overturn the no-marriage rule, and deregulation, which eventually transformed them into commuters. Within this context, the AFA's servicing logic developed, activated by a relatively supportive environment: Its technical and legal environments were relatively stable and supportive and management accepted AFA as the flight attendants' representative. As we have seen elsewhere, the servicing logic can sustain the union's instrumental legitimacy and members' segmented commitment in such a supportive environment. Unfortunately, AFA's environment remained stable for a brief period, time enough for the mutual-aid logic to atrophy and the servicing logic to become established. Consequently, when deregulation hit the airline industry and AFA's environment turned increasingly hostile, the flight attendants were at a loss. Without their old mutual-aid logic to sustain them, the flight attendants were unable to cope with management's speedup in the air and suffered a high degree of work and emotional distress. Within this context, veteran flight attendants were responsible for reviving their mutual-aid logic, arguing that AFA's servicing logic was inconsistent with the new hostile working environment and that its future was dependent on involving members once again in a community of workers, which supported flight attendants on and off the job.

Our data also suggest that AFA's MAP has been successful in helping to revive the union's mutual-aid logic. Through the work of the peer counselors, the mutual-aid logic is being reembedded within AFA's culture and structure as well as the routines of members' work and social lives. More important, however, our data also suggest that flight attendants' involvement with the MAP is helping to renew AFA's normative legitimacy and the attendants' core commitment to the union. Through the MAP, flight attendants are learning the value of sisterhood, are coming to regard the mutual-aid logic as a legitimate way of organizing AFA, and are choosing to become increasingly involved in other AFA activities such as running for office and organizing new AFA locals on un-unionized airlines.

While the AFA case generally supports our theoretical model, it also deepens our insights into several factors. First, our discussion in chapter 2 suggested that regulative legitimacy was a crucial activating factor in the rapid growth of the labor movement after 1935. The AFA case suggests that regulative legitimacy conferred on unions may be a necessary condition but is not a sufficient condition for the development of an independent union. Indeed, the AFA case highlights the detrimental effects of paternalism within the labor movement. While management's paternalism was particularly evident from the occupation's inception, it was the labor movement's paternalism that had the most debilitating impact on AFA's development as an independent union. ALPA represented the air line pilots who, until very recently, were men. ALPA assumed that the flight attendants were incapable of representing themselves because they were women and pressed to be their representative, even though its economic interests were opposed to the attendants' interests. Within this context, the flight attendants were never taken very seriously even when they did successfully act in their own interest. Indeed, it took another piece of federal legislation, the Civil Rights Act, to provide the flight attendants with enough regulative legitimacy to be taken seriously and the ability to act on their own interests. In this sense, the AFA case also further deepens our understanding of the fragmentation stage of the labor movement, suggesting that labor leaders must regard those whom they seek to organize as legitimate actors capable of running their own affairs in order for a strong labor movement to reemerge.

Finally, the AFA case demonstrates how quickly the mutual-aid logic can atrophy. Indeed, AFA emerged as an independent union in 1973; yet, by 1978, the mutual-aid logic was barely visible within AFA's culture and structure and the routines of its members. Within the context of the larger changes in the airline industry and the pressing day-to-day activities of AFA administration, leaders and members simply forgot about the mutual-aid logic's importance in their communal lives. Still, the AFA case also highlights the extent to which the mutual-aid logic can be revived by members' willingness to assert its importance in their lives and their willingness to befriend one another. Within this context, the AFA case also suggests that keeping the mutual-aid logic alive and well requires constant vigilance.

5 Renewing Community in an Industrial Union

Unlike the railroad brotherhoods and AFA, which were initially organized around individual crafts, the Transport Workers Union (TWU) is an industrial union. Industrial unions represent all workers in a particular industry, regardless of craft. In this chapter, we examine the logics of union-member relations in the TWU's New York City local, which represents all subway and bus workers in New York City. The TWU is an interesting comparative case because, unlike the brotherhoods and AFA, the union did not have a natural workers' community on which to build. The workers did not share a common occupation, a common ethnic heritage, or a common geographic community on which to construct its mutual-aid logic. The TWU story, then, is about the workers' struggle to develop a sense of community and a mutual-aid logic on which to build a union. Still, like the brotherhoods and the AFA, the TWU's mutual-aid logic was activated within the context of a transportation management that rejected unions, a hostile legal environment, and a rapidly changing technical environment. Similarly, the TWU's mutual-aid logic atrophied and its servicing logic was activated within a context of a co-opting transportation management, a supportive legal environment, and stable technical environment. In the 1980s, TWU's community of memory also began to argue for a return to its old mutual-aid logic. Once again, the mechanism for renewing members' core commitment and TWU's normative legitimacy is the member assistance program (MAP). However, TWU's program differs greatly from that of the brotherhoods and AFA. In contrast to those programs, TWU's peer counselors are "professionals," that is, the peer counselors are union members who are paid to work full time counseling coworkers. This difference highlights an important constraint in their efforts

128

to reconstruct their mutual-aid logic, one that the MAP is struggling to overcome by involving more TWU members in the program voluntarily.

The Struggle to Construct Feelings of Community

The transportation industry of the late nineteenth and early twentieth century was not the monolith that the Metropolitan Transportation Authority (MTA) later became. Across the five boroughs, bus and subway services were operated by a variety of small companies who employed a largely immigrant workforce drawn from across New York City (McGinley 1949). Early efforts to create a union in New York City's transportation industry failed because the workers, unlike the brotherhoods and AFA, lacked a naturally occurring community on which to construct a union with a mutual-aid logic. In addition, the transit workers faced a very hostile organizing environment. Management vehemently rejected unions as legitimate actors in the transit industry, even after Congress passed the National Labor Relations Act. Economically, the workers were also at a disadvantage because there were also more immigrant workers available than there were transportation jobs, and technological improvements continuously reduced the number of workers required to operate the transportation system. Within this environment, employers felt free to intimidate workers, play workers off against one another, and summarily fire union organizers. Workers' sense of powerlessness is evident in the historical record and in the memories of veteran transportation workers.

Working conditions were particularly brutal before the TWU won recognition from the Interborough Rapid Transit Line (IRT) in 1937 to represent all of the workers, regardless of craft, employed on that subway line. Workers complained about the filthy, unsanitary conditions in which they were forced to work (Freeman 1989). Ticket agents were forbidden to go to the bathroom, unless relieved by a relief worker, the scarcity of whom resulted in few if any relief breaks for the ticket agents. A similar fate was experienced by trolley and subway operators, many of whom solved the problem by resorting to "the motorman's friend," a urine collection tube and bottle that were strapped to the operator's leg. Within this degrading context, transport workers felt that they were treated like slaves. A bus operator who was active in organizing the TWU in the 1930s aptly expressed this sentiment:

> People talk about slavery, working for them [the bus lines], in 1934 and 1935, you were nothing but a number. They didn't even recognize your

name. . . . They never referred to you as [Joe Delaney], as a person; they referred to me as 308.

In addition to feeling like slaves, transport workers also felt abused by the riding public and powerless to do anything about it for fear of losing their jobs. For instance, in her biography of Mike Quill, a founder of the TWU and its most illustrious president, Shirley Quill describes his experience as a young ticket agent (1985, 46):

> [Mike was] assaulted by a parade of anonymous, tense faces, petulant and strident voices, hands impatiently tapping coins on the counter of the booth . . . [he] was bombarded with questions. "What color is the green light?" "Is this my train?" "Have you seen my wife?" "Is my husband in the lavatory?" . . . "Do you sell stamps? Well, why don't you? You're working for the public aren't you?"

Transport workers were forced to work long hours for little pay. In the 1930s, the seven-day week was standard and workdays were often scheduled for as long as twelve to eighteen hours. On the IRT, for example, ticket agents generally worked seventy-two hours a week, porters worked seventy hours, and shop men worked fifty hours a week. A transport worker who worked as an ironworker on the elevated lines in the thirties described his typical workweek:

> Working hours was nine hours per day, seven days per week. If you didn't come in Sunday, you were sent home Monday. I was there eight years before I got a vacation. We were off every holiday without pay and sent home on rainy days.

Most transport workers were paid subsistence wages that kept them and their families hovering just above the poverty line (Freeman 1989).

In addition to the long hours and poor pay, the transit system's disciplinary process was harsh and unforgiving. The companies had extensive rules covering every aspect of the job as well as employees' personal behavior. Minor infractions of those rules were severely punished. As one bus driver, who began work in 1932, put it:

> No matter what you did, you were wrong. . . . If you didn't follow the book of rules you were wrong. If you followed the book of rules and got into a disagreement or any kind of an altercation, you were wrong. You should have used your judgment, but the book of rules says you don't have a right to a judgment. So you are wrong no matter what you do.

In circumstances where transport workers could not be directly supervised, the companies hired "beakies," plainclothes agents to spy on workers. The companies regarded unfavorable reports from the beakies as sufficient grounds to fire or otherwise discipline workers. A bus driver described his experience with the beakies in the 1930s:

> If you were out, the boss would have these inspectors out in the street. And if they didn't find fault, . . . he would call them in [and say,] "How come I don't get any citations or complaints from you?" Well you say, "But gee Mr. Mulligan, I don't find any fault. I got a good crew working." He says, "Listen, let me tell you something. If I go out on a Saturday morning, I will find things wrong with them. Understand me?" So to be an inspector, you had to be a weasel. Go looking for problems. . . . Or create them.

As a result of the transit system's harsh disciplinary practices, workers were thoroughly intimidated. Moreover, before the TWU, one had little choice except to submit to the bosses' arbitrariness because there were few, if any other jobs available, particularly during the depression years. This sense of intimidation and insecurity was enhanced by managerial efforts to introduce new labor-saving technologies such as turnstiles and multidoor unit controls. Able to employ fewer and fewer workers, management consistently threatened to replace current employees with the growing reserve of immigrants. Indeed, despite the need to hold on to their jobs, few men survived the grueling working conditions for very long. As one TWU member noted:

> You start at forty-two cents an hour; after ten years of service, you would get sixty-two cents an hour. I never knew any man that I worked with that lasted ten years to get sixty-two cents an hour. . . . If you had five years and you were getting fifty-two cents an hour and you come in and your tie wasn't up, or you didn't have two dollars and fifty cents in your changer or you needed a shave, you got suspended or fired.

According to Mike Quill, "Before the TWU appeared . . . the boss had the right to hire and fire at will. No charges of wrongdoing were necessary. . . . Even the most insignificant lackey of the employer had life and death control over a worker's destiny" (quoted in Quill, 1985, 47).

In order to understand both the transport workers' failed attempts to organize and the emergence of the TWU, it is also necessary to comprehend their relationship to New York City's Irish community and its mutual-aid ethic, which was both the workers' strength and weakness. The transit system employed native-born Protestants as well as a wide range of first- and second-generation workers of other ethnicities, including Germans, Italians, Hispanics, English, African-Americans, Norwegians, and Russians; nevertheless, Irish immigrants dominated the work force (Freeman 1989). The transit companies hired them in large numbers in the transportation departments where workers had to speak English in order to interact with the public. Also, newly arrived Irish immigrants generally found their first jobs in the United States with the help of relatives and friends who got them employment where they worked. Thus, through their ethic of mutual aid, the Irish became concentrated in such industries as construction, shipping, trucking, and transit.

New York's Irish community emphasized a social order remarkably consistent with the one the immigrants left behind — a social order built around deference to traditional authority and a communal ethic of mutual aid (Greeley 1972; Bayor 1978; Stivers 1985). The Irish community was constructed around a number of interlocking traditional institutions, which demanded and rewarded compliance, including the Catholic church, fraternal organizations, and the machine politics of Tammany Hall. "It was the duty of the faithful to follow the priest and to be faithful [to the clergy] — just as it was the duty of the precinct worker to follow the direction of the district leader" (Cross 1978, 183). In return, the church and the political party provided their followers with whatever spiritual or temporal rewards were deemed appropriate.

The church also exerted a great deal of influence over employers' and workers' attitudes toward unionism. Its doctrine of Social Catholicism called for a harmonious relationship between capital and labor, recognizing the right of workers to a living wage and the obligation of employers to act in accordance with the common good. This doctrine reinforced the Irish community's values of deference to authority and inhibited the Irish immigrants' involvement with unionism.

Within this context, Irish workers, struggling to survive the brutality of the transit companies, tended to look to the Irish community for solutions to their problems rather than to creation of independent unions. For instance, one TWU organizer described the relationship between Irish workers and the Democratic politics of Tammany Hall in the 1920s and 1930s:

> The Irish owned all of the . . . districts. . . . They had Democratic clubs all over the City of New York. . . . You were out of a job so your family used to go out and campaign for them. You needed a ton of coal, and they would have a ton of coal shipped to you. . . . You were being taken care of.

That was the pay off. Instead of giving you money . . . the coal company was just sending you coal which was a payoff for the politician.

During the depression, those who lost their jobs turned to their neighbors for help. For instance, a retired bus driver described how the neighbors in his apartment building helped other families without work:

One neighbor would have a loaf of bread. The kids got half of it and you had to save two slices. "Mrs. Murphy's kids has nothing to eat up there. You wait last." You gave your own kids less to try and help somebody else.

Likewise, it was natural for the workers, on arriving in New York, to turn to the Irish community for help. For instance, single transit workers lived as boarders with Irish families, and married transit workers usually had one boarder. In addition, the immigrants turned to such fraternal organizations as the Ancient Order of Hibernians and the United Irish Counties Association to satisfy their social needs. Here, they drank inexpensive beer, attended weekend dances, and participated in such traditional Irish sports as soccer. If they needed medical care and could not afford it, they also turned to the Irish community as Mike Quill did when he needed a thousand dollars for an operation:

[Mike's brothers] energetically plunged into fund raising activities. A labor of love for their kid brother. . . . They went to friends, relatives, in-laws, and neighbors from home. Nobody turned Mike down; the crumpled two-dollar, five-dollar and ten-dollar bills grew to a respectable nest egg. His brothers took bank loans, scrimped and saved every penny. In three months Mike had the money. (Quill 1985, 51)

Thus, while there existed a strong, ethnically based mutual-aid ethic among the Irish immigrants, many of whom were employed as transit workers, this ethic was not cognitively linked to the workplace. Indeed, the mutual-aid ethic, linked as it was with Irish deference to authority and the church's doctrine of Social Catholicism, was a powerful counterweight to workers' unionizing efforts. Combined with their employers' power to intimidate and a lack of legislative support for unionizing, it is little wonder that the workers' early efforts at organizing failed and they felt like slaves. Indeed, they were poorly organized and lacked a sense of community and a mechanism for coordinating organizing activities across the entire transit system. Consequently, when one group struck, there was little support from the other transit workers. Inevitably, the strike failed and the workers were replaced, making workers skeptical about the practicality and benefits of forming an independent union. Nevertheless, TWU and its mutual-aid logic would emerge from a more militant version of Irish beliefs in mutual aid.

Mutual Aid and the Establishment of the TWU

TWU's mutual-aid logic developed out of members' struggle to create and sustain the union. As we have already seen, passage of the National Labor Relations Act conferred regulative legitimacy on unions and set off a wave of organizing. The immediate catalyst leading to the formation of the TWU was the economic crash of 1929. Ridership on the city's transit systems fell by 424 million riders between 1930 and 1933. In order to cut costs, the IRT and BMT cut workers' pay by at least 10 percent (Freeman 1989). As in the past, the workers attempted to organize a union around the discontent set off by this management decision. Within this hostile economic and managerial context, the transport workers would eventually emerge victorious because two groups, the Clan na Gael and the Communist party, combined their resources in order to build the TWU on a more militant mutual-aid ethic than that offered by the traditional Irish community.

Clan na Gael, Gaelic for "We stand together," is a secret fraternal society of Irish-Americans that was formed in 1858 by John O'Mahony to unite the American Fenians (Bell 1970). Until the 1920s, it was a traditional fraternal organization fostering mutual aid within the Irish community and encouraging deference to authority among its members. That changed when the Irish Free State released thousands of Irish Republican Army (IRA) prisoners, thousands of whom immigrated to New York where they found jobs throughout the transit system and joined Clan na Gael. They transformed the clan from an Irish-American organization to an immigrant organization and created within the transit system a network of militant workers that could be organized across companies (Bell 1970). Up to this point, the membership of the Clan na Gael were older men who had been in transit for many years. The younger Irish-Americans and especially the Irish immigrants were drawn to the clan because of its secretive nature and its strong support for the IRA cause that they had recently left. The younger members' republican experiences in Ireland made them tough men. They had fought against the British, faced imprisonment, injury, and the death of their peers; therefore, they were less intimidated by the beakies and transit management's normal threats.

These experiences also taught them to work as a group and the value of a more militant, Irish mutual-aid ethic.

Whereas the Clan Na Gael provided transit workers with a militant network for organizing workers across the transit systems, the Communist party provided them with organizational expertise and financial backing (Freeman 1989). As we argued in chapter 2, the Communist party became very involved in union organizing during the Great Depression. It was particularly involved in organizing transportation workers, seeing them as a critical case for demonstrating to Americans the communal power of the working class. Although many of the Irish transport workers distrusted the Communist party, many felt, as one TWU organizer told us, "What we were fighting was worst than Communism." Likewise, Mike Quill later told those who asked about the union's early days:

> Sure I worked with the Communists. In 1933, I would have made a pact with the Devil himself if he could have given us the money, the mimeograph machines and the manpower to launch the Transport Workers Union. The Communist party needed me, and I knew them. I knew what the transport workers needed. The men craved dignity, longed to be treated like human beings. The time had come to get off our knees and fight back. (Quoted in Quill 1985, 63)

On April 12, 1934, a small group composed of Communist party members and transit workers who were also members of Clan na Gael, met to formally announce the formation of the Transport Workers Union. They distributed thousands of copies of the *Transport Workers Bulletin*, announcing the union's formation:

> Our aim is to at all times safeguard, protect, and improve the working conditions and living standards of all transport workers regardless of race, color, creed, nationality or political views or affiliations. We are based firmly on the principle of industrial unionism and militant struggle and against company unionism and craft unionism.

As one TWU organizer active in the 1930s told us, industrial unionism gave the workers power:

> Whether you were cleaning the floor in a bus garage, washing parts, or a number-one motorman, you were all the same. You paid the same dues. You went to the same meetings and sections. One for all and all for one. That's what made the TWU. . . . No one is any better than anybody else.

The process of establishing and maintaining the TWU was difficult. In 1934, the IRT was the first transit company to be organized; the BMT and the ISS followed in 1936 and 1937. In the summer of 1937, the TWU gained recognition across all of the major transit companies and also became affiliated with the Committee for Industrial Organization (CIO). On October 4, 1937, with the TWU claiming victory throughout the transit industry, it held its first international convention, electing four of its founding members as international officers. In 1940, when the city took over the Rapid Transit System, Mayor La Guardia refused to recognize the union but the TWU slowly triumphed over the city and won back its recognition. By 1948, however, the TWU was strong enough to stand on its own; thus it broke with the Communist party and moved toward a stronger relationship with the national CIO and the Democratic party. During the 1950s and 1960s, the TWU fought against a number of dissident labor organizations, which sought to undermine the TWU. However, by the time of Quill's death in 1966, the TWU had won exclusive bargaining rights for almost all New York transit workers, institutionalized collective bargaining for municipal transit workers, and established itself as one of the most powerful labor organizations in the country.

TWU's Mutual-Aid Logic

Clan na Gael and the Communist party successfully provided workers with a militant framework for developing TWU. However, workers' involvement in building the union embedded the mutual-aid logic into its culture and structure and members' routines. Within this context, workers developed a core commitment to the TWU, regarding it as normatively legitimate.

Although stories of TWU's success depict leaders such as Mike Quill and Austin Hogan as the heroes responsible for vanquishing their employers, the rank-and-file members who participated in the routine organizing of the TWU and its long-term maintenance are the union's real heroes. As one retired TWU organizer told us, "We were all leaders then. There were other locations where you had leaders too. You had a lot of angry men at that time." With each organizing and contract success, members became more and more aware that they had succeeded in besting their employers by being able to stick together, and the mutual-aid logic became more deeply embedded within the TWU.

The mutual-aid logic was embedded in members' routine work activities. For example, the early leaders routinely made sacrifices to build the union. One TWU organizer told us about the difficulties of trying to organize the workers while having to drive a bus ten hours a day under the beakies' watchful eyes:

> The problem was getting to the people because, under the Labor Relations Act at that time, the Wagner Act, they did every goddamn thing to try and fire these five guys [who were organizing]. . . . And they did fire us on and off. I was fired three different times . . . supposedly for violations.

Even after the TWU, with the aid of the National Labor Relations Act, won its first major victory, there were many organizing battles to be fought after New York City took over the transit system and refused to recognize the TWU's right to bargain for workers. Here too it was the transport workers who tirelessly organized their departments and eventually won for the TWU the right to be their exclusive bargaining agent. TWU members were routinely encouraged to avoid nonmembers, who were portrayed as undermining workers' sense of community. For instance, one organizer described how he would put pressure on "freeloaders" to join the union:

> He was in the union and I asked him, "Why is it that you are playing cards with a man that is not in the union? All the others are in the union." . . . So, this union fellow says to the man, "I didn't know you weren't in the union. . . . If you want to play cards here from now on, sign that card." He signed it.

Another organizer told us:

> In the year 1940, the city took over the roads. Mayor LaGuardia said, "You don't need the union. We are all one happy family." Thousands left the Union in every department. The Union had to decide how we were going to get those people back. So one man went around from gang to gang in his own department one day a week without pay . . . We got insults from those who didn't pay dues. They told me I was a communist. I said, "It's a little better than a freeloader!" Then we got Mayor O'Dwyer elected. We got a memorandum of understanding that, if a man signed a union card, he was in for the life of the contract. Under Mayor Wagner, we were able to get a union shop.

Such victories made the transport workers feel as though they had been liberated from slavery. As one TWU member aptly put it, "On account of this organization coming into existence, we were able to go to our bosses and talk to them like men, instead of . . . like slaves" (quoted in Freeman 1989, 127).

If talking like men did not succeed with their bosses, transportation workers saw that the union had other ways to take job actions and win. For instance, a mechanic described how he and his co-workers reacted to a supervisor who attempted to discipline a worker unfairly:

> One of our co-workers was fired on the spot. Nobody knows why because he was in the hole. So we had to stop and look. [We told the supervisor] "You want to give him a trial, fine, but you can't fire him right away." . . . The shop steward come over and said, "We don't work until he is rehired!" . . . Nobody went back to work. He was rehired and we went back to work. . . . That's what it means to have a union.

The early leaders also embedded the mutual-aid logic into TWU's structure in a variety of ways. The local chairmen made sure that members attended meetings, were involved with the union's day-to-day activities and were knowledgeable about the contract and their obligations. For instance, one TWU organizer described how, in the early years of the union, local chairmen took attendance at the meetings:

> When you went to your union meeting, you signed the ledger going in. . . . If you had ten meetings in a year and these guys attended ten meetings in the year, well they were all special union guys. They were special.

The early leaders also embedded the mutual-aid logic into the union's structure by educating the membership about the contract and the set of mutual obligations specified by that contract, that is, the obligations members owed to one another as well as those they owed to management under the contract. As one member told us, "Mike believed in a fair day's work for a fair day's pay. If we wanted to be treated fairly, we had to live up to the contract." The stewards explained the contract to members and made certain that their members and the transit authority lived up to their obligations to one another. As one former steward explained to us:

> [Being a steward is tough because] any little grievance that workers have, they run to the shop steward. You [the steward] don't always have the answers. But you do the best you can. Sometimes the best you can do is not good enough for the guy who is bringing the grievance. So, there is an argument. . . . If you [the worker] are wrong, you are wrong.

As in the railroad brotherhoods, the early leaders also embedded the mutual-aid logic into the TWU's structure by organizing an auxiliary for members' wives. As one TWU member remarked to us:

They formed a ladies auxiliary in the union there. It was very effective. It was good for the morale of the men that these women were very union minded. . . . They used to hold their own meetings, the ladies auxiliary. And I can assure you they had a hell of an effect on their husbands. If they went to the meetings, it would give them a sense of security. His wife is supporting him 100 percent. He is proud of her and she is proud of him.

Culturally, TWU's mutual-aid logic was embedded in stories about the early years, the telling of which reinforced its cognitive and normative legitimacy. Many of these stories depict Mike Quill or some other TWU leader such as Danny Gilmartin or Austin Hogan as the hero who stands for the essential value of brotherhood. For instance, TWU members tell many stories about Quill's hatred of discrimination, which he believed sapped workers' sense of community. Other stories highlight the union's obligation to take care of its members and their families. A retiree told us the following story about taking care of a member's family:

Nancy's father was a motorman. And Nancy's father had a drinking problem. . . . Nancy's mother died. Nancy at the time was fourteen years of age and she had a three-year-old brother. . . . Nancy's father was found dead. . . . Now what do you do with a fourteen-year-old girl with a three-year-old brother? . . . Mike Quill found her a job here answering the switchboard. He worried about her and took care of her. She worked here for years. . . . She was one of the top secretaries here. Died after forty years of service here. . . . This is a man with a heart and compassion.

Culturally, TWU's mutual-aid logic was reinforced by a variety of ceremonies and rituals. For instance, just as the railroaders paid their respects to their dead members and comforted their grieving families, the transport workers also participated in the funerals their brothers and sisters. One retiree told us:

Let's say one fellow's father passed away. In those days, they would give us a bus, and we would go down in groups and we would pay our respects. . . . Then, we were close.

Drinking Rituals and TWU's Mutual-Aid Logic

As in railroading, drinking among transport workers is a ritual that generates feelings of solidarity and highlights members' obligations to protect one another. Several members discussed the communal nature of drinking experiences among transport workers. One bus driver, for instance, noted that it was common practice for bus drivers to leave work early on pay day and meet at an uptown bar for an afternoon of drinking. Similarly, a retired splicer told us, "The cable section was known for being heavy drinkers. We worked in small groups and we were like a small, second family." Like railroaders, transport workers also provide a variety of excuses for drinking and the principal reasons given for drinking are to relieve the physical and psychological pains associated with their work and in order to belong to the group. For instance, bus driving is described as "a very, very stressful job" because it does not require a great deal of intelligence and is, therefore, considered by the drivers as being "boring." At the same time, drivers must contend with a variety of potentially dangerous situations over which they must exercise split-second judgments in order to insure the safety of their passengers and themselves. In addition, drivers must contend with passengers' numerous questions and a public who generally looks on their work with a great deal of disdain. As one driver put it, "Bus driving stimulates drinking."

Just as the railroad management punished railway workers for their drinking behavior, the transit companies summarily discharged transport workers for drinking. For instance, a TWU organizer in the 1930s remarked:

> In those days . . . if you were a bus driver and you had a drinking problem, that was the end of the road for you. Or motormen! . . . When it was the private bus companies, there was no redemption for you. You were gone.

Within this context, as in the railroads, drinking among transport workers became a symbol signifying who was a trusted community member. In order to be accepted into the group, members drank and were expected to protect one's co-workers who drank on the job. As a car cleaner explained:

> At the depot, it was like a fraternity. It was almost the original reason I started drinking in high school . . . group pressure and to get accepted into the group. . . . You were in with the crowd now. As long as you didn't fuck up — didn't bring the heat on anybody — you were all right! . . . When I

started, seventy-five percent of the workers at the depot were drinking. [Those workers who did not drink] were all right if they would mind their own business and they would accept your drinking. . . . Don't turn you in [to the Transit Authority]!

According to another transport worker, "If someone didn't drink, you very seldom trusted him." He went on to explain how crews would make it uncomfortable for nondrinkers considered untrustworthy:

We got a new man in there. Another helper from another section who was very nosy and started walking around with a notebook. He was in a manhole one day. The manhole cover was closed, and we "forgot" he was in the manhole. The trucks rolled. The crew finally came back, opened the manhole, and let him out. . . . [On another occasion], he came down one day and found his brake lines cut.

Not surprisingly, then, transit workers learned early on in their careers that their continued employment was dependent on complying with the norm of covering up for one another. The extent to which transport workers felt compelled to cover up one another's drinking is aptly illustrated by the following story recounted by a local union chairman who is also a recovering alcoholic:

We covered a lot for each other. I remember one time I was splicing and had been out all night. I really couldn't splice because I was so hung over. One of the helpers could splice. He went down into the hole and worked on the splice while I was laid up in the truck. . . . Just before I retired, I was driving a truck back to the shop because the rest of the crew had been drinking. I was driving because I was in recovery and didn't drink. . . . So I was still covering, even though I don't drink anymore. . . . We always cover for each other. Yes, if a man needs to be covered, you covered him. Cable section had one of the lowest incidents of ever being turned in for drinking. . . . If someone got caught for drinking on the job, someone outside the cable section turned him in.

Likewise, union officers also felt compelled to cover up for workers. In its efforts to help members charged with drinking violations, the union would attempt to keep one step ahead of management, by arranging for the members to be transferred to another location or shift. If that failed, they would take the worker's case to grievance. For instance, one TWU organizer noted how, during the 1930s, he attempted to cover up for a co-worker who had been drinking and had an accident:

As a union organizer, I tried to get him off regardless of what happened. I had one fellow one time driving a truck. He hit a column; he bent the structure. . . . I told [the supervisor], he [the driver] would have hit the child if he didn't sway. I says, "I would rather he hit the column than hit the child." . . . [The supervisor gave him] three days off. Well, I says, "I can't accept that." Then I had to turn it over to the union. . . . [The local chairman] says: "You are here a long time and everybody wants to help you. Did you have a drink that day?" And we told him, "Don't say you had a drink."

The mutual-aid logic of union-member relations, then, grew out of members' efforts to build the TWU. Indeed, by the 1940s the logic was deeply embedded in the union's culture and structure and members' routines. Members had a core commitment to TWU and regarded it as normatively legitimate. Through their routine actions on the job, workers enacted the logic, by demonstrating their support for one another. TWU's leaders embedded it within the union structure, encouraging all members to become active participants in running the union and enforcing the contract. The mutual-aid logic was also deeply embedded within TWU culture; for example, members' stories about the early union and members' drinking rituals highlighted it. Within this context, TWU's members developed their core commitment to the TWU. This sentiment was well expressed by several retired TWU members. A former car mechanic told us, "Years ago, when you called a guy, 'Brother,' he was your brother! . . . You protected one another. There was that closeness."

TWU's Servicing Logic

As in the brotherhoods and AFA, the TWU's mutual-aid logic went into abeyance and was replaced by a servicing logic of union-member relations in which members no longer felt a reciprocal obligation to work for the union. Instead, they developed a segmented commitment to TWU, believing that their only obligation to the union was to pay dues, which entitled them to the benefits of membership. For instance, one token clerk, who had been hired in the late sixties and had taken early retirement, told us:

I never really got involved with the union. I paid my dues and, as far as the meeting was concerned, I went to a couple of meetings. But, I was never involved with it. . . . The benefits. We have medical, eyeglasses . . . the credit union. . . . If something went wrong, they [the union] were there for you. But I didn't need them because I didn't drink on the job and I didn't steal no money.

As in the AFA and brotherhoods, the TWU's shift to a servicing logic was precipitated by a series of impressive bargaining successes throughout the 1950s and 1960s. In 1966, the TWU won a settlement worth an estimated $45–$75 million dollars, most of which was devoted to a 15 percent wage hike spread over the next two years. Two years later, the TWU successfully negotiated for additional wage increases plus a generous retirement package that provided for half pay after twenty years of service at age fifty and up. As in AFA and the brotherhoods, these successes had the unanticipated consequence of radically changing the communal patterns from which the mutual-aid logic and members' core commitment were constructed. In the case of the TWU, there was a mass exodus of senior workers from the system, including nearly all those who remained from the generation that had organized and nurtured the TWU (Freeman 1989). As a result, the Transit Authority hired a whole new generation of workers who were unfamiliar with the earlier generation's struggle to develop the union.

All of the retirees whom we interviewed felt that "things have come too easy" to the younger generation and that these workers did not understand the role that mutual obligations played in winning the benefits they enjoyed. One retired worker described this shift in values in the following manner:

> The younger men do not realize the struggle that was made. Forget where they are today. You take a bus driver today. Makes a thousand dollars a week without breaking his can . . . five weeks vacation! Good health coverage! Eleven holidays a year! Don't have to take any abuse from the biggest boss in the business.

Others complained that the younger workers did not "understand brotherhood." As one retired TWU member remarked, "I think the people got to a point where it is 'me.' In those days it was 'we.' . . . We were all in the same category. We had nothing. . . . Today, they got two cars, a boat, three houses, maybe. It's me and what I have to lose." Similarly, a retired bus driver complained that the younger workers were uninvolved with their co-workers:

> It's just how much money can I get and as fast as I can get it. I don't want to be bothered with you or anybody. . . . I can remember some of the guys

I drove buses with. They would tell you about situations out there. . . . "Be careful over there at Thirty-fourth and Fifth. There's a pothole you can't see."

. . . Today, he gets off and walks away. You get on and go.

As in AFA and the brotherhoods, the shift to a servicing logic could not have occurred at a worse time for TWU. In the 1970s, the union's economic and managerial environments turned increasingly hostile. New York City experienced a fiscal crisis, during which it postponed capital expenditures and slashed payrolls. Within this cost-conscious climate, the Transit Authority reverted to its older "rule by intimidation" management style. In order to control costs, management sought to take all discretion out of workers' hands by centralizing its authority and standardizing what workers did. Within this context, management promulgated rules to cover every contingency and instructed supervisors to strictly enforce them. Both retired and employed interviewees lamented that, in contrast to the past, workers were not given sufficient training and knowledge to make decisions because the Transit Authority wants "to do the impossible . . . run the whole thing from one place." All felt that the Transit Authority was too quick to discipline workers for minor infractions. A recently retired bus driver, who had begun driving in the late sixties, told us:

> The rules and regulations have changed. . . . Like that little accident that I had when I first came on the job. My supervisor looked at me and said, "Come on, get out of here! That is no big deal. It was a fender bender." Today, if you put a little scratch on the bus, you go for a hearing and are subject to suspension.

In contrast to the past, supervisors are no longer promoted from the ranks. Rather, the Transit Authority hires young inexperienced supervisors who have not worked in the system. From management's perspective, these supervisors are more susceptible to following the rules than are the older, experienced supervisors who were promoted from the ranks and felt some loyalty to their old co-workers. Inevitably, the hiring of inexperienced supervisors has caused friction with older workers accustomed to exercising judgment on the job. These sentiments were well expressed by a recently retired railroad clerk:

> The new supervision doesn't have the relationship with you that the old supervisor had. . . . They were more like a family. The new supervisors, it's

just a job. They are afraid of their job so it's like a chain reaction. Their boss gives them the devil so they got to give you the devil.

Rule by intimidation has taken its toll on the workers. Not surprisingly, they feel compelled to work to the rules and complain about being stressed out. For instance, one driver explained that he no longer tried to accommodate older passengers by stopping where it might be easier for them to get on and off the bus; instead, he only stopped in designated areas in order to avoid problems:

Some guys become dispatchers . . . I would love to find out if they are brainwashing them, "The operator is the enemy. You have to treat them as strict as possible." They are looking to give you a violation whatever the situation might be. Condemn you for any little thing.

Similarly, the retired token clerks told us that supervisors' petty rule enforcement stressed workers:

These railroad clerks are stressed. Really! They are more stressed than we were. . . . Supervision! Supervision! That's all they talk about. . . . If their bow tie is not straight, or if they don't button the tie up. . . . If you come into a job and you know you are gonna be reprimanded for little petty stuff, you are gonna get all worked up with your passengers.

In addition, the Transit Authority has made work even more stressful by turning workers against one another. An older steward explained that in the old days, crewmembers stuck together but today the Transit Authority encourages them to turn in one another when something goes wrong:

[The union] tries to tell these people, "Look, you are a crew. You are married. You have got to take care of one another, which is something we did in the old days. . . . [In the past] if any kind of trouble arose on the road, the motorman and conductor got together and got their stories straight before they even went before supervision. They don't do that today . . . because management intimidates them.

The consequences of this managerial strategy of intimidation and "divide and conquer" on the union have been profound. First, it has increased the workers' reliance on the union officers as hired professional agents responsible for protecting them as individuals from managerial abuse. While such protective services have always been a union obligation, in the past members recognized that the ability of their union to provide such services was contingent on the membership's willingness to abide by *their* obligations as specified in the collective bargaining agreement. In the past, members viewed their union less as a group of hired legal experts protecting members' individual interests and more as the organizational framework representing and promoting the collective interests of the membership as a whole. Second, it placed the union in a no-win situation with respect to its membership. On the one hand, given the nature of the servicing logic, members expected the union to protect them regardless of the nature of their particular case. When the union was unable to successfully do so, members complained that the union sold them out and failed to "fight hard enough for them." On the other hand, many members, particularly union veterans, increasingly felt that, by going out of its way to protect members that take advantage of the contract, the union was losing credibility and bargaining power and, thus, hurting the interests of the membership as a whole. One retired bus driver expressed these sentiments in the following manner:

> Why is the union protecting this man that is not doing his job? What about my protection? I'm paying the same dues. But the policy of the union is you protect your workers. . . . Fine. . . . I don't feel its up to the Transit Authority to punish this man. I feel that it is the union's because he is messing up the job for the next guy.

Within this context, many TWU members no longer regard the servicing logic as instrumentally legitimate. Thus, as we have seen in AFA and the brotherhoods, the TWU is also experiencing a crisis of instrumental legitimacy.

TWU's MAP and Its Reemergent Mutual-Aid Logic

As in the AFA and brotherhoods, the mutual-aid logic is reemergent within the TWU. As in AFA and the brotherhoods, TWU veterans argue that, in order for the union to survive in its hostile environment, it must reconstruct the mutual-aid logic by revitalizing members' core commitment and renewing its normative legitimacy. Retired workers, for example, repeatedly told us that TWU's survival depended on members becoming more involved in the union and caring about one another. A conductor who currently serves as a union steward summed up the retirees' sentiments about his own generation:

If they don't change their attitudes, the future of this generation is right down the tubes. . . . I'm talking about the majority of them. Whether they are educated or uneducated, they both have the same types of attitudes. That attitude is "Give it to me!"

As in the AFA and brotherhoods, the TWU is using its MAP as a mechanism for reconstructing the mutual-aid logic. The federal government's war on drugs precipitated the development of TWU's MAP by creating a more hostile managerial environment than the one existing in the 1970s. Increasingly concerned about drug use among young people, the government encouraged employers to be tough on users and pressed them to implement drug-screening programs. Because of a number of high-profile accidents, the government focused its drug reduction efforts on the transportation industry.

The Transit Authority, always sensitive to government demands, responded by getting tough with workers and turning its employee assistance program (EAP) into a mechanism for identifying and disciplining workers suffering from alcohol and other drug problems. The Transit Authority's EAP was established in 1956. Like other alcoholism programs of that era, the EAP was an informal partnership between company physicians and recovering employees who were members of AA. In 1980, as part of the national trend toward the adoption of professionally staffed, management-based EAPs, the Transit Authority eliminated the peer-based component of its traditional alcoholism program. The company hired a social worker as the director of its new EAP, and she, in turn, replaced the AA volunteers with clinical professionals. The program quickly lost its original reputation and increasingly became known among workers as a management ploy to fire workers. The following comments from one of the TWU's current peer counselors illustrates how workers felt about management's EAP:

Inside of two years, she [the new program director] built up so much mistrust that nobody volunteered to go to the employee assistance program any more. Employee assistance became an extension of discipline. It was there to catch people; it wasn't there to rehabilitate or help people. The situation just got worse and worse.

Recovering TWU members urged their leaders to implement a peer-based MAP to help alcoholic and drug addicted co-workers. At the same time, the TWU found itself spending a considerable amount of time and resources in grievance disputes about workers discharged because of alcohol and other drug problems and under increasing government and management pressure to implement drug testing. In 1988, the president of Local 100 negotiated an agreement with the Transit Authority, allowing the union to operate its own peer-based alcohol and drug program.

> It was originally started because people who were ready to admit their problem were not by any significant number going into the management program. Fear of punishment — admitting their problem and having it on their record. So, we convinced the Authority to do a pilot program. . . . There were so many of our co-workers — even some front line supervisors — thinking they were doing the right thing by covering up for people. . . . We wanted to come up with a way they could help without jeopardizing people's jobs. . . . We added some more counselors. . . . Their role was to go out into the field, to do prevention, . . . and to bring in more volunteers.

The Culture and Structure of the TWU's MAP

TWU's MAP, like those in the brotherhoods and AFA, is reembedding the mutual-aid logic in the union's culture and structure and members' routines. Culturally, the MAP is framed around the belief that peer counselors, because they share many of the same experiences of their troubled co-workers, are best equipped to help them. Consequently, all of the TWU peer counselors are union members who are in recovery and have demonstrated their ability to maintain their own long-term sobriety, generally by affiliating with a twelve-step program (e.g., AA, NA) and helping others. The idea that recovering peers are best equipped to help their addicted co-workers was well expressed by the comments of one recovering member:

> He [the peer counselor] made me feel very comfortable. . . . Only a person that has gone through that hell can know what you feel like when you come in [the program]. . . . He was part of the peer group. Yes, that definitely helped too. Here was a person who survived what I was going through. He had come out on the other side whole. So he was a good example to see that it worked — that something worked — because I had no idea what worked.

The emergent mutual-aid logic is also embodied in the MAP's structure; that is, the structure highlights members' obligations to help one another. In contrast to the brotherhoods and AFA, however, the structure of TWU's MAP is highly professionalized and bureaucratized. By professionalized, we mean that, although the program is based on the belief that peer counselors are uniquely situated to help their co-workers, it requires its peer counselors to supplement this common sense knowledge with professionally sanctioned knowledge. Peer counselors study for and eventually pass the New York Federation of Alcoholism Counselor's certification exam for alcoholism counselors in order to retain their position within the program. In addition, the Employee Assistance Professional Association certifies some peer counselors; a few are also pursuing more traditional degrees within university settings. The program is also professionalized in the sense that its peer counselors perform their role as paid full-time work rather than as a voluntary part-time task performed in the course of their regular job. That is, unlike the peer counselors in the brotherhoods and AFA, who work at the customary tasks of their occupations, TWU peer counselors no longer perform the customary tasks of transit workers. Consequently, rather than counseling members while also performing such customary tasks as driving or cleaning buses, the peer counselors perform most of their duties in the privacy of the program's offices, which are removed from the work sites.

TWU's program is also highly bureaucratized. By bureaucratized, we mean that individual peer counselors, rather than performing all of the tasks associated with peer counseling, are assigned discrete tasks which they perform according to a prescribed routine. Some of the peer counselors perform outreach, which consists of educating members about substance abuse and the program. In their education efforts, they highlight the differences between the peer-based MAP and the Transit Authority's EAP, emphasizing the program's voluntary nature and encouraging members to seek help before management catches them. A peer counselor explained:

> One of the tools we have is to let them know their alternatives. "If you don't stop now, management will get you. That experience will not be as good as this experience. We are voluntary and everything is confidential. It doesn't go into your yellow jacket. . . . There are at least eight different ways management can catch you; eventually your time will be up. We are giving you a choice. We are not mandating that you come here. . . . Just remember what I said is going to happen if you get caught by management."

They also teach shop stewards about the follies of continuing to cover up members' problems and how to refer those members to the program; they also conduct education programs for their co-workers. After the presentation, the peer counselors remain at the location, generally making themselves available to members with questions about either their co-workers' or their own behavior. At this time, they also hand out cards, encouraging members to call if they know of a friend with a problem. A peer counselor describes the typical outreach program provided to co-workers:

> At this point, we have outreach counselors in the field five to six days a week. They are continuously in the field. They are not looking for people [with problems]; they are telling them what is available if they feel they have a problem. . . . They do that with films. The counselors try to see if the members can identify with the film. They explain the characters' roles in the film. [The cover up by supervisors and co-workers. The addict's denial of his problem and his willingness to change his behavior once confronted by his supervisor and co-workers.] At that point, it is the individual's choice whether to come forward and ask for help.

Other peer counselors perform assessment and referral, which consists of efforts to assess co-workers' problems and refer those individuals who suffer from alcoholism or other drug addictions to appropriate forms of treatment. Assessment and referral are two of the most difficult tasks faced by all clinicians, especially when their clients deny their problems. Consequently, clinicians have difficulty arriving at an accurate assessment of the client's problem and matching the diagnosis with an appropriate treatment. Within the MAP, the clinical intake is organized around the expectations that, at least initially, union members will deny their problems and that peer counselors must overcome their denial before the members will accept a diagnosis of addiction and willingly seek help from a treatment program. This is an additional benefit of peer counselors being either recovering alcoholics or drug addicts — because of their own experiences they feel that they are better able to see through the addict's denial and overcome it. As the director aptly stated it:

> Look, you can't bullshit a bullshitter. All of these guys have been there. So, when someone comes in here and starts running a line of shit, they can spot it right away.

The assessment and referral component of the TWU MAP is more formal and standardized than in AFA's program. As we argued earlier, the AFA peer counselors use a variety of facilitative counseling skills (e.g., empathy, confrontation, genuineness) in order to establish a working relationship with the troubled flight attendants and to encourage them to talk about their problems. Assessment often consists of accepting the flight attendant's account of his or her problem and directing them to an appropriate resource. In contrast, the TWU peer counselors are trained to be suspicious of union members' accounts, which are assumed to be part of the addict's denial system.

In order to break down the addict's denial, the peer counselors rely on a well-organized intake form that summarizes information about members' drinking and drugging history and its impact on their lives, including their family and personal relations, job performance, and physical health. During intake, the peer counselors also assess the members' suitability for particular types of treatment. One peer counselor stated:

> I am trying to find out about his environment — whether or not it is conducive to his becoming sober. Does he need to be placed in an inpatient program because of his immediate surroundings? I am trying to find out if his wife uses drugs or if he has a child that uses drugs. I am also trying to find out if he is trying to avoid a disciplinary situation by coming here to hide out.

Once the peer counselors have completed the intake, they use the information to break down the member's denial and convince him that drinking and drugging have made his life unmanageable and that he must accept treatment.

Still other TWU peer counselors conduct follow up, which consists of a variety of activities geared to keeping members sober after they return to work from treatment. One component consists of regularly scheduled counseling sessions with peer counselors and recovering members. A second component consists of an informal association of recovering alcoholics and addicts called the Alumni Group who meet once a month. In addition to these activities, members are expected to actively participate in a twelve-step program and are encouraged to become involved with other forms of aftercare such as individual and marital counseling. These various forms of follow up are intended to reinforce one another by providing members with multiple social supports for learning to live a sober life.

Follow-up meetings with the peer counselors are highly formalized; members returning to work from treatment are required to meet with the peer counselors regularly to discuss how they are managing the recovery process. During the first month after treatment, the peer counselors see recovering members once a week in order to ensure that they are remaining abstinent, attending a self-help group, going to aftercare, and having relatively few difficulties either on the job or with their families. These meetings continue for at least six months. A recovering member describes how the peer counselors helped keep him sober during the first six months of his sobriety:

> The peer counselors reinforced what you learned about AA and NA in rehabilitation. Some of the old-timers describe rehab as AA kindergarten. It was like that. It gave you time to think about a lot of things . . . to learn about yourself and how to behave. Some people go through the program and never learn who they are because they are too busy feeling sorry for themselves. I consider myself lucky that I developed some awareness about myself. . . . [After I returned] I was involved with the aftercare with the union. . . . I also started going to family counseling. . . . Most of the time my wife was angry at me. . . . I was feeling pretty bad about myself because of how she felt, but the counselors helped me so that I didn't feel bad enough to drink.

If after six months the recovering member is doing well, he is given an "atta-boy letter" and encouraged to join the Alumni Group, which meets once a month. Over the years, the Alumni Group has evolved from being a surrogate AA/NA meeting for members to including members' spouses in the program and holding a variety of social functions such as picnics and trips. Still, the program is modeled after the philosophy of AA and NA that the best way to maintain one's sobriety is to help others maintain theirs. One Alumni member described the program as a "brotherhood" for the prevention of relapse:

> There is the fraternity of the program. The counselors [who are responsible for coordinating the Alumni program] are recovering with us, and they show us that recovery is an every day thing. We have our get-togethers — fishing trips and picnics — which are also helpful in keeping one another sober because it is sober people doing sober things and having fun together. I think that is one of the greatest causes for people to relapse, boredom.

In other words, members keep one another sober by sharing their common experiences with one another, and thus reinforce the belief that one does not have to drink in order to cope with one's problems. As one Alumni member stated it:

> The good thing about the Alumni is that we all have two things in common. We are all addicts and we are all transit workers. . . . When someone has a problem, we can sit down and talk about it together because we understand one another.

The mutual-aid logic is also embedded in the routines by which TWU's peer counselors help their co-workers. Despite the program's bureaucratic and professional structure, the helping processes are firmly grounded in the peer philosophy of Alcoholics Anonymous. The TWU peer counselors feel that substance-abuse treatment has been unnecessarily complicated by the bureaucratic procedures of too many managed-care providers and treatment professionals who are really ignorant of alcohol and drug problems. From their perspective, peer-based MAPs represent a return to the simple beliefs of AA:

> The peer programs are basically a sign that it is necessary to keep it as simple as you can. Our basic treatment is a very simple treatment — a lot of love and a lot of care are given here. We have people that are just damn good counselors because they care.

Similarly, an Alumni member's comments underscore the importance of AA's peer beliefs within the program:

> Helping others is a part of my own recovery process. It is part of me. It is as the [AA] program says, "The more I receive, the more I have to give back." It makes me feel good!

According to the peer counselors, the TWU's MAP, in contrast to the Transit Authority's EAP is voluntary and, therefore, they do not overcome members' denial by threatening them with termination. Rather, within the context of their AA beliefs, they argue that co-workers are attracted to the MAP by the sober examples set by themselves and other recovering transport workers and that this attraction occurs when individuals are "hurting enough." Both the peer counselors and members of the Alumni Group are aware of their role as examples and its importance in attracting co-workers to the program. For instance, a peer counselor commented on his role:

> Before I got sober, I had a lot of respect in the work site — macho-type shit. . . . After I started getting sober, other people with problems who saw my behavior change came to me and asked, "Hey, what is going on? You know I was thinking about this AA stuff myself." They know when you get sober. Everybody knows and the word gets around. , . . So I was a role model in different ways.

The following remarks from a recovering TWU member illustrate how he was first attracted to the program by the example of his co-worker, who had been suddenly transformed by treatment:

I saw what the program did in 1988. . . . What happened was that another guy who was drinking and drugging [got sober through the program]. He was also a bus driver and I hadn't seen him in about two to three months. When I finally saw him, he said, "Hey man, I'm not going to do any more of that shit! I just came from a rehab." He was looking pretty good, and he talked to me about it. The conversation sort of stuck in my head for a while. Then, thinking about it and looking at him, I decided to check it out.

Although the program depends on attracting alcoholic and drug-addicted members by the examples of recovering co-workers, the peer counselors do not passively sit back waiting for members to voluntarily seek help from the program. Rather, they will target individuals and work areas known to have drinking and drugging problems for outreach. One outreach counselor described how they targeted the cleaning crew:

The steward called me . . . . "I am having a problem with the wash team [which scrubs down the subway stations]. They are getting drunk and high." So I target that area. I call a superintendent in charge of the area and tell him I want to educate these people. I don't tell him that they are a problem or anything. . . . Then we go in and do the presentation. If I have a particular name, I don't target him directly. I do my presentation and wait for him to come forward.

The peer counselors have a variety of strategies for attracting reluctant co-workers to the program. These strategies seek to "befriend" the targeted individual; however, in each instance, the peer counselors attempt to persuade rather than coerce the individual into accepting help. One strategy often used by the peer counselors is to offer their own lives up as examples of how AA has changed their lives for the better:

The best way that I know to help somebody with their drinking is to talk about your own drinking. If you talk to them about their own drinking, they will shut right down. If you talk to them about your own drinking and what goes on in your own life, they will listen and consider it.

Another strategy is to catch the targeted individual's attention and interest by asking him to distribute education materials. A peer counselor explained the tactic:

If I know someone needs help but he doesn't come forward, I'll say to him, "Listen, do me a favor. You look like a pretty decent guy. I know that you are concerned about your fellow employees. If you know someone who is having a problem, could you do me a favor and give them some of my cards? Just hand them to a few people. You don't have to say anything; just spread it around where they can see it."

Despite the program's best efforts to attract alcoholic and drug-addicted members, many remain resistant to seeking help from the program. Peer counselors take a more direct tact with these members. They forthrightly discuss the workers' alternatives with them and let them know that they are responsible for their choices. The reluctant members can either voluntarily seek help from the member assistance program or they can get caught by management and lose their jobs. Either way, the choice is theirs and they are responsible for their actions.

The peer counselors go to great lengths in order to help their co-workers to live sober lives. In order to ensure their sobriety, they provide members with a variety of supports, including follow-up counseling and a readily available Alumni network, all of which are intended to reinforce the essential lessons of AA: For alcoholics like us, sobriety is possible by following the twelve-steps and, by following the twelve steps, alcoholics learn to accept responsibility for their actions. As one counselor noted:

We are available to members at any time. We have traditional appointments, but we also have the tradition of recovering people and the tradition of a union that really cares about its members. We will see a member at any given time in order to ensure their sobriety.

In this section, we have seen that, through its MAP, TWU is renewing its mutual-aid logic. The logic is embedded within the culture of the MAP, which emphasizes workers helping workers, and within the structure of the MAP, which is built around the role of peer counselors. Although the structure of the TWU's MAP is highly bureaucratic and professional, the mutual-aid logic remains embedded in the roles of the peer counselors and the routines by which they help co-workers become sober. The counselors emphasize that, unlike the professionals in the EAP, they too are union members, they have an obligation to help co-workers recover from their substance abuse problems, and they are willing to go to great lengths to help them. However, because of the professional orientation of the TWU MAP, the emergent mutual-aid logic is not as deeply embedded in members' work routines as it is in the brotherhoods and AFA. This occurs because the peer counseling is still regarded as a professional role. The MAP is aware of this limitation and is seeking to overcome it by expanding the Alumni network and making its members lay counselors.

Constraints and Consequences

TWU's MAP is relatively new and far from fully implemented within New York. Within this context, the peer counselors feel that they have a long way to go to change the union's drinking culture. For instance, one peer counselor observed:

> The same shit is still going on today — the drinking and drugging. . . . It's not as blatant, but they still have coolers and everything out there. . . . Collectively the cable section doesn't drink like it used to, but there are still people there who drink heavy and most of them work together in the same crews.

In addition, the peer counselors recognize that the program, in order to be completely successful, needs to expand beyond its current focus on substance abuse to include helping members with other personal problems. For instance, while praising the success of the program, one peer counselor noted:

> The union is providing one hell of a service to the point that it needs to be expanded — not only dealing with alcohol and drugs but with stress. We do some of these kind of cases. We deal with people who may have problems with their kids.

Nevertheless, it is possible to glimpse some of the MAP's social consequences for members' core commitment and TWU's normative legitimacy. As we have seen in both the brotherhoods and AFA, involvement in the MAP creates within members a sense of gratitude toward the union while also fostering a greater sense of responsibility to the union. Involvement also increases their willingness to volunteer their time and energy as peer counselors in order to help their co-workers. These same effects can be seen at work within the TWU's MAP. According to the TWU peer counselors the primary beneficiary of the program's efforts is the union because, as a consequence of their work, members know that "we [TWU] care for our membership." As the following comment from one recovering TWU member suggests, members who have been helped by the program feel eternally grateful to the union for having saved their jobs, families, and their lives:

> People who go through this program show a lot of gratitude to the union. . . . Thank God, this program was there for me to go into. Thank God, I still have my job and that there was no discipline attached to my records for being an alcoholic or drug addict. The gratitude for having been able to change my life, which is becoming A-plus again. . . . I have a lot of gratitude to the union for what this program has done for me.

Similarly, another remarked:

> I owe my job to the union because twelve years ago management tried to do me in [for my drinking] and a couple of old organizers saved my job. I don't ever forget that, and it is the same with the guys who go through this program. They don't forget either; they take it back to the other members and share it by helping others.

In appreciation of the program's help, members are more willing to assume responsibility for union activities. For instance, all of the recovering members to whom we spoke said that they felt they became better union members after they became sober. Some, as the following quote from one recovering member suggests, go on to become local union officers:

> After recovery I became a chairperson and became even more active with the union. I'm not the only one who has done this; most people when they sober up, start realizing they have an obligation. . . . All of a sudden you start taking an active part in the union because sobriety makes you responsible. . . . I believe that it makes them a more solid union member.

In addition to acting more responsibly, recovering members also are willing to extend themselves by voluntarily helping their alcoholic and drug-addicted co-workers become sober. For instance, one peer counselor commented on the willingness of recovering members to help their co-workers:

> Some of them have been in rehab, aftercare, or outpatient treatment together, and they notice that so-and-so isn't around. They'll come in here and ask questions about him. . . . They aren't doing it out of malice; they really aren't trying to blow the whistle on somebody. They are concerned about whether the person is doing what is good for himself. That is the big change — going from being an active alcoholic or drug addict to somebody in recovery — when they start caring for somebody other than

just themselves. . . . It makes me realize that everything is starting to work; it is all becoming a whole.

Indeed, it is the willingness of recovering members to reach out to one another that is the mainstay of the MAP and its efforts to revitalize the TWU. As one of the founding members of the program noted:

> If anything ever happened to this program, the Alumni will always carry on the tradition helping and moving ahead. They are the ones, who will be out on the roads, in subway tunnels, and in the barns, helping members in the best traditions of unions and twelve-step programs. . . . It would be a group of alcoholics and addicts making themselves available to each other, which would start the whole process over again.

Although TWU's MAP is highly professional and bureaucratic, members' involvement in the program yields similar social consequences to those we observed in the brotherhood and AFA programs. Through their involvement in the program, transport workers are likewise reconstructing the TWU's mutual-aid logic by revitalizing members' core commitment and the union's normative legitimacy. Still, there is also a significant difference between those programs and TWU's MAP. In contrast to the brotherhoods and AFA, TWU's MAP has made little headway embedding the mutual-aid logic into the culture and structure of the union as a whole. Within AFA, for example, the peer counselors have worked hard to embed the mutual-aid logic into the workings of other local committees, including organizing, professional standards, and grievance. Several constraints help to explain this difference. First, the TWU peer counselors have been caught up within the union's servicing logic. This is well illustrated by their emphasis on becoming professionals and by their efforts to bureaucratically structure the program. To their credit they recognize that the MAP's growth is dependent on involving more members in the Alumni network, which is expected to embed the MAP's mutual-aid logic more deeply into the New York local. Still, the peer counselors have made fewer efforts to create ties with other local programs than the AFA has made. These ties appear critical for embedding the mutual-aid logic into the culture and structure of the union as a whole.

Another constraint acting to inhibit the MAP's efforts to embed the mutual-aid logic into the union as a whole is TWU leadership. In contrast to the leaderships of the brotherhoods and AFA, TWU's national leadership has been relatively timid about supporting the MAP. Within AFA and the brotherhoods, union leaders did not initially support the MAPs as mechanisms for transforming the servicing logic. They, however, did support their dissemination as another service offered to members. Only later did it become evident that, through the work of the MAPs, the mutual-aid logic was beginning to reemerge. Within the TWU, national leadership has been reluctant to expand the MAP beyond its New York City base, even as another service offered to members. Indeed, it continues to see the MAP as a worthwhile program, which locals ought to adopt after careful consideration of its benefits to members.

Examination of the MAP's social consequences, then, highlights two lessons for our understanding about the reemergence of the mutual-aid logic. On one hand, we see that, involving members of an industrial union in caring for each other generates core commitment in individuals and enhances the union's normative legitimacy. On the other, we see that the reemergence of the mutual-aid logic is constrained by the perceptions of both union leaders and members.

Concluding Remarks

In this chapter, we attempted to deepen our understanding of the logics of union-member relations by focusing on them in the TWU. As with our analyses of the brotherhoods and AFA, this analysis generally supports the theoretical framework presented in chapter 2. Within the context of a hostile organizing environment, transit workers activated the mutual-aid logic. This environment consisted of management that rejected workers' legitimate right to establish a union, a legal environment that continued to see unions as a conspiracy, and a technical environment that was changing very rapidly. Within this context, the development of the mutual-aid logic enabled workers to unite and survive in their struggle to establish the TWU. It also enabled the TWU to negotiate a highly lucrative benefits package for its members. However, as in the brotherhoods and AFA, TWU's bargaining successes also had unanticipated consequences. They likewise created a highly bureaucratized union and undercut members' communal interaction patterns and core commitment on which the mutual-aid logic was constructed. TWU's servicing logic was activated by the union's increasingly stable environment, characterized by a co-opting management, supportive legal environment, and stable technical environment. As TWU's environment became more stable, its mutual-aid logic atrophied and the servicing logic came to dominate union-member relations. During this period the servicing logic served TWU leaders and members well. TWU leaders steadily improved members' working conditions and compensation, and members continued to perceive their authority as instrumentally legitimate. Unfortunately, in the 1970s and 1980s, as management began to implement stricter discipline and introduce new labor-saving technologies into the workplace, TWU's servicing logic began to break down. Within this hostile environment, TWU found it increasingly difficult to provide the benefits expected by its members. Within this context, veteran transit workers were responsible for reviving the TWU's mutual-aid logic, once again arguing that the union's survival required that members develop a core commitment to the union and that the TWU enhance its normative legitimacy.

The analysis of TWU has also deepened our understanding of the logics of union-member relations by highlighting how participation in constructing the union generates the mutual-aid logic. Unlike the AFA and brotherhoods, there was no natural community and mutual-aid ethic on which the transport workers could construct a union. Consequently, transit workers struggled for many years to construct a permanent union. Before passage of the Labor Relations Act, their employers crushed their efforts. While the veterans of the Irish Republic Army and the Communist party provided workers with a militant mutual-aid ethic on which to build, it was the workers' participation in constructing the union that generated TWU's mutual-aid logic of union-member relations. Through their involvement, transport workers understood that they were the union. As the TWU retirees so aptly expressed it, "The union is us!" Members' involvement provided the mutual-aid logic with a potent cognitive and normative legitimacy that sustained the TWU into the 1960s.

Our analysis of the TWU and its MAP also highlights the role of members' participation in renewing the mutual-aid logic. This analysis is less hopeful than our analyses of the brotherhoods and AFA. As in the brotherhoods and AFA, we found that the MAP was constructed around the reemergent mutual-aid logic and that members' participation in the MAP was revitalizing members' core commitment and renewing the TWU's normative legitimacy. However, we also found that the TWU had made less progress embedding the mutual-aid logic into the union's culture and structure and members' routines. We attributed this difficulty to the MAP's emphasis on professionalism and its bureaucratic structure as well as leadership's reluctance to diffuse the program throughout the union. Unlike the AFA and brotherhood peer counselors, the TWU's peer counselors are not working at the tasks typically performed by members of their occupation. Consequently, the MAP's helping processes are more removed from members' work and social lives, and the mutual-aid logic is less likely to be diffused to other union members as it is in the brotherhoods and AFA. To their credit, the TWU MAP recognizes this problem and is working to overcome it by strengthening its Alumni Group and turning its members into lay counselors. Still, the MAP has made relatively little progress in embedding its mutual-aid logic into other local programs and diffusing it to other TWU locals. These constraints indicate that the transformation from its servicing logic to its mutual-aid logic is likely to be a long, difficult task. Indeed, given the extent to which the servicing logic remains entrenched in the TWU, it is possible that the mutual-aid logic may never be reestablished within the union. Thus, the TWU case should temper our enthusiasm about the ease of reconstructing the mutual-aid logic within the labor movement.

6 Union Renewal

American unions are struggling to renew themselves. In this book, we argued that unions are confronting a crisis of instrumental legitimacy and that in order to renew themselves some unions are reconstructing their traditional mutual-aid logic. We defined labor's logic of union-member relations as the cognitive framework guiding union strategies for legitimizing the union to its members, securing the commitment of its members, and attracting new members to the union. More specifically, we argued that unions are currently organized around the servicing logic, which emphasizes utilitarian authority. Within the context of this logic, unions maintain their legitimacy by providing services to their members, who are instrumentally oriented toward the union and develop segmented commitment to it. Because many unions have been unable to deliver the services some members have come to expect, they are experiencing a legitimacy crisis. Specifically some members are questioning the instrumental authority of unions. In response to this challenge, some unions are working to reconstruct their traditional mutual-aid logic, which emphasizes familial authority.

More specifically, we argued that the mutual-aid logic is characterized by union members' intensive involvement with one another and by their participation in the life of the union, which generate strong feelings of core commitment and normative legitimacy. During periods when the technical, management, and political environment is hostile to labor, unions are using the mutual-aid logic as a mechanism to gain members' commitment and sustain themselves in hard times. In contrast, the servicing logic of union-member relations is characterized by members' limited involvement with one another and limited participation in the life of the union, which generates segmented commitment and instrumental legitimacy. Unions use the servicing logic as a mechanism of gaining members' commitment when the technical, managerial, and political environment is supportive of labor. Currently, American unions are primarily organized around the servicing logic of union-member relations, which has become a questionable mechanism for gaining members' commitment in labor's current hostile environment. Consequently, in order to solve their crisis of instrumental commitment, unions are attempting to reconstruct their mutual-aid logic, which is consistent with their hostile environment. By implementing a variety of strategies such as member assistance programs (MAP), unions are reactivating their traditional mutual-aid logic and thus revitalizing members' core commitment and renewing their normative legitimacy.

Throughout our argument, it is important to note that the emergent mutual-aid logic is not being created out of whole cloth. Rather, it is a reactivation of a component of the union's earlier history. Thus, programs such as MAPs, while appearing to be new, are based on abeyance structures, memories and practices that have become dormant. Abeyance structures are repositories for a group's collective memory; they are the enclaves within an institution where members retain old cultural beliefs and sustain a community of memory. Labor's community of memory consists of those members who have a normative orientation and a core commitment to the union. These normatively oriented members remember when unions were organized around the mutual-aid logic. They recall when "brothers" and "sisters" meant that union members were a fictive family with mutual obligations toward one another. They argue for the reconstruction of the mutual-aid logic in order to renew their unions. In doing so, they construct practices of commitment, which involve members in reconstructing feelings of family, brotherhood, and sisterhood. Thus, they renew their own sense of core commitment and their union's normative legitimacy.

In order to understand the process of union renewal, we examined the cycle of logics of union-member relations within the American labor movement and within three unions. In each of these cases, we defined the logics of union-member relations as embedded within labor's culture and structure and the routines of members' work and social lives, and we examined how the logics were constructed in reaction to its managerial, technical, and legal environments. Generally, the four cases conformed to our conceptual model. When labor's environment was hostile, unions used the mutual-aid logic as a mechanism for gaining members' commitment; when labor's environment was less hostile, unions used the servicing logic as a mechanism for generating members' commitment.

As we examined the three institutional carriers (i.e., culture, structure, and routines), we discovered that, at each stage of the cycle, they interact differently with one another. During the early nineteenth century, labor's environment was hostile and the mutual-aid logic was critical for the development of permanent unions. According to M. Douglas (1986), institutions are initially constructed on analogies. In constructing the early unions, nineteenth-century workers used analogy to frame their experiences; they claimed that early unions were like other fraternal experiences and ought to be organized around the same mutual-aid logic of intensive involvement and active participation. In the workers' communities of the nineteenth century, workers' intensive involvement with one another and their participation in union activities was cognitively regarded as the legitimate way to organize their relationship to one another. Through their day-to-day participation with one another, members developed a core commitment and regarded the unions as normatively legitimate. Within this context, the mutual-aid logic was deeply embedded in the work and social routines of their workers' communities and the early union structures were an extension of those communal relationships in which everyone was expected to lend a hand for the common good. Within the rail and mining industries, these relationships sustained members, enabling them to develop strong unions during one of the bloodiest periods of labor-management relations. Similarly, in the mid-twentieth century, the communal relationships comprising the stew zoos sustained the flight attendants in their efforts to overcome the paternalism of both airline executives and labor leaders and form an independent union, the AFA.

However, once permanent unions were established, the mutual-aid logic atrophied, receding into abeyance and giving way to the servicing logic. The servicing logic developed as a consequence of labor's success in pressuring the federal government to enact the National Labor Relations Act, which created a supportive political environment by conferring regulative legitimacy on independent unions. The act enabled many new unions to be established in the 1930s and 1940s. Additionally, it fostered growth of a labor oligarchy and an explosion in workers' wages and benefits that transformed members' relationships with one another and the union. Union leaders and a cadre of experts provided services to members whose participation in their unions was limited to a small number of roles. Members were primarily expected to be the reserve troops who would strike when called on by their leaders. As a result of their newly acquired middle-class status, many workers abandoned their old communities for the suburbs, where they found themselves isolated from their own kind. Just as the new oligarchical structure undercut members' participation in their unions, their movement to the suburbs also undercut their involvement with one another, creating new work and social routines in which members often barely knew one another let alone interacted with one another off the job. Thus the cultural frame of the servicing logic emerged from the union's oligarchical structure and members' limited involvement with one another.

In the 1970s and 1980s, the labor movement's technical and managerial environment became increasingly hostile and unions found that the servicing logic was an increasingly ineffective mechanism for gaining members' commitment, which precipitated labor's current legitimacy crisis and reemergence of the mutual-aid logic. Within this context, labor's community of memory, recalling its hostile environment of the past, argued that the union's present situation was analogous and that, in order to assure its long term survival, members had to become reinvolved with one another and assume responsibility for the affairs of the union. These older workers argued that members' core commitment had to be renewed and the normative legitimacy of the union had to be revitalized. However, unlike the earlier period of the mutual-aid logic, the union could not build a new structure on the communal work and social routines of members. Rather, in order for workers to become involved with one another and relearn how to participate in union life, they had to consciously design new participatory structures and routines. To embed the reemergent mutual-aid logic in members' work and social routines, they had to reconstruct new mutual-aid practices of commitment, which would renew members' core commitment and revitalize unions' normative legitimacy.

We examined MAPs as one practice that is revitalizing the mutual-aid logic as a mechanism for enhancing members' core commitment and revitalizing the normative legitimacy of unions. Specifically, in order to further our understanding of the relationship of the mutual-aid logic's reemergence, we examined MAPs in three unions. While all of the programs were peer-based, there were some significant differences in the way the unions structured the role of peer counselors. The MAP of the railroad brotherhoods was composed of peer counselors who were volunteers, and at least initially, the program focused on the prevention of substance abuse and helping railroaders with alcohol and other drug problems find treatment. In contrast, the AFA's MAP, which was also composed of volunteers, focused on an array of members' personal problems. In addition to referring members to treatment, the AFA peers also counseled troubled flight attendants on and off the job. The TWU's MAP, however, was structured very differently. Whereas the brotherhood and AFA counselors were volunteers who performed their MAP roles while working at their normal jobs, TWU's peer counselors were paid to perform their MAP roles full-time. Despite these differences, each of the programs is based on the mutual-aid logic, that is, the programs highlight that the union is a corporate entity whose members have multiple obligations to one another and share a collective responsibility for the well-being of one another. Whether it is the communalism of the MAP of the railroad brotherhoods or the facilitative counseling of the AFA's MAP or the emergent professionalism of the TWU's MAP, each of these programs was based on the assumption that helping meant more than servicing.

Members' participation in their MAPs renewed their core commitment and revitalized their union's normative legitimacy. This was true for those who acted as peer counselors and those who received help from them. Many who received help became more active in the union by becoming peer counselors and taking on other leadership roles. MAP participants also became involved in developing other union-related activities such as teaching community education programs, assisting other unions to implement MAPs, and organizing picnics, raffles, and dances for union members and their families. In addition to renewing members' core commitment to their unions, the MAPs provided other benefits. Within all of the programs, members expressed appreciation for what the peer counselors were doing to help them solve their personal problems. These consequences further enhanced the unions' normative legitimacy.

Comparing the three cases also enriched our understanding of the cycle of union-member relations in several ways. First, we found that, in the early stages of any union, the mutual-aid logic plays a critical role. This was true for the brotherhoods, which developed in the nineteenth century, as well as the AFA and TWU, which developed in the twentieth century. It was also true for both craft and industrial unions, regardless of whether their membership was composed primarily of men or women. In each case, members' core commitment and the unions' normative legitimacy sustained members' relationships with one another and enabled the union to become established as their legitimate representative. Second, we discovered that regulative legitimacy was not sufficient for the establishment of independent unions. This was particularly evident in AFA and TWU. In their struggles to become recognized as workers' legitimate representatives, the mutual-aid logic was a critical resource in sustaining their members' commitment to organizing. Third, we also discovered that the mutual-aid logic atrophies very quickly once members stop enacting its practices of commitment. This was particularly evident in the AFA, where changes in their communal interaction patterns were precipitated by their successes at the bargaining table and by management responses to deregulation. Within this changed environment, members developed a segmented commitment to the union and the union legitimated its authority instrumentally. However, the case of the brotherhoods highlights the extent to which the mutual-aid logic may endure long after the workers are organized as a union as long as conditions are supportive of members' communal interactions.

Our observations have several implications for the labor movement and its reemergent mutual-aid logic. Within organizational theory, there has been an ongoing debate about whether effective change occurs from the top down or from the bottom up (Wardell 1992). This study suggests that labor's community of memory will continue to play a critical role in renewing the movement's mutual-aid logic of action. Because the community of memory is composed of both rank-and-file members and union officials, change can occur from both directions. Veteran rank-and-file members remain important resources for recapturing the mutual-aid logic and reframing it for today's struggles. They have real stories to tell about their unions, especially the sacrifices made by members to gain recognition from their employers. Veterans also remember the old practices of commitment and, as the discussion of MAPs illustrates, they are able to adapt them to labor's current environment. Such stories and practices highlight the essential meaning of community for members: becoming involved with one another and participating in union activities. At the same time, many labor leaders may also remember the old ways and have their own stories to tell. John Sweeney exemplifies that type of leadership. Articulating his vision of a renewed sense of worker community, Sweeney (1996, 156) writes, "We can reshape the world in which we live in the image of our dreams and values." In writing about that vision, he tells stories of workers, like his father at the Transport Workers Union, and how they constructed their workers' communities and secured for themselves union recognition and the good life. The challenge for labor's community of memory is to transform the terms "brothers" and "sisters" from rhetorical flourishes of a bygone era into the basis of a new workers' community.

Historians trace the beginning of the American labor movement to the Philadelphia Typographical Society's strike of 1786; some contemporary observers wonder whether it will survive far into this century. Many Americans believe that unions have achieved their goals, outlived their usefulness, and become corrupt; many union members, feeling that their leaders are no longer responsive to their needs, question the legitimacy of their unions and are withholding their support from them. According to Aronowitz (1992), the movement's problems are due to leadership's unwillingness to make labor's history part of their contemporary strategy for renewing Americans' belief in unionism. Instead of using its collective history as a mechanism for renewing workers' beliefs in unionism and members' sense of community, leaders continue to focus on workers' instrumental concerns. In contrast, the women's and the civil rights movements have reclaimed their histories and subsequently attracted a new generation to their causes (Harding 1981; Morris 1985; Aronowitz 1990). Thus, Aronowitz (1992, xix) argues that the labor movement must develop a useable past:

> Without a useable past, which becomes part of the collective memory, workers are condemned — not only to remain ignorant of the dangers undiscovered by their predecessors — but to repeat some of their mistakes.

In his seminal study, *Collective Memory*, Maurice Halbwachs (1950) argued that every group develops a unique memory of its past that highlights its identity in relationship to others. Collective memory provides the group with an account of its origins and development, which allows it to view itself through time. Halbwachs originally made a distinction between historical and collective memory, conceiving of history as an objective science detached from sociopolitical pressures and collective memory as an organic part of social life that is continuously transformed in response to society's current needs. Today, few social theorists accept this sharp distinction; rather, they argue that the historical record and current social and political agendas are entwined as a group reconstructs its collective memory (Zerubavel 1995). Accordingly, collective memory is neither completely transmutable to current circumstances nor completely constrained by historical facts (Schwartz 1991). For instance, George Washington was an aristocrat, who has become a revered figure, symbolizing Americans' abiding faith in democracy. Within our collective memory, his image has shifted with historical circumstances. Between 1800 and 1865, he was remembered as a man of remoteness, gentility, and flawless virtue; after 1865, he began to be remembered as an ordinary, imperfect man with whom common people could identify. Yet, Americans have never forgotten his original aristocratic image.

Collective memory has become a major arena for interdisciplinary study. Research has focused on several areas. Some researchers, for example, have studied the institutional processes that maintain or suppress information as part of public culture (Fine 1996; Griswold 1986; Lang and Lang 1988). Still, others have examined group struggles to define the ways in which members interpret widely shared information about their past (Schudson 1992; Schwartz 1991; Maier 1988; Zerubavel 1995). This study contributes to the literature on collective memory by examining its role in the transformation of social action. Like Aronowitz, we are concerned about labor's collective memory; however, in contrast to his pessimistic view, we argue that labor's collective memory contains a mutual-aid logic of action, which has been in abeyance and may be reemerging to renew the movement.

In our optimistic view, labor's community of memory is a large, untapped resource. While, we have discussed the role of veteran rank-and-file members in the community of memory, retirees belong to this enclave as well. Today, retirees make up the largest proportion of the labor movement and are an important resource for its revitalization. Roszak (1999) makes a similar observation about retirees within American society:

> [A]n increasing number of us will be living decades longer than our parents or grandparents. . . . Think of those years as a *resource* — a cultural and spiritual resource. . . . During any one of those years, somebody who no longer has to worry about raising a family, pleasing a boss, or earning more money will have the chance to join with others in building a compassionate society [emphasis in the original].

With the aging of America's workforce and the changing nature of retirement, many unions are — for the first time — facing a situation in which their retiree membership is becoming equal to, if not greater than, their "active" membership. Within the framework of the servicing logic, unions have long tended to the financial needs of their retiring members. However, some — like a United Auto Workers local in upstate New York — have begun to use their retirement activities as a means by which to renew members' core commitment and strengthen their normative legitimacy. These UAW retirees have an active retirement club, with approximately 25 percent of all members attending monthly meetings. The club's committees provide a framework for continued union involvement based on the principle of mutual aid. Thus, for example, a number of UAW retirees are involved in a committee whose primary responsibility it is to make sure that hospitalized or home-bound union members receive visits from other members. In this way, mutual aid serves as a basis for retaining member solidarity even in retirement and provides the union with a readily mobilized and highly committed retiree membership. Thus, for example, retirees are often counted on to staff union phone banks during vital state and national political campaigns and have played an important role in backing up local job actions. Of course, retirees can perform a variety of roles within the union as well. The point is that, by staying involved in the union and interacting with the next generation of members to solve their shared problems, they enact the mutual-aid logic and demonstrate its continuing importance in the labor movement. However, the most important role that retirees play is the storyteller. By telling stories about the union's development, they recount the crucial role of members' core commitment in its founding and the centrality of normative legitimacy for its continuation. Thus, as part of labor's community of memory, retirees connect members with the past, present, and future of their union.

We also argue that labor's community of memory extends well beyond the boundaries of individual unions. The mutual-aid logic need not be solely dependent on members of a union local for its reconstruction. This is evident in the efforts of MAP peer counselors to develop peer programs in other unions. By teaching members of other locals about MAP practices, they are reawakening the mutual-aid logic across the labor movement. Similarly, many unions have published historical accounts of their struggles and are collecting oral histories from rank-and-file members and retirees in order to preserve their past. For instance, the United Federation of Teachers and New York State United Teachers have ongoing oral history projects. In addition, many unions are finding creative ways to share this information with their members and the public. These include plays like "Marching to Union Square," photo exhibits like "Ordinary People, Extraordinary Lives: A Century of Labor in New York City," and web sites like "Cartoonists Unions: A Legacy of Artists Helping Artists." These are valuable resources for diffusing the mutual-aid logic across the labor movement and attracting new members to unions.

It is one thing to tell stories about the old days, it is another to embed the mutual-aid logic in a union's structure and workers' routines. After all, that means creating participatory union structures and getting members involved. On the surface, that looks like an insurmountable task. Within today's oligarchical union structure, labor leaders are unaccustomed to telling members that they are the union and must become participants in rebuilding a strong labor movement. Some have attempted to do so. For instance, a number of AFL-CIO affiliates, following Sweeney's admonition, have attempted to reconstruct themselves as organizing unions. According to Fletcher and Hurd (1998b), this transformation is not easy because leaders, who are often politically conflicted over internal union politics, lack the managerial skills to create such a change and because staff members resist it. At the same time, rank-and-file members argue that they do not have the time to become involved with others and participate in union affairs. As study after study attests, workers are working longer hours, have less time to spend with their families and on community affairs, and are spread over larger geographic areas than they were fifty or seventy years ago. These are real barriers to workers becoming involved in rebuilding their unions and communities. Still, as this study suggests, many are willing to participate and, once they become involved, are likely to expand their efforts into other communal projects. Again, Sweeney's (1996, 156) comments are germane:

> As I like to remind leaders of our movement, the labor unions still have more than thirteen million members across the country. If we mobilized only 2 percent of those members, we would have an army of more than a quarter million Americans from every background and walk of life, ready to devote their energies to social justice and community service.... Imagine if a half million — or better yet, a million — working men and women devoted some of their spare time to organizing exploited workers, raising their wages, and helping them support their families without food stamps.

Yet, one question persists, "What does the new participatory structure look like?" From our data, we cannot prescribe its shape but we can suggest that it will be built, at least initially, from members working together to solve their common problems. From that perspective, there are many common problems confronting workers today. These include developing more participatory forms of collective bargaining and grievance handling as well as participatory solutions to problems such as work-family conflict and child and elder care. They also include larger social issues such as the environment, education, social security, and campaign reform. Like the MAP solution to alcohol and drug problems, solutions to these problems will come from workers finding innovative ways of helping one another and teaching those solutions to one another. Shostak (1991, 1995) documents many of these participatory innovations for creating a robust unionism. Many are similar to the small groups developed by American churches to revitalize their congregations (Wuthnow 1994); others call for creating creative coalitions with other social movements and community groups (Clawson and Clawson 1999). All, however, encourage greater involvement of members in solving their collective problems. Nevertheless, the one thing that we can assert with a great deal of confidence is that building these new participatory structures will take a great deal of time and energy. There are no quick fixes for renewing members' core commitment and unions' normative legitimacy. Embedding the mutual-aid logic in labor's culture and structure and workers' routines will be hard work and may take decades. Indeed, the process of reconstructing new workers' communities is just beginning.

This study also has implications for unions in other countries. As we stated in chapter 1, the decline in union density is not merely a United States phenomenon. Visser (1994, 1992) examined union density in twenty-four countries that belong to the Organization for Economic Cooperation and Development (OECD, i.e., in North America, Europe, and Asia), between 1980 and 1989. Union density remained stable in five countries, where union density was greater than 50 percent of the national labor force: Sweden, Finland, Norway, Luxembourg, and Iceland. Two factors explain the stability of union density in these countries: (1) the highly concentrated and specialized nature of their economies and (2) greater societal homogeneity. As a result of these factors, unions in these countries continue to operate in a supportive environment; thus, they have less interunion competition, greater union concentration, and wide bargaining coverage, which enables them to be more efficient in their recruitment and retention of members. Thus, in these OECD countries, unions have been able to maintain members' commitment and their own legitimacy despite the predominance of large and highly bureaucraticized, industrial unions (Korpi 1983). In contrast, union density declined in the nineteen remaining OECD countries by approximately a third. Unions in these countries are experiencing hostile environments similar to those experienced by unions in the United States (Davis 1994; Peetz 1990; Freeman and Pelletier 1990). They too are ensnared in the web of the global economy, changing work processes, and shifting legal actions. At the same time, they too find themselves confronting managers less willing to work with labor and more likely to export jobs abroad. And, like their counterparts in the United States, they too are unable to rely on members' core commitment to the union when facing down employer opposition and confronting legal obstacles. Within this context, Visser concluded that unions in these OECD countries "must live with lower levels of protections and benefits than can be provided to workers and members" and, therefore, must "count on a higher degree of ideological identification and motivation" (1994, 173–174) from their members. Thus, unions in these OECD countries are facing the same crisis of instrumental legitimacy faced by unions in the United States.

Does our theory of cycles of logic apply to unions in other countries? Indeed, each of the labor movements in these countries have their own unique institutional history and whatever logic of action is embedded in those unions is likely to reflect aspects of that unique history as well as aspects of their national culture. Nevertheless, we believe that our theory — with some modifications and refinements — may apply to these labor movements as well. The mutual-aid ethic, which we identified as a basic building block of the logic's emergence in the United States, is also evident in the history and culture of many OECD countries. For instance, Friendly Societies were common throughout Europe in the eighteenth and nineteenth centuries and were diffused to America, where their mutual-aid ethic was continued by the crafts, enabling them to develop the first unions (Clawson 1989; Thompson 1963). We suspect that, as in the United States, this mutual-aid logic has atrophied because of strong European social welfare policies and highly bureaucratized unions. For instance, Turner's (1998) discussion of German rank-and-file members' efforts to create innovative organizing campaigns is remarkably congruent with the AFL-CIO's current organizing campaigns and suggests that a new mutual-aid logic may be emergent in Europe as well. Turner (1998, 134) concludes:

> Case studies of union organizing success and failure at home and abroad suggest that ongoing and extensive rank-and-file participation, rather than a faucet to be turned on and off by employers or unions, is a necessary ingredient for the revitalization of contemporary workplaces, communities, and labor movements.

Likewise, the concept of mutual aid is deeply embedded within East Asian "Confucian" societies. For instance, unions in these societies appear to have developed a strong servicing orientation on top of a deeply embedded mutual-aid ethic, which is manifested in a variety of union programs, including extensive welfare plans, recreational and educational services, and cooperative housing (Chiu and Levin 1999). However, it remains an empirical question whether the mutual-aid logic and servicing logic are embedded in the labor movements of other countries. If they are, we should like to know whether the mutual-aid logic is reemerging there and revitalizing the labor movements of those countries. We encourage other social scientists to examine these questions in order to refine our theoretical analysis.

This study also has theoretical implications for institutional theory and the study of organizations. It highlights the usefulness of conceptualizing institutions as multidimensional. Neoinstitutional theorists have focused primarily on the cultural or cognitive dimension of institutions, giving the regulative and normative dimensions relatively short shrift. By conceptualizing logics of union-member relations as being embedded in culture, structure, and routines, we have been able to develop a more comprehensive understanding of the processes of institutionalization and deinstitutionalization than we would have developed by focusing on any one of these carriers exclusively. As Selznick has argued, to institutionalize means infusing with value beyond the requirements of the task at hand. By focusing on the different carriers of the logics of union-member relations, we were able to observe that the process of infusing value entailed a layering of culture, routines, and structure. Thus within the early unions the mutual-aid logics of unions were deeply embedded or highly institutionalized in the members' lives so they took it for granted cognitively and normatively. Later the federal government conferred regulative legitimacy on the mutual-aid logic, at least initially embedding it further into the lives of workers and their union. Similarly, deinstitutionalization of the mutual-aid logic and its replacement by a servicing logic entailed the loss of value by a different layering of the institutional carriers (i.e., structure, routines, and culture). In this layering sequence, cognitive legitimacy follows, rather than precedes, regulative legitimacy. Indeed, it is a post-hoc justification members use to account for their transformed patterns of interaction. As members struggle to reconstruct the mutual-aid logic, the interplay of carriers shifts once again as veterans assert the cognitive and normative legitimacy of this logic and attempt to embed it within their union's culture and structure.

Second, this study also highlights the potential of using logics of action as a bridging concept between the overly socialized actor of institutional theory and the overly rational actor of rational-actor models of organizational theory. On one hand, logics of action are rational solutions to collective problems; on the other hand, they also constrain action. In the nineteenth century, for instance, the mutual-aid logic of union-member relations was a rational solution to the early unionists' problems. As it became embedded in the culture and structure of unions as well as the routines of members, the members were increasingly constrained, both cognitively and normatively, to act in their communal best interest. Similarly, the shift to the servicing logic of union-member relations was a rational response to the structural changes wrought by the National Labor Relations Act, freeing members from the old communal constraints to act on their self interests. The shift to a reemergent mutual-aid logic is likewise rational; it remains an empirical question whether members will come to see it as, once again, the cognitively and normatively legitimate way to organize their relationships.

Third, this study highlights the importance of studying the interplay between member commitment and organizational legitimacy. Social scientists generally examine one or the other. Seeing member commitment within the context of an organization's legitimacy deepens our understanding of the social processes. Thus, for example, we may see the current discussion about employers' abandonment of the social contract as a crisis for both employees and the organization. On one hand, the discussion reflects the feelings of betrayal experienced by employees who were committed to their employers because they believed in the social contract. On the other hand, the discussion reflects an organizational crisis, in which employers have lost their legitimacy. This crisis will not be solved by managerial efforts to develop high-commitment organizations, which use simple-minded techniques to manipulate employees' motivation. Its solution requires employers and employees to develop a new logic of action, which emphasizes their mutual obligations to one another. Only then will employees become recommitted to their employing organizations and employers regain their legitimacy.

Fourth, this study illustrates the utility of studying institutional cycles and the role of agency in perpetrating them. Institutions are not static phenomena and may change in predictable cycles as actors react to shifts in their environment. Actors may take them for granted, forget them, or remember them. As we have argued in this book, many structures and practices, which are assumed to have been forgotten, may be in abeyance and may reemerge in response to environmental shifts. An important aspect of examining institutional change is the examination of cycles of institutions. Specifically, how do institutions emerge from the abeyance of collective memory and become part of everyday practice? As yet, neoinstitutional theorists know little about these cycles and the role of collective memory in sustaining them.

While this study has examined the logics of organization-member relations within unions, it would be useful to study them in other settings to discover whether similar cyclical patterns apply there as well. Other types of social movements would be particularly interesting to study. Like labor, they are characterized by professional social movement organizations, which ask little of their members; in contrast to labor, however, social movement members are free to withdraw their membership at any time. Researchers have begun to identify cycles of protest that characterize social movements (Staggenborg 1998; Taylor 1989; Mauss 1975). Are these cycles similarly composed of mutual-aid and servicing logics? If so, how are they embedded in these social movement cycles? Do the logics emerge in relation to hostile and hospitable environments? What role do collective memory and collective amnesia play in perpetrating the cycle? Likewise, it would be useful to examine the logics of organization-member relations in business organizations. Recent research, for instance, suggests that managers also forget and remember cyclical strategies for motivating employees (Barley and Kunda 1992)

In closing it is worth remembering that, once before, the labor movement was declared dead. It was in 1932, shortly before President Roosevelt signed the National Labor Relations Act and set off an explosion of union organizing. Once again, labor is struggling to renew itself. History is not always a predictable guide to the future. However, this book suggests that labor's successful renewal is predicated on the ability of its community of memory to vividly recall the mutual-aid logic and embed it within labor's culture and structure and members' work and social routines, renewing members' core commitment and revitalizing the normative legitimacy of unions.

References

Appelbaum, Eileen, and Rosemary Batt. 1994. *The New American Workplace*. Ithaca, N.Y.: ILR Press.

Aronowitz, Stanley. 1992. *False Promises: The Shaping of American Working Class Consciousness*. Durham, N.C.: Duke University Press.

———. 1990. "Radicalizing Labor Education." In *The Re-education of the American Working Class*, edited by Steven London, Elvira Tarr, and Joseph Wilson, 21–33. Westport, Conn.: Greenwood Press.

Bacharach, Samuel B., Peter Bamberger, and William J. Sonnenstuhl. 1996. "The Organizational Transformation Process: The Micropolitics of Dissonance Reduction and the Alignment of Logics of Action." *Administrative Science Quarterly* 41: 477–506.

———. 1994. *Member Assistance Programs in the Workplace*. Ithaca, N.Y.: ILR Press.

Bacharach, Samuel, and Joseph Shedd. 1998. "Institutional Change in Exchange Relations." Working paper ILR School, Cornell University.

Bamberger, Peter, Avraham Kluger, and Ronenna Suchard. 1999. "Antecedents and Consequences of Union Commitment: A Meta Analysis." *Academy of Management Journal* 42 (3): 304–19.

Bamberger, Peter, and William J. Sonnenstuhl. 1996. "Tailoring Union-Wide Innovations to Local Conditions: The Case of Member Assistance Program Implementation in the Airline Industry." *Labor Studies Journal* 21 (1): 19–39.

———. 1995. "Peer Referral Networks and Utilization of a Union-Based EAP." *Journal of Drug Issues* 25 (2): 291–312.

Barley, Stephen R., and Gideon Kunda. 1992. "Design and Devotion: Surges of Rational and Normative Ideologies of Control in Managerial Discourse." *Administrative Science Quarterly* 37: 363–99.

Barley, Stephen R., and Pamela Tolbert. 1997. "Institutionalization and Structuration." *Organizational Studies* 18 (1): 93–116.

Barling, Julian, Clive Fullagar, and Kevin Kelloway. 1992. *The Union and Its Members: A Psychological Approach*. New York: Oxford University Press.

Bayor, R. H. 1978. *Neighbors in Conflict: The Irish, Germans, Jews, and Italians of New York City, 1929–1941*. Baltimore: John Hopkins University Press.

Bell, Bowyer J. 1970. *The Secret Army: History of the IRA*. Cambridge: Cambridge University Press.

Bellah, Robert, Richard Madsen, William M. Sullivan, Ann Swidler, and Steven M. Tipton. 1991. *The Good Society*. New York: A. A. Knopf.

———. 1985. *Habits of the Heart*. Berkeley: University of California Press.

Benson, Herman. 1985. "The Fight for Union Democracy." In *Unions in Transition*, edited by Seymour Martin Lipset, 323–70. San Francisco: ICS Press.

Berger, Peter, and Thomas Luckmann. 1967. *The Social Construction of Reality*. New York: Doubleday Anchor.

Bernstein, Irving. 1960. *The Lean Years*. Cambridge: Riverside Press.

Blau, Peter M. 1964. *Exchange and Power in Social Life*. New York: John Wiley.

Blau, Peter, and W. Richard Scott. 1962. *Formal Organizations: A Comparative Approach*. San Francisco: Chandler Publishing.

Blocker, Jack. 1989. *American Temperance Movements: Cycles of Reform*. Boston: Twayne Publishers.

Blum, T. C., D. L. Fields, S. H. Milne, and C. S. Spell. 1992. "Workplace Drug Testing Programs: A Review of Research and a Survey of Sites." *Journal of Employee Assistance Research* 1 (2): 315–49.

Blumberg, Leonard. 1991. *Beware the First Drink: The Washington Temperance Movement and Alcoholics Anonymous*. Seattle: Glen Abbey Books.

Bok, Derek C., and John T. Dunlop. 1970. *Labor and the American Community*. New York: Simon and Schuster.

Bourdieu, Pierre. 1990. *The Logic of Practice*. Stanford: Stanford University Press.

Brandes, Stuart. 1970. *American Welfare Capitalism, 1880–1940*. Chicago: University of Chicago Press.

Brinton, Mary, and Victor Nee, eds. 1998. *The New Institutionalism in Sociology*. New York: Russell Sage.

Bronfenbrenner, Kate. 1993. "Seeds of Resurgence: Successful Union Strategies for Winning Certification Elections and First Contracts in the 1980s and Beyond." Ph.D. diss., Cornell University.

Bronfenbrenner, Kate, Sheldon Friedman, Richard W. Hurd, Rudolph A. Oswald, and Ronald L. Seeber, eds. 1998. *Organizing to Win: New Research on Union Strategies*. Ithaca, N.Y.: ILR Press/Cornell University Press.

Bronfenbrenner, Kate, and Tom Juravich. 1998. "It Takes More Than House Calls." In *Organizing to Win: New Research on Union Strategies*, edited by Kate Bronfenbrenner, Sheldon Friedman, Richard W. Hurd, Rudolph A. Oswald, and Ronald L. Seeber, 19–36. Ithaca, N.Y.: ILR/Cornell University Press.

Caplan, G. 1964. *Principles of Preventive Psychiatry*. New York: Basic Books.

Cappelli, Peter. 1987. "Airlines." In *Collective Bargaining in American Industry*, edited by David Lipsky and C. Donn, 135–86. Lexington, Mass.: Lexington Books.

———. 1985. "Competitive Pressures and Labor Relations in the Airline Industry." *Industrial Relations* 24: 316–88.

Carkhuff, Robert R. 1969. *Helping and Human Relations*. Vol. 2. New York: Holt, Rinehart, and Winston.

Carver, Charles B. 1993. *Can Unions Survive?* New York: New York University Press.

Chiu, S., and Levin, D. A. 1999. "Colonialism and Labor Relations the Last Colony." In *Colonialism, Nationalism and the Institutionalization of Industrial Relations in the Third World*, edited by Sarosh Kuruvilla and Bryan Mundell, 231–70. Stamford, Conn.: JAI Press.

Clawson, Dan, and Mary Ann Clawson. 1999. "What Has Happened to the U.S. Labor Movement? Union Decline and Renewal." *Annual Review of Sociology* 25: 95–119.

Clawson, Mary Ann. 1989. *Constructing Brotherhood: Class, Gender, and Fraternalism*. Princeton, N.J.: Princeton University Press.

Cleary, Edward. 1992. "Labor Keynote." *EAPA Exchange* 22: 30.

Clemens, Elisabeth S. 1996. "Organizational Form as Frame: Collective Identity and Political Strategy in the American Labor Movement, 1880–1920." In *Comparative Perspectives on Social Movements: Political Opportunities, Mobilizing Structures, and Cultural Framings*, edited by Doug McAdam, John D. McCarthy, and Mayer Zald, 205–26. New York: Cambridge University Press.

Clemens, Elisabeth S., and James M. Cook. 1999. "Politics and Institutionalism: Explaining Durability and Change." *Annual Review of Sociology* 25: 441–66.

Cohen-Rosenthal, Edward, and Cynthia E. Burton. 1993. *Mutual Gains: A Guide to Union-Management Cooperation*. Ithaca, N.Y.: ILR Press.

Commons, John R. 1970. *The Economics of Collective Action*. Madison: University of Wisconsin Press.

———. 1924. *The Legal Foundation of Capitalism*. New York: Macmillan.

Commons, John R., et al.(1916) 1966. *History of Labour in the United States*. New York: A. M. Kelley.

Conroy, David W. 1991. "Puritans in Taverns: Law and Popular Culture in Colonial Massachusetts, 1630–1720." In *Drinking: Behavior and Belief in Modern History*, edited by Susanna Barrows and Robin Room, 29–60. Berkeley: University of California Press.

Cook, Alice. 1984. Introduction to *Women and Trade Unions in Eleven Industrialized Countries*, edited by Alice Cook, Vail Lorwin, and Arlene Daniels, 3–36. Philadelphia: Temple University Press.

———. 1982. Introduction to *From Sky Girl to Flight Attendant: Women and the Making of a Union*, by Georgia Panter Nielsen. Ithaca, N.Y.: ILR Press.

Cooper, Cary L. 1987. *Retirement in Industrialized Societies: Social, Psychological, and Health Factors*. New York: Wiley.

Cornfield, Daniel B. 1999. "Shifts in Public Approval of Labor Unions in the United States, 1936–1999." September 2, 1999. Princeton, N.J.: Gallup Organization.

———. 1989. *Becoming a Mighty Voice: Conflict and Change in the United Furniture Workers of America*. New York: Russell Sage Foundation.

Cornfield, Daniel B., and Randy Hodson. 1993. "Labor Activism and Community: Causes and Consequences of Social Integration in Labor Unions." *Social Science Quarterly* 74 (4): 590–602.

Cornfield, Daniel B., Holly McCammon, Darren McDaniel, and Dean Eatman. 1998. "In the Community or in the Union? The Impact of Community Involvement on Non-union Worker Attitudes About Unionizing." In *Organizing to Win: New Research on Union Strategies*, edited by Kate Bronfenbrenner, Sheldon Friedman,

Richard W. Hurd, Rudolph A. Oswald, and Ronald L. Seeber, 247–58. Ithaca, New York: ILR Press/Cornell University Press.

Crane, Diana. 1994. *The Sociology of Culture*. Cambridge: Blackwell.

Cross, R. D. 1978. "The Irish." In *Ethnic Leadership in America*, edited by J. Highman, 176–97. Baltimore: John Hopkins University Press.

D'Andrade, Roy. 1984. "Cultural Meaning Systems." In *Cultural Theory*, edited by Richard A. Shweder and Robert A. LeVine, 88–119. Cambridge: Cambridge University Press.

Davis, Edward M. 1994. "Trade Unionism in the Future." In *The Future of Industrial Relations: Global Change and Challenges*, edited by J. R. Niland, R. D. Lansbury, and C. Verevis, 123–63. Thousand Oaks, Calif.: Sage.

Davis, Gerald, Kristina Diekmann, and Catherine Tinsley. 1994. "The Decline and Fall of the Conglomerate Firm in the 1980s." *American Sociological Review* 59: 547–70.

Department of Labor. 1997. *Register of Reporting Labor Organizations*. Washington, D.C.: Office of Labor-Management Statistics.

Derber, Milton. 1970. *The American Idea of Industrial Democracy, 1865–1965*. Urbana: University of Illinois Press.

Derickson, Alan. 1988. *Workers' Health, Workers' Democracy: The Western Miners' Struggle, 1891–1925*. Ithaca, N.Y.: Cornell University Press.

DiMaggio, Paul J. 1997. "Culture and Cognition." *Annual Review of Sociology* 23: 263–87.

DiMaggio, Paul J., and Walter W. Powell. 1983. "The Iron Cage Revisited." *American Sociological Review* 48: 147–60.

Douglas, Mary. 1986. *How Institutions Think*. Syracuse, N.Y.: Syracuse University Press.

Douglas, Sara U. 1986. *Labor's New Voice: Unions and the Mass Media*. Norwood, N.J: Ablex.

Dublin, Thomas. 1992. *Lowell: The Story of an Industrial City: A Guide to Lowell National Historical Park and Lowell Heritage State Park, Lowell, Massachusetts*. Washington, D.C.: U.S. Department of the Interior.

Ducker, James H. 1983. *Men of the Steel Rails: Workers on the Atchison, Topeka & Santa Fe Railroad, 1869–1900*. Lincoln: University of Nebraska Press.

Dulles, Foster Rhea, and Melvyn Dubofsky. 1984. *Labor in America: A History*. 4th ed. Arlington Heights, Ill.: Harlan Davidson.

Durkheim, Emile.[1893] 1949. *The Division of Labor in Society*. Glencoe, Ill.: Free Press.

———. (1912) 1961. *The Elementary Forms of Religious Life*. New York: Collier.

Eaton, A., M. Gordon, and J. Keefe. 1992. "The Impact of Quality of Working Life Programs and Grievance System Effectiveness on Union Commitment." *Industrial and Labor Relations Review* 45 (3): 591–604.

Edelman, Lauren. 1992. "Legal Ambiguity and Symbolic Structures." *American Journal of Sociology* 97: 1531–76.

———. 1990. "Legal Environments and Organizational Governance." *American Journal of Sociology* 95: 1401–40.

Edelstein, J., and Malcolm Warner. 1979. *Comparative Union Democracy: Organisation and Opposition in British and American Unions*. New Brunswick, N.J.: Transaction Books.

Edwards, Richard. 1979. *Contested Terrain*. New York: Basic Books.

Eichler, Stephen, Clifford M. Goldberg, Louise E. Kier, and John P. Allen. 1988. *Operation: Redblock*. Rockville, Md.: U.S. Department of Transportation.

Epstein, Abraham. 1926. "Industrial Welfare Movement Sapping American Trade Unions." *Current History Magazine* 24 (4): 520.

Erikson, Kai T. 1976. *Everything in Its Path: Destruction of Community in the Buffalo Creek Flood*. New York: Simon and Schuster.

Faler, Paul. 1974. "Cultural Aspects of the Industrial Revolution: Lynn, Massachusetts, Shoemakers and Industrial Morality, 1826–1860." *Labor History* 393: 367–94.

Filippelli, Ronald L. 1984. *Labor in the USA: A History*. New York: Alfred A. Knopf.

Fine, Gary A. 1996. "Reputational Entrepreneurs and the Memory of Incompetence." *American Journal of Sociology* 101 (5): 1159–93.

Fiorito, Jack, Paul Jarley, and John Thomas Delaney. 1995. "National Union Effectiveness in Organizing: Measures and Influences." *Industrial and Labor Relations* 48 (4): 613–35.

Fletcher, Bill, and Richard W. Hurd. 1998a. "Beyond the Organizing Model: The Transformation Process in Local Unions." In *Organizing to Win: New Research on Union Strategies*, edited by Kate Bronfenbrenner, Sheldon Friedman, Richard W. Hurd, Rudolph A. Oswald, and Ronald L. Seeber, 37–53. Ithaca, N.Y.: ILR Press/Cornell University Press.

———. 1998b. "Overcoming Obstacles to Transformation: Challenges on the Way to a New Unionism." Unpublished paper presented at an ILR conference: The Revival of the American Labor Movement? Ithaca, N.Y.: Cornell University.

Freeman, Richard, and Jeffrey Pelletier. 1990. "The Impact of Industrial Relations Legislation on British Union Density." *British Journal of Industrial Relations* 28: 141–64

Freeman, Joshua. 1989. *In Transit: The Transport Workers Union in New York City, 1933–1966*. New York: Oxford University Press.

Friedland, Roger, and Robert R. Alford. 1991. "Bringing Society Back In: Symbols, Practices, and Institutional Contradictions." In *The New Institutionalism in Organizational Analysis*, edited by Walter W. Powell and Paul J. DiMaggio, 232–63. Chicago: University of Chicago Press.

Galenson, Walter. 1985. "The Historical Role of American Trade Unionism." In *Unions in Transition*, edited by Seymour Martin Lipset, 39–74. San Francisco: ICS Press.

Gapasin, Fernando. 1998. "The Intersection of Labor Movement Activism and Sociology." *Contemporary Sociology* 27 (2): 133–36.

Geertz, Clifford. 1973. *The Interpretation of Cultures*. New York: Basic Books.

Gerber, Robin. 1998. "Defining a New Labor Politics." Unpublished paper presented at an ILR conference: The Revival of the American Labor Movement? Ithaca, N.Y.: Cornell University.

Giddens, Anthony. 1984. *The Constitution of Society*. Berkeley: University of California Press.

Glaser, Barney, and Anselm Strauss. 1967. *The Discovery of Grounded Theory*. Chicago: Aldine.

Goffman, Erving. 1974. *Frame Analysis: An Essay on the Organization of Experience*. Cambridge: Harvard University Press.

Gompers, Samuel. (1925) 1984. *Seventy Years of Life and Labor*. Edited by Nick Salvatore. Ithaca, N.Y.: ILR Press.

———. 1898. "The Next Step toward Emancipation." *American Federationist* 6 (10): 248–49.

———. 1900. "Establish Union Benefits." *American Federationist* 8 (1): 10–11.

Gordon, M. E., J. Barling, and L. E. Tetrick. 1995. "Some Remaining Challenges." In *Changing Employment Relations: Behavioral and Social Perspectives*, edited by L. Tetrick and J. Barling, 349–66. Washington, D.C.: American Psychological Association.

Gordon, M. E., J. W. Philpot, R. E. Burt, C. A. Thompson, W. E. Spiller. 1980. "Commitment to the Union: Development of a Measure and an Examination of Its Correlates." *Journal of Applied Psychology* 65: 474–99.

Grabelsky, Jeffrey, and Richard Hurd. 1994. "Reinventing an Organizing Union: Strategies for Change." *Proceedings of the Forty-sixth Annual Meeting*, 95–104. Madison, Wis.: Industrial Relations Research Association.

Greeley, Andrew M. 1972. *That Most Distressful Nation: The Taming of the American Irish*. Chicago: Quadrangle Books.

Grenier, Guillermo J. 1987. *Inhuman Relations: Quality Circles and Anti-unionism in American Industry*. Philadelphia: Temple University Press.

Griswold, W. 1986. *Renaissance Revivals: City Comedy and Revenge Tragedy in the London Theatre, 1756–1980*. Chicago: University of Chicago Press.

Gritzer, Glenn, and Arnold Arluke. 1985. *The Making of Rehabilitation: A Political Economy of a Medical Specialization*. Berkeley: University of California Press.

Gross, James A. 1995. *Broken Promise: The Subversion of U.S. Labor Relations Policy, 1947–1994*. Philadelphia: Temple University Press.

———. 1974. *The Making of the National Labor Relations Board: A Study in Economics, Politics, and the Law*. Albany: State University of New York Press.

Gutman, Herbert George. 1975. *Work, Culture, and Society in Industrializing America: Essays in American Working-class and Social History*. New York: Knopf.

Halbwachs, Maurice. 1950. *The Collective Memory*. New York: Harper and Row.

Harding, Vincent. 1981. *There Is a River: The Black Struggle for Freedom in America*. New York: Harcourt, Brace and Jovanovich.

Hartwell, Tyler D., Paul Steele, Michael T. French, F. J. Potter, N. F. Rodman, Gary A. Zarkin. 1996. "Aiding Troubled Employees: The Prevalence, Cost, and Characteristics of Employee Assistance Programs in the United States." *American Journal of Public Health* 86 (6): 804–8.

Hattie, John A., Christopher F. Sharpley, and H. Jane Rogers. 1984. "Comparative Effectiveness of Professional and Paraprofessional Helpers." *Psychological Bulletin* 95 (3): 534–41.

Heckscher, Charles. 1998. "Taking Union Transformation Seriously." Unpublished paper presented at an ILR conference: The Revival of the American Labor Movement? Ithaca, N.Y.: Cornell University.

Hewitt, John P. 1989. *Dilemmas of the American Self*. Philadelphia: Temple University Press.

Hitchkock, Lyman C., and Mark S. Sanders. 1976. *A Survey of Alcohol and Drug Abuse Programs in the Railroad Industry*. Crane, Ind.: The Center, 1976.

Hochschild, Arlie Russell. 1983. *The Managed Heart: Commercialization of Human Feeling*. Berkeley: University of California Press.

Horwitz, Allan V. 1990. *The Logic of Social Control*. New York: Plenum Press.

———. 1977. "The Pathways into Psychiatric Treatment: Some Differences between Men and Women." *Journal of Health and Social Behavior* 18: 169–78.

Hurd, Richard W. 1998. "Contesting the Dinosaur Image — The Labor Movement's Search for a Future." *Labor Studies Journal* 22 (4).: 5–30.

———. 1996. "Union Free Bargaining Strategies and First Contract Failures." *Proceedings of the Forty-eighth Annual Meetings*, 145–52. Madison, Wis.: Industrial Relations Research Association.

———. 1994. *Assault on Workers' Rights*. Washington, D.C.: Industrial Union Department, ALF-CIO.

Irwin-Zarecka, Iwona. 1994. *Frames of Remembrance: The Dynamics of Collective Behavior*. New Brunswick: Transaction Publishers.

Jacobs, James B., and Lynn Zimmer. 1991. "Drug Treatment and Workplace Drug Testing: Politics, Symbolism, and Organizational Dilemmas." *Behavioral Sciences and the Law* 9: 345–60.

Jepperson, Ronald L. 1991. "Institutions, Institutional Effects, and Institutionalization." In *The New Institutionalism in Organizational Analysis*, edited by Walter W. Powell and Paul J. DiMaggio, 204–31. Chicago: University of Chicago Press.

Johnson, Candice. 1994. "Organizing Innovations Boosting Union Efforts." *AFL-CIO News* 39 (11): 4.

Johnson, Paul. 1978. *A Shopkeeper's Millennium: Society and Revivals in Rochester, N.Y., 1815–1837*. New York: Hill and Wang.

Johnston, Paul. 1998. "Social Movement Unionism: Labor as a Citizenship Movement." Unpublished paper presented at an ILR conference: The Revival of the American Labor Movement? Ithaca, N.Y.: Cornell University.

Juravich, Tom. 1998. "Toward a Revived Sociological Practice." *Contemporary Sociology* 27 (2): 136–39.

Katz, Alfred H. 1993. *Self-Help in America: A Social Movement Perspective*. New York: Twayne.

Kennedy, James B. 1908. *Beneficiary Features of American Trade Unions*. Baltimore: Johns Hopkins University Press.

Klandermans, B. 1986. "Psychology and Trade Union Participation: Joining, Acting, and Quitting." *Journal of Occupational Psychology* 59: 189–204.

Kochan, Thomas A. 1980. *Collective Bargaining and Industrial Relations*. Homewood, Ill.: Richard D. Irwin.

Kochan, Thomas A., Harry C. Katz, and Robert B. McKersie. 1994. *The Transformation of American Industrial Relations*. Ithaca, N.Y.: ILR Press.

Kochan, Thomas A., and Paul Osterman. 1994. *The Mutual Gains Enterprise: Forging a Winning Partnership, Among Labor, Management, and Government*. Boston: Harvard Business School Press.

Kolko, Gabriel. 1965. *Railroads and Regulation, 1877–1916*. Princeton, N.J., Princeton University Press.

Korpi, W. 1983. *The Democratic Class Struggle.* London: Routledge and Kegan Paul.

Kriesky, Jill. 1998. "Structural Change in the AFL-CIO: A Regional Study of Union Cities' Impact." Unpublished paper presented at an ILR conference: The Revival of the American Labor Movement? Ithaca, N.Y.: Cornell University.

Kropotkin, Petr Alekseevich. (1903) 1989. *Mutual Aid: A Factor of Evolution.* New York: Black Rose Books.

Lang, Gladys Engel, and Kurt Lang. 1988. "Recognition and Renown: The Survival of Artistic Reputation." *American Journal of Sociology* 94 (1): 79–109.

Leblebici, Husayin, Gerald R. Salancik, Anne Copay, and Tom King. 1991. "Institutional Change and the Transformation of Organizational Fields." *Administrative Science Quarterly* 27: 227–42.

Lender, Mark E., and James Kirby Martin. 1987. *Drinking in America: A History.* New York: Free Press.

Lester, Richard. 1958. *As Unions Mature: An Analysis of the Evolution of American Unionism.* Princeton, N.J.: Princeton University Press.

Licht, Walter. 1983. *Working for the Railroad.* Princeton, N.J.: Princeton University Press.

Lipset, Seymour Martin. 1998. "American Union Density in Comparative Perspective." *Contemporary Sociology* 27 (2): 123–25.

———. 1996. *American Exceptionalism: A Double-Edged Sword.* New York: W. W. Norton.

Lipset, Seymour Martin, Martin A. Trow, and James S. Coleman. 1956. *Union Democracy: The Internal Politics of the International Typographical Union.* Glencoe, Ill.: Free Press.

McDonald, Charles. 1992. "U.S. Union Membership in Future Decades: A Trade Unionist's Perspective" *Industrial Relations.*

McGinley, J. J. 1949. *Labor Relations in the New York Rapid Transit System, 1904–1944.* New York: King's Crown Press.

McWilliams, Wilson C. 1973. *The Idea of Fraternity in America.* Berkeley: University of California Press.

Maier, C. S. 1988. *The Unmasterable Past: History, Holocaust, and German National Identity.* Cambridge: Harvard University Press.

Maines, David R. 1977. "Social Organization and Social Structure in Symbolic Interactionist Thought." *Annual Review of Sociology* 3: 235–59.

Mannello, T. A., and F. J. Seaman. 1979. *Prevalence, Costs, and Handling of Drinking Problems on Seven Railroads.* U.S. Department of Transportation, Federal Railroad Administration: Washington, D.C.

March, James G., and Herbert A. Simon. 1958. *Organizations.* New York: John Wiley.

Markowitz, Linda. 1998. "After the Organizing Ends: Workers, Self-Efficacy, Activism, and Union Frameworks." *Social Problems* 45 (3): 356–82.

Martin, Albro. 1992. *Railroads Triumphant.* New York: Oxford University Press.

Masters, Marick F., and Robert S. Atkin. 1999. "Union Strategies for Revival: A Conceptual Framework and Literature Review." *Research in Personnel and Human Resource Management* 17: 283–314.

Mauss, Armand L. 1975. *Social Problems as Social Movements.* New York: J. P. Lippincott.

Meyer, John W., and Brian Rowan. 1977. "Institutionalized Organizations: Formal Structure as Myth and Ceremony." *American Journal of Sociology* 83:340–63.

Michels, Robert. (1911) 1949. *Political Parties: A Sociological Study of the Oligarchical Tendencies of Modern Democracy*. New York: Free Press.

Milkman, Ruth. 1998. "The New Labor Movement: Possibilities and Limits." *Contemporary Sociology* 27 (2): 125–29.

———. 1997. *Farewell to the Factory: Auto Workers in the Late Twentieth Century*. Berkeley: University California Press.

Montgomery, David. 1979. *Workers' Control in America: Studies in the History of Work, Technology, and Labor Struggles*. New York: Cambridge University Press.

Morgan, Edward P. 1991. *The '60s Experience: Hard Lessons about Modern America*. Philadelphia: Temple University Press.

Morris, Aldon. 1985. *Origins of the Civil Rights Movement*. Chicago: University of Chicago Press.

Morris, James O. 1958. *Conflict Within the AFL*. Ithaca, N.Y.: New York State School of Industrial Relations.

Muehlenkamp, Robert. 1991. "Organizing Never Stops." *Labor Research Review* 17 (10): 1–5.

Murphy, John. 1995. "Offering a New Politics." In *For Labor's Sake*, edited by Arthur B. Shostak, 244–46. New York: University Press of America.

Nelson, Richard R., and Sidney G. Winter. 1982. *An Evolutionary Theory of Economic Change*. Cambridge: Harvard University Press.

Newton, L. A., and L. M. Shore. 1992. "A Model of Union Membership: Instrumentality, Commitment, and Opposition." *Academy of Management Review* 17: 275–98.

Nielsen, Georgia. 1982. *From Sky Girl to Flight Attendant*. Ithaca, N.Y.: ILR Press.

Nissen, Bruce. 1998. "Building a Minority Union: The CWA Experience at NCR." Unpublished paper presented at an ILR conference: The Revival of the American Labor Movement? Ithaca, N.Y.: Cornell University.

Oliver, Christine. 1992. "The Antecedents of Deinstitutionalization." *Organizational Studies* 3: 563–88.

Orenstein, Jeffrey R. 1990. *United States Railroad Policy: Uncle Sam at the Throttle*. Chicago: Nelson-Hall.

Orren, K. 1992. "Metaphysics and Reality in Late Nineteenth-Century Labor Adjudication." In *Labor Law in America: Historical and Critical Essays*, edited by C. L. Tomlins and A. J. King, 160–79. Baltimore: Johns Hopkins University Press.

———. 1991. *Belated Feudalism: Labor, the Law, and Liberal Development in the United States*. Cambridge: Cambridge University Press.

Ostrom, E. 1986. "An Agenda for the Study of Institutions." *Public Choice* 48: 3–25.

Parker, Mike. 1985. *Inside the Circle: A Union Guide to QWLU*. Boston: South End Press.

Peetz, D. 1990. "Declining Union Density." *Journal of Industrial Relations* 32 (2): 197–223.

Perkins, George. 1894. "True Trade Unionism." *American Federationist* 1 (8): 168–69.

Perlow, Charles. 1979. *Complex Organizations*. New York: McGraw.

Plaganis, Paul. 1995. "Challenging Business as Usual." In *For Labor's Sake*, edited by Arthur B. Shostak, 231–42. New York: University Press of America.

Popp, Michael W. 1993. "In the Mailbag: Comment from Labor About Treatment Costs." *EAPA Exchange* 23 (May): 35.

Porter, L., R. Steers, R. Mowday, and P. Boulain. 1974. "Organizational Commitment, Job Satisfaction and Turnover among Psychiatric Technicians." *Journal of Applied Psychology* 59: 603–9.

Powell, Walter W., and Paul J. DiMaggio, eds. 1991. *The New Institutionalism in Organizational Analysis.* Chicago: University of Chicago Press.

Puchala, L. 1980. "Deregulating in the New Decade." *Flight Log* 21 (2): 10–11.

Puette, William J. 1992. *Through Jaundiced Eyes: How the Media View Organized Labor.* Ithaca, N.Y.: ILR Press.

Quill, Shirley. 1985. *Mike Quill: Himself.* New York: Transport Workers Union.

Reinhardt, Richard. 1970. *Workin' on the Railroad: Reminiscences from the Age of Steam.* Palo Alto, Calif.: American West Publishing.

Rogers, Joel. 1995. "A Strategy for Labor." *Industrial Relations* 34, (3): 367–81.

Rorabaugh, W. J. 1986. *The Craft Apprentice: From Franklin to the Machine Age in America.* New York: Oxford University Press.

———. 1979. *The Alcoholic Republic: An American Tradition.* New York: Oxford University Press.

Roszak, Theodore. 1999. *America the Wise.* Boston: Houghton Mifflin.

Rumbarger, John J. 1989. *Profits, Power, and Prohibition: Alcohol Reform and the Industrializing of America, 1800–1930.* Albany: State University of New York Press.

Rundle, Jim. 1998. "Winning Hearts and Minds: Union Organizing in the Era of Employee Involvement Programs." In *Organizing to Win: New Research on Union Strategies,* edited by Kate Bronfenbrenner, Sheldon Friedman, Richard W. Hurd, Rudolph A. Oswald, and Ronald L. Seeber, 213–31. Ithaca, New York: ILR Press/Cornell University Press.

Sackman, Morris. 1949. *Welfare Collective Bargaining in Action.* Ithaca, N.Y.: New York State School of Industrial and Labor Relations.

Salaman, Greame. 1974. *Community and Occupation: An Exploration of Work/Leisure Relationships.* London: Cambridge University Press.

Schlesinger, Arthur. 1986. *The Cycles of American History.* Boston: Houghton Mifflin Company.

Schmidt, Alvin J. 1980. *Fraternal Organizations.* Westport, Conn.: Greenwood Press.

Schmitt, L. Max. 1995. "Reaching Out to the Entire Membership." In *For Labor's Sake,* edited by Arthur B. Shostak, 36–49. New York: University Press of America.

Schudson, M. 1992. *Watergate in American Memory: How We Remember, Forget, and Reconstruct the Past.* New York: Basic Books.

Schuman, Howard, and Jacqueline Scott. 1989. "Generations and Collective Memories." *American Sociological Review* 54: 359–81.

Schwartz, Barry. 1991. "Social Change and Collective Memory: The Democratization of George Washington." *American Sociological Review* 56: 221–36.

Scott, W. Richard. 1995. *Institutions and Organizations.* Thousand Oaks, Calif.: Sage.

Seeber, R. L., and M. L. Lehman. 1989. "The Union Response to Employer-Initiated Drug-Testing Programs." *Employee Responsibilities and Rights Journal* 2 (1): 39–48.

Selznick, Philip. 1992. *The Moral Commonwealth: Social Theory and the Promise of Community.* Berkeley: University of California Press.

———. 1969. *Law, Society, and Industrial Justice.* New York: Russell Sage Foundation.

————. 1957. *Leadership in Administration*. New York: Harper and Row.

Shore, L. M., and L. A. Newton. 1995. "Union-member Relations: Loyalty, Instrumentality, and Alienation." In *Changing Employment Relations: Behavioral and Social Perspectives,* edited by L. Tetrick and J. Barling, 189–208. Washington, D.C.: American Psychological Association.

Shore, L., L. Tetrick, R. Sinclair, and L. Newton. 1994. "Validation of a Measure of Perceived Union Support." *Journal of Applied Psychology* 79 (6): 971–77.

Shostak, Arthur B., ed. 1995. *For Labor's Sake.* New York: University Press of America.

————. 1991. *Robust Unionism: Innovations in the Labor Movement.* Ithaca, N.Y.: ILR Press.

Sinclair, Robert R., and Lois E. Tetrick. 1995. "Social Exchange and Union Commitment: A Comparison of Union Instrumentality and Union Support Perceptions." *Journal of Organizational Behavior* 16: 669–80.

Sloane, Arthur A., and Fred Witney. 1985. *Labor Relations.* 5th ed. Englewood Cliffs, N.J.: Prentice-Hall.

Sonnenstuhl, William J. 1996. *Working Sober: The Transformation of an Occupational Drinking Culture.* Ithaca, N.Y.: ILR Press.

————. 1986. *Inside an Emotional Health Program: A Field Study of Workplace Assistance for Troubled Employees.* Ithaca, N.Y.: ILR Press.

Staggenborg, Suzanne. 1998. "Social Movement Communities and Cycles of Protest: The Emergence and Maintenance of a Local Women's Movement." *Social Problems* 45: 180–204.

Staudenmeier, William J., Jr. 1989. "Urine Testing: The Battle for Privatized Social Control During the 1986 War on Drugs." In *Images of Issues,* edited by Joel Best, 207–20. New York: Aldine.

————. 1985. "Alcohol and the Workplace: A Study of Social Policy in a Changing America." Ph.D. diss. Washington University.

Stinchcombe, Arthur. 1997. "On the Value of the Old Institutionalism." *Annual Review of Sociology* 23: 1–18.

Stivers, R. 1985. "Historical Meanings of Irish-America Drinking." In *The American Experience with Alcohol,* edited by Linda Bennet and Genevieve Ames, 109–30. New York: Plenum.

Stover, John. 1970. *The Life and Decline of the American Railroad.* New York: Oxford University Press.

Strauss, Anselm. 1987. *Qualitative Analysis for Social Scientists.* New York: Cambridge University Press.

Strauss, George. 1995. "Is the New Deal System Collapsing? With What Might It Be Replaced?" *Industrial Relations* 34 (3): 329–349.

Stromquist, Shelton. 1987. *A Generation of Boomers: The Pattern of Railroad Labor Conflict in Nineteenth-Century America.* Urbana: University of Illinois Press.

Sutton, John R., and Frank R. Dobbin. 1996. "The Two Faces of Governance: Responses to Legal Uncertainty in U.S. Firms, 1955–1985." *American Sociological Review* 61: 794–811.

Sutton, John R., Frank R. Dobbin, John W. Meyer, and W. Richard Scott. 1994. "The Legalization of the Workplace." *American Journal of Sociology* 99: 944–71.

Sverke, Magnus, and Sarosh Kuruvilla. 1995. "A New Conceptualization of Union Commitment: Development and Test of an Integrated Theory." *Journal of Organizational Behavior* 16: 505–32.

Sverke, Magnus, and Anders Sjoberg. 1995. "Union Membership Behavior: The Influence of Instrumental and Value-based Commitment." In *Changing Employment Relations: Behavioral and Social Perspectives*, edited by Lois E. Tetrick and Julian Barling, 229–54. Washington, D.C.: American Psychological Association.

Sweeney, John. 1996. *America Needs a Raise*. Boston: Houghton Mifflin.

Swidler, Ann. 1986. "Culture in Action: Symbols and Strategies." *American Sociological Review* 51: 273–86.

Tannenbaum, Frank. 1921. *The Labor Movement: Its Conservative Functions and Social Consequences*. New York: G. P. Putnam's Sons.

Taylor, Verta. 1989. "Social Movement Continuity: The Women's Movement in Abeyance." *American Sociological Review* 54: 761–75.

Tetrick, Lois E. 1995. "Development of Organizational Behavior." *Journal of Organizational Theory* 16: 583–95.

Thompson, E. P. 1963. *The Making of the English Working Class*. New York: Vintage Books.

Tolbert, Pamela, and Lynne Zucker. 1983. "Institutional Sources of Change in the Formal Structure." *Administrative Science Quarterly* 30: 22–39.

Tomlins, C. L. 1992. "Law and Power In the Employment Relationship." In *Labor Law in America: Historical and Critical Essays*, edited by C. L. Tomlins and A. J. King, 71–98. Baltimore: Johns Hopkins University Press.

Trice, Harrison M. 1993. *Occupational Subcultures in the Workplace*. Ithaca, N.Y.: ILR Press.

Trice, Harrison M., and Janice M. Beyer. 1993. *The Cultures of Work Organizations*. Englewood Cliffs, N.J.: Prentice Hall.

———. 1982. "A Study of Union-Management Cooperation in a Long Standing Alcoholism Program." *Contemporary Drug Problems* 11: 295–317.

Trice, Harrison M., and Paul M. Roman. 1972. *Spirits and Demons at Work: Alcohol and Other Drugs on the Job*. Ithaca, N.Y.: New York State School of Industrial and Labor Relations, Cornell University.

Turner, Lowell. 1998. "Rank-and-File Participation in Organizing at Home and Abroad." In *Organizing to Win: New Research on Union Strategies*, edited by Kate Bronfenbrenner, Sheldon Friedman, Richard W. Hurd, Rudolph A. Oswald, and Ronald L. Seeber, 123–34. Ithaca, N.Y.: ILR Press/Cornell University Press.

Tyrell, Ian R. 1979. *Sobering Up: From Temperance to Prohibition in Antebellum America, 1800–1860*. Westport, Conn.: Greenwood Press.

Ulman, Lloyd. 1961. *American Trade Unionism*. Berkeley: Institute of Industrial Relations, University of California.

———. 1955. *The Rise of the National Trade Union: The Development and Significance of Its Structure, Governing Institutions, and Economic Policies*. Cambridge: Harvard University Press.

U.S. Bureau of Labor Statistics. 1928. *Beneficial Activities of American Trade Unions*. Washington, D.C.: United States Government Printing Office.

U.S. Department of Labor. 1970. *National Union Benefit Plans*. Washington, D.C.: United States Government Printing Office.

Visser, Jelle. 1994. "Union Organization: Why Countries Differ." In *The Future of Industrial Relations: Global Change and Challenges*, edited by J.R. Niland, R.D. Lansbury, and C. Verevis, 164–84. Thousand Oaks, Calif.: Sage.

———. 1992. "The Strength of Union Movements in Advanced Capitalist Democracies: Social and Organizational Variations." In *The Future of Labour Movements*, edited by Marino Regini, 17–52. Newbury Park, Calif.: Sage Publications.

Vogel, Lise. 1977. "Heart to Fell and Tongues to Speak: New England Mill Women in the Early Nineteenth Century." In *Class, Sex, and the Woman Worker*, edited by Milton Cantor and Bruce Laurie, 64–82. Westport Conn.: Greenwood Press.

Voss, Kim. 1996. "The Collapse of a Social Movement: The Interplay of Mobilizing Structures, Framing, and Political Opportunities in the Knights of Labor." In *Comparative Perspectives on Social Movements*, edited by Doug McAdam, John D. MacCarthy, and Mayer N. Zald, 227–60. Cambridge: Cambridge University Press.

Walsh, David J. 1988. "Accounting for the Proliferation of Two-Tier Wage Settlements in the U.S. Airline Industry, 1983–1986." *Industrial and Labor Relations Review* 42: 50–62.

Wardell, Mark. 1992. "Changing Organizational Forms from the Bottom Up." In *Rethinking Organization: New Directions in Organizational Analysis*, edited by Michael Reed and Michael Hughes, 144–64. Newbury Park, Calif.: Sage Publications.

Weber, Max. (1922) 1964. *The Theory of Social and Economic Organization*. New York: Free Press.

Weiler, Paul. 1991. "Hard Times for Unions: Challenging Times for Scholars." *University of Chicago Law Review* 58: 1015.

Whitehead, Pamela Ann. 1997. "The Impact of Managed Care on Workplace Substance Abuse Programs: An Examination of Internal EAP and MAP Programs within New York State." Senior Honors Thesis, Cornell University, College of Industrial and Labor Relations.

Wilner, Frank N. 1991. *The Railway Labor Act and the Dilemma of Labor Relations*. Omaha, Neb.: Simmons-Boardman Books.

Wolfe, Alan. 1998. *One Nation After All*. New York: Viking.

Wuthnow, Robert. 1994. *Sharing the Journey: Support Groups and America's New Quest for Community*. New York: Free Press.

———. 1987. *Meaning and Moral Order: Explorations in Cultural Analysis*. Berkeley: University of California Press.

Zald, Mayer, and Roberta Ash. 1966. "Social Movements Organizations: Growth, Decay and Change." *Social Forces* 44: 327–40.

Zerubavel, Eviatar. 1997. *Social Mindscapes: An Invitation to Cognitive Sociology*. Cambridge: Harvard University Press.

Zerubavel, Yael. 1995. *Recovered Roots: Collective Memory and the Making of Israeli National Tradition*. Chicago: University of Chicago Press.

Zientek, Bob. 1993. "Working Through Managed Care Roadblocks." *EAPA Exchange* 23 (February): 28–29.

Zucker, Lynne. 1977. "The Role of Institutionalization in Cultural Persistence." *American Sociological Review* 42: 726–43.

Index

Irish Republican Army (IRA), 134, 160
IRT (Interborough Rapid Transit Line), 129, 134, 136
Irwin-Zarecka, Iwona, 9
Isomorphism, 35

Jacobs, James B., 53
Jarley, Paul, 15
Jepperson, Ronald L., 26
Job relocation, 1, 48
Job security, 45
Johnson, Candice, 15
Johnson, Paul, 56
Journeymen, 31–32
Juravich, Tom, 15

Katz, Alfred H., 28
Katz, Harry C., 10, 49
Keefe, J., 11
Kelloway, Kevin, 4
Kennedy, James B., 36
Kinship networks, 33–34
Klandermans, B., 31
Kluger, Avraham, 5
Kochan, Thomas A., 4, 10, 11, 49
Kolko, Gabriel, 64
Korpi, W., 172
Kropotkin, Petr Alekseevich, 28
Kunda, Gideon, 176

Labor Assistance Professionals, 16, 20
Labor-management cooperation, 11
Labor market, 27, 47
Labor movement: coalescence with mutual aid, 35–40, 50; conservatism, 45; cycles of union-member relations, 30–35, 163, 173, 175; fragmentation, 46–50, 126–27; as institution, 26–27; international arena, 172–73
Ladies auxiliaries, 63, 139
LaGuardia, Fiorello, 136, 137
Lang, Gladys Engel, 169
Lang, Kurt, 169
Legal environment, 27, 32, 34, 37, 50; airline industry, 105, 106, 107; transportation industry, 159
Legitimacy, 2–3, 45, 51–52, 167–68; AFA and, 105–6; familial principle, 7–8, 89, 162–63; government and, 4, 27, 37, 174;

logics of, 6–9; railroad brotherhoods and, 56, 85–89; union-member relations, 23, 26; utilitarian principle, 7, 10, 162. *See also* Normative legitimacy; Regulative legitimacy
Lehman, M. L., 53
Lender, Mark E., 29, 58
Lester, Richard, 14
Levin, D. A., 173
Licht, Walter, 58, 59, 61, 63
Lipset, Seymour Martin, 44
Locomotive Engineer's Journal, 58
Logics of action, 6–9, 174; individualism and communalism, 28–30; interaction of, 19, 26–27. *See also* Mutual-aid logic; Servicing logic
Lowell textile mills, 32–33
Luckmann, Thomas, 2, 65

Maier, C. S., 169
Maines, David R., 24
Management, 1, 11, 27, 44, 50; benefits paid by, 40, 43; co-optation by, 37–39, 49, 128, 159; cycles, 176; flight attendants and, 102–3; legitimacy and, 175; pro-employer legislation, 48–49, 52; railroad brotherhoods and, 76–78; threats by, 48–49; transport workers and 128, 144–48, 159; capitalism and, 37–40
Managerial environment, 48–49, 165; airline industry, 94, 102–3, 106–8, 125–26, 167; transportation industry, 128, 144–48. *See* Hostile environment
Mannello, T. A., 77
Manufacturing sector, 47–48
MAPs. *See* Member assistance programs
March, James G., 25
Mark-offs, 78, 82–83
Markowitz, Linda, 16
Martin, Albro, 67
Martin, James Kirby, 29, 58
Masters, Marick F., 10
Mauss, Armand L., 46, 176
McDonald, Charles, 11, 12
McKersie, Robert B., 10, 49
McLaughlin, Brian, 13
McWilliams, Wilson C., 29
Meany, George, 45, 47